THE LIFE OF THE MADMAN OF Ü

DAVID M. DiVALERIO

OXFORD
UNIVERSITY PRESS

OXFORD
UNIVERSITY PRESS

Oxford University Press is a department of the University of Oxford. It furthers the University's objective of excellence in research, scholarship, and education by publishing worldwide. Oxford is a registered trade mark of Oxford University Press in the UK and certain other countries.

Published in the United States of America by Oxford University Press
198 Madison Avenue, New York, NY 10016, United States of America.

CIP data is on file at the Library of Congress
ISBN 978–0–19–024402–6 (hbk.); 978–0–19–024403–3 (pbk.)

9 8 7 6 5 4 3 2 1

Paperback printed by Webcom, Inc., Canada
Hardback printed by Bridgeport National Bindery, Inc., United States of America

The Life of the Madman of Ü

Dedicated to the memory of Dawa

Contents

List of Illustrations

Acknowledgments

THIS TRANSLATION REFLECTS the combined efforts of the many excellent language instructors I learned from during my education, in the Upper Darby School District, at New York University, Wesleyan University, the University of Virginia, the University of Chicago, Tibet University, and elsewhere. I hope that my work fulfills some small part of my kind teachers' intentions. This book is dedicated to the remembrance of a dear friend and professor, Dawa, who lived and tragically died as a bodhisattva.

There are two individuals who must be recognized for their key contributions to the present work: Khenpo Tsülnam Rinpoché, of Sherap Ling monastery in Bir, India, and Sangyé Tendar Naga, of the Library of Tibetan Works and Archives in Dharamsala. I spent many hours discussing the *Life of the Madman of Ü* with each of them during my dissertation fieldwork in 2009. My translation would be much less informed and accurate if not for the knowledge and experience they were generous enough to share with me. I was a complete stranger when I arrived introductionless before them, but felt meaningfully bonded before our time together was through. Each of them has my deepest graditute and respect. I have also discussed parts of the *Life* with many other kind and learned people, in India and elsewhere. I appreciate the role each of them has played in helping me to translate this text. My most heartfelt congratulations to Tülku Ngawang Sönam on the completion of his Geshé Lharampa degree.

I thank Cynthia Read and the entire team at Oxford University Press for providing me with the means to realize my vision for this pair of books on Tibet's holy madmen. Two anonymous readers gave a number of helpful suggestions as part of the press's review of my translation. Terence Barrett, Nick Fleisher, Massimo Rondolino, and Jann Ronis provided feedback on a late draft of the manuscript—all are valued friends, and helpful collaborators. The two maps were made by the excellent Tsering Wangyal Shawa. I thank the National Archives of Nepal for allowing me to include images drawn from texts preserved in their invaluable collection of microfilm.

Fieldwork for this project was made possible by a fellowship from the American Institute for Indian Studies and a grant from the University of Wisconsin–Milwaukee.

Technical Note

IN THE TEXT that follows, Tibetan words and names are written out in a manner that approximates how they would be pronounced in the central Tibetan dialect, using the phonetic transcription scheme developed by the Tibetan and Himalayan Library. To indicate how Tibetan words and names are spelled, I use the orthographic transliteration system first developed by Turrell V. Wylie and revised somewhat in recent years. For instance, the Tibetan word for the advanced tantric practice of inner-fire meditation is pronounced "tum-mo," which is rendered in this book as *tummo*; its proper spelling, using Wylie's system, is *gtum mo*. Transliterated spellings of Tibetan personal names, place names, and text titles are given in two keys provided at the end of the book.

The Tibetan phoneme represented in this book as ü, as in the Madman of Ü, should be pronounced like a German umlauted u, such as in the word *für*. Its pronunciation is similar to the vowel sound in the French *rue*. "The Madman of Ü" is pronounced roughly similar to "the madman of goo," minus the g, with the vowel sound umlauted. An umlauted o, as in the name Chödrak (spelled *chos grags*), should be pronounced like a German umlauted o, as in the first vowel sound in the name of the poet Goethe, which is similar to the vowel sound in the French *peu*. É should be pronounced like the "ay" in the English "day," so that Taktsé is pronounced "tak-tsay," and Dorjé "door-jay." Shényen is pronounced "shay-nyen" (not shen-yen). Lotsāwa is pronounced "lo-tsa-wa" (as opposed to lot-sa-wa). The Tibetan phoneme that we represent with Lh is actually pronounced like "hl." The name of the capital city, typically rendered as Lhasa, is pronounced "hla-sa."

The Sanskrit letter represented with *Ś* should be pronounced "sh," as in the god Śiva. *Ṭ*, *ḍ*, and *ṇ* are pronounced as retroflexes, with the tip of the tongue folded back, touching the top of the mouth. *Ṣ* is a retroflex "sh."

In Sanskrit words, *th* should not be pronounced as it would in the English word "the," but as a hard "ta." Thus the name of the buddha of our world age, Siddhartha, is pronounced "Siddharta," with the final *ta* heavily aspirated, rather than "Siddhar-tha." *Ca* should be read as "cha," with Cakrasaṃvara pronounced "Chakrasamvara," *bodhicitta* pronounced "bodhichitta," and so on. A line over a vowel indicates a slight lengthening of its sound, as in the word *mudrā*.

In the body of the translation, a number in {curly brackets} indicates the beginning of the corresponding page in the 1972 edition of the Tibetan text.

The Life of the Madman of Ü

Introduction

THE HAGIOGRAPHY OR religious biography translated in this volume shows how a boy born to an ordinary Tibetan family in 1458 became, over the course of decades, a famous tantric master known as "the Madman of Ü."

During childhood he was known as Kyepo Dar. He was given the new name of Künga Zangpo when he became a Buddhist monk during his teens. In his mid-twenties he renounced his monkhood and assumed a highly tantric lifestyle that was much less common. This entailed dressing in human remains, drinking alcohol, making threats to powerful lords, and even consuming the brains of a corpse. During visits to Nepal he is said to have desecrated Hindu temples and to have urinated on the head of a minor king. On account of this behavior, he quickly became renowned far and wide as *Ü-nyön* (*dbus smyon*), "the Madman from Ü." In this usage, the sobriquet "madman" carries a number of meanings and connotations, being potentially praiseful and pejorative simultaneously.

From the time he entered the religious life until his death, Künga Zangpo performed a remarkable asceticism. He spent at least a quarter of his seventy-five-year life meditating in isolated retreat. During some of these retreats he would be literally sealed inside his chamber, his interaction with the world limited to what could pass through a small window. He also made a religious practice out of defying the elements, enduring many winters in Himalayan caves wearing little or no clothing, eating next to nothing.

But between these lengthy periods of withdrawal—one retreat lasted for a continuous *decade*—Künga Zangpo would leave the tranquility of his mountain refuges and descend into the world of men. These encounters were, with surprising frequency, occasions of violence against the yogin. The descriptions of the ways he was attacked and tortured by these many uncouth unbelievers—bound, hanged, burned, hacked to bits by every conceivable type of weapon—are among the most detailed and imaginative passages in the biography. Künga Zangpo's miraculous ability to survive these attacks serves to reassert, again and again, the greatness of his accomplishment.

On account of the potency of the religious lineage he was initiated into, his many years of meditation and asceticism, his norm-overturning behavior, his divine visions, the miracles that were attributed to him, and the quality of his own teaching, many people considered the Madman of Ü to be an enlightened *siddha*. Thus he attained, during his lifetime and after, a status we might usefully refer to as sainthood.

Throughout his education, his years of meditation, and his career as a teacher, Künga Zangpo's extensive engagement with the subcurrent within Buddhism that we commonly call tantra exemplifies important features of religious life in old Tibet. But some of the more striking aspects of Künga Zangpo's tantric activity are not representative of the practices of most other Tibetan Buddhists. These include his dressing in ornaments fashioned out of bones, publicly consuming repulsive substances, undertaking periods of ascetic wandering, provoking others to violence—indeed, much that would contribute to his being dubbed a "madman." This particular behavior resulted from Künga Zangpo's attempt (along with a circle of other fifteenth-century Kagyüpas, including the Madman of Tsang) to enact a literalist reading of the late, transgressive tantric scriptures. In this way they defined themselves against other Tibetan religious practitioners, who maintained that by nature these texts were to be taken figuratively.

The biography translated here was written in two parts, by two primary authors. The first part, by Nyukla Peṇchen Ngawang Drakpa (1458–1515), was composed and printed in 1494, when the Madman of Ü was about thirty-six years old. The second part, by Lhatong Lotsāwa Shényen Namgyel (born in 1512), was composed and printed in 1537, five years after the yogin's death. In spite of the forty-three years separating the composition of its two parts, the *Life of the Madman of Ü* is from start to finish a single flowing prose narrative, punctuated by short but densely packed sections of poetic verse. In its nine brief chapters, the biography offers telling details about every phase of its subject's life. From the miraculous omens preceding his birth to the moment the great lama transcends this broken realm of existence, from his decision to renounce his monkhood to the way he fostered his own disciples, the entire portrait is painted with evocatively colorful language. The two authors have created a loving depiction of the master, intended to endure as a record of his spiritual perfection.

The following translation is meant to be accessible and useful to lay readers and Tibetologists alike. *The Life of the Madman of Ü* can serve as an introduction to the Buddhism, culture, literature, and history of Tibet. The biography also documents and celebrates the life of a notable Kagyüpa, yielding an abundance of information about a well-trained and well-connected member of the Kagyü sect during one of the most formative periods in its thousand-year history. What's more, the biography can prove extremely useful in reconstructing the political and religious dynamics of Tibet during the fifteenth and sixteenth centuries, concerning which a good deal of research still remains to be done.

The *Life* also serves as a useful example of hagiographic literature. From the first awakening of our protagonist's religious sensibility to his perfect death, the narrative exemplifies many of the traits characteristic of biographies of saintly figures, irrespective of which religious tradition they belong to. The composition of the *Life* also exemplifies the sort of collaborative process out of which many traditional hagiographies were composed. We see that the contents of the biography are a combination of the yogin's own firsthand descriptions of his life, tales told about him by others, and original passages penned by the authors themselves. Examining the text, the way it was formulated, and the effect its dissemination had on the public standing of the Madman of Ü can allow us an especially comprehensive understanding of the career arc of a saint. The Madman of Ü's is a highly instructive case, as the means and the trajectory of his rise to religious prominence are in important respects representative of those of many other saintly figures in the premodern world.

Considering the life of Madman of Ü can also help us in our attempt to understand the revered Buddhist *siddhas* of India, who lived during the last centuries of the first millennium. The details of their individual lives will always remain a mystery to us, but perhaps we can establish some basic facts about who they were by extrapolating from the careers of other tantric saints.

The Madman of Ü (1458–1532) is the third best known of Tibet's "holy madmen" (*smyon pa*), after Drukpa Künlé, "the Madman of the Drukpa [Kagyü]" (born in 1455), and Sangyé Gyeltsen, the "Madman of Tsang" (1452–1507). Drukpa Künlé's wild antics have long been a favorite subject of Tibetan and Bhutanese oral traditions. The Madman of Tsang is remembered primarily for his role as the author of the famous *Life* and *Collected Songs* of Milarepa, which he completed and published in 1488. By contrast, the Madman of Ü has been nearly forgotten in the centuries since his death, but not completely. For a good deal more information on all three of these figures and the time in which they lived, as well as other religious "madmen" and "madwomen" from throughout Tibetan history, see my monograph on the subject, *The Holy Madmen of Tibet*. The present work should serve equally well as a prequel or a sequel, as preparatory or supplemental to that book.

This Introduction is intended to provide orientation for readers of the translation. To understand the life of the Madman of Ü requires some familiarity with Buddhist philosophy. But no less important is having an awareness of certain Tibetan beliefs and traditions that were not derived from the Buddhism imported from India, and of the immediate social and material circumstances of Künga Zangpo's life. Toward developing a more holistic understanding of the Madman of Ü, in the space available in this Introduction I will briefly address the familial circumstances Kyepo Dar was born into; the basics of Buddhism; some defining features of the form that Buddhism has taken in Tibet; tantric thought and practice; the Kagyü sect and its particular presentation of tantra; some key political and religious developments in fifteenth- and sixteenth-century Tibet; and how the Madman of Ü was positioned with respect to the religious culture of his day. The Introduction will then turn to describing the original Tibetan text of the *Life*, the process by which the translation was carried out, and the conventions used in the translation. The final section of the Introduction will explain a few further aspects of Tibetan culture that are referenced in the biography. The translation is followed by an epilogue offering a brief description of the Madman of Ü's legacy among Tibetan people over the five hundred years since his death.

Social Background

Kyepo Dar was born to a family based in the area of Ölkha, which is in the Ü region, the eastern part of central Tibet (Tsang being its western part; Kharak is sometimes said to mark their border). The biography states that the boy's family was either of the lower ranks of the nobility or of the higher ranks of commoners (page 60 in the following translation; page 387 in the 1972 edition). The family had the status of *trelmi* (*'khral mi*), which translates literally as "tax people." This does not indicate the fact that they paid taxes, for indeed most households paid taxes—typically in the form of days of labor, or of produce or material goods created through earlier labor. Rather, "tax people" were called as such because they had significantly greater tax obligations than those better or worse off than them. Unlike other commoners and bound serfs, who often rented it on a temporary basis, "tax people" owned land. But they could maintain possession of their lands only by fulfilling a perpetual series of tax obligations, paid to nobles, to monasteries, or to the central government by way of local representatives. Most of these taxes came due on an annual cycle. These obligations were based on formal contracts that applied to whoever was in control of a particular parcel of land. Parents passed these burdens on to their children. In effect, "tax people" families owned their lands by means of mortgages that could never be paid off.

At times throughout the year, the household would be obligated to send one or more able-bodied persons to perform unpaid labor, usually in the form of agricultural work, such as sowing, reaping, and repairing irrigation works. In addition, when goods or eminent people were passing through the area, the household could be called upon to transport them from one appointed wayplace to another, without payment or even reimbursement for the expenses incurred. Because of this, a supply of animals, for riding and for portage, had to be kept on hand, as well as persons capable of traveling with and overseeing them. According to the *Life of the Madman of Ü*, the demands of these corvée tax obligations (*'u lag*) caused the boy's family great hardship. Although they may have been better off than some families, there was still an enormous gap between them and the truly wealthy and powerful in this feudal society.

Families in the position of "tax people" traditionally formed polyandrous marriage relations, in which a generation of brothers would welcome a woman into the home, whom they married collectively. Whereas establishing separate households for each son would entail having to divide up the family's resources and labor capacities, a polyandrous relationship enabled a family to keep most of its capital intact. Allowing its members to work together as a team, this arrangement made the economic unit more effective and flexible in meeting its tax obligations, some of which could fall at any time with no warning.

When Kyepo Dar was a teenager, he and his four older brothers entered into just such a matrimonial arrangement with a young woman. Then, for reasons that are not specified in the biography, they brought a second wife into the household. The two wives did not get along with one another, which caused significant discord in the home.[1]

These were not the only hardships that Kyepo Dar and his family had to endure. His mother had passed away when he was still a boy. The young Kyepo Dar was also on one occasion physically assaulted by a drunken minor lord. According to the biography, experiencing this injustice caused the youngster to perceive a great unfairness in the standing social order, in which members of the upper classes seemed to have the impunity to mistreat anyone beneath them.

On account of these and other experiences, in his teenage years Kyepo Dar began to grow disillusioned with life as he knew it. He realized that despite his family's toils, they labored not in order to get ahead, but merely to survive. In spite of their efforts and careful planning, a family could be made bankrupt by a few bad harvests, a disease among their livestock, or by the whim of someone holding power over them. According to his biography, Kyepo Dar observed that like bees, we humans work tirelessly to get by. And as it is with bees, the fruits of our labors can be snatched away from us at any moment. Kyepo Dar did not see the struggles endured by humans as being unique, but rather as putting us on a continuum with beings suffering in the three lower forms of rebirth—those of animals, hungry ghosts, and hell-beings. Suffering, the common denominator in all forms of life, unites every being trapped within the realm of perpetual rebirth, or *saṃsāra*.

Worst of all was knowing that this nightmare would not end at the moment of death, but would begin anew in every subsequent rebirth, just as it had in all of Kyepo Dar's previous lives, countless in number. Realistically, the very best that Kyepo Dar could hope for was to be reborn as a human in a similar station—and thus be fated to experience these same tribulations all over again. Even if he somehow managed to be reborn into one of the two highest of the six realms of saṃsāra—those of the demigods and the gods—that lifetime, like all things, would eventually come to an end, after which he would inevitably fall back into a state of continual suffering.

The only way to escape from this condition would be to break the cycle of rebirth once and for all. This could become possible only after many years of intensive Buddhist training and practice. Completely resolved in his purpose of freeing himself from the chains of existence in order to help liberate others as well, the teenage Kyepo Dar announced his intention of leaving the village to become a Buddhist monk.

Kyepo Dar's father and brothers did not share the view that he should go forth into the monkhood, and for two years they prevented him from leaving. The biography does not state whether this was because of their affection for Kyepo Dar or because his departure was certain to increase the household's burdens for decades to come, for, regardless of a family's ideals, giving up an able-bodied young man to the religious life was a palpable loss to the economic unit. Not to be deterred by the wishes of those mired in the world, at the age of sixteen in the Tibetan way of determining ages (fifteen in the Western manner of counting) Kyepo Dar fled from his home. He joined up with some people who were returning home to Tsari, the great holy mountain some days' rugged travel south from Ölkha. Shortly after arriving at Tsari, Kyepo Dar met his first guru. When he took his pre-novitiate monks' vows and assumed the maroon robes for the first time, he was given the name of Künga Zangpo, which marked the beginning of his new religious life.

Basic Buddhism

When Kyepo Dar exchanged the repetitive (in)stability of domestic life for the uncertainty and freedom known by the ascetic, he was following in the footsteps of countless other Buddhist renunciants from across Asia. In going forth into homelessness, each was himself emulating the life of the buddha of our world age, Siddhartha Gautama, the north Indian princeling born around 480 BCE. After renouncing his kingdom and worldly obligations at the age of twenty-nine, Siddhartha embarked on a religious quest, searching for a way to escape from the realm of perpetual rebirth and suffering. After six years of asceticism and experimentation, Siddhartha came to realize the deepest truths about existence. He now knew that there was no enduring soul and no supreme deity. He realized that we are in fact impermanent and constantly changing beings, held together by nothing more than our *karma*. Whatever happens to us, good or bad, has been precipitated out of all our previous actions. The fact that we lack a true self ensures the possibility of release from all of this.

Tradition maintains that once Siddhartha had this deep realization about the true nature of existence, he was no longer subject to its laws. He was now the Buddha, or "Awakened One." For the next forty-five years he would travel around northern India teaching others the truths he had discovered, the Dharma. After his death at the age of eighty, the Buddha would not be reborn, but would enter into *nirvāṇa*. By definition, the nature of the state of nirvāṇa is incomprehensible to the unenlightened. It is not of saṃsāra in any way, and thus cannot be described or understood using our worldly, unenlightened categories.

It would be a millennium before the religion of Śākyamūṇi, "the sage of the Śākya people," was brought from India to Tibet. In the intervening years, his teachings underwent a marked evolution. A new form of Buddhism, calling itself the Mahāyāna or "great vehicle," came into being over the first centuries of the Common Era. The Mahāyāna offered revised takes on many concepts and practices of defining importance to Buddhism.

Most fundamental among the changes brought on by the Mahāyāna, many now saw the Buddha's insight about the lack of a true self as applying to all the phenomena of existence—not just to our human bodies and lives. Any object, any thing, any idea could be seen as lacking its own inherent existence, produced ultimately by factors external to itself. Take, for example, a chariot. While it can be used as an animal-drawn cart for transporting people, we may call a certain object a "chariot." But if it were disassembled and its parts left in a heap, we would no longer call it a "chariot," even though the same physical parts are all still present. Therefore, the quality of being a chariot must be said not to reside in the parts themselves. We only happen to call those parts a "chariot" when they are arranged in such a way that they function as what we recognize as a chariot. On the level of conventional appearances and human interaction, we may refer to "chariots" without complication or apparent confusion. But from the perspective of what truly exists, we must conclude that the concept of a "chariot" is imposed upon reality, not derived from it. "Chariot" is a human construct, a category produced by language, which is man-made, and by its very nature imperfect. This line of reasoning exemplifies one facet of the radically deconstructive understanding of the world known by the shorthand of *śūnyatā* in Sanskrit (*stong pa nyid* in Tibetan), which is translated into English as "emptiness" or "voidness."

While the classical example of the chariot demonstrates some of the logic at the heart of the Mahāyāna Buddhist idea of emptiness, it does not convey its full scope or significance. Emptiness is the nature of all things, whether they exist in the physical realm or the mental. Imagine an object one might perceive as large, such as a full-grown tree, or even a skyscraper. When that same tree or skyscraper is compared to the size of the earth itself, it becomes impossibly small—proving the idea that it is "large" to be ultimately foundationless and false. Most of our subjective impressions can be undermined just as easily. To consider something from more than one perspective simultaneously has a profoundly destabilizing effect. Ultimately, all that we may experience is empty. The incessant ripening of previous negative karma causes us to continue to misunderstand this reality.

The idea of time, crucially, is completely undermined by the reasoning of emptiness. Our typical conception of time relies on distinguishing between past, present, and future. But a definition of "past," "present," or "future" can only ever be formulated by making direct reference to the other two—the present is that which is not the past or the future; the future is that which is not the past or the present; and so on. Thus, rather than being ultimately separable from one another, "past," "present," and "future" must be part of some greater whole. What's more, that which one might consider to constitue "the past" has not always been the past: at some point it was the present, and before that, the future. Likewise, that which we now consider to be the future must necessarily become the present, and then the past. Paradoxically, time as we conventionally conceive of and experience it comes into being only through the utter instability of the "past," the "present," and the "future." If each was fixed and real, temporal progression could not take place. Our mistaken, saṃsāric notion of "time" results from our faith in these ultimately foundationless categories.

Existence as we know it is comprised by causes and effects. To be of the system of causes and effects, something cannot be unchanging and permanent; nor can it be ontologically autonomous from everything else. Things are impermanent, and they exist in dependence on other things. They exist "interdependently," are "dependently arisen," "dependently originated." What's more, at any given moment, anything that we might perceive or conceive of—a form—arises as a distinct thing by being differentiated—physically, mentally—from everything else, as well as from utter nonexistence. Things *are,* based on what they are not. Based on what they are, things *are* not. Anything that we might see or hear or smell or taste or feel or think or dream or imagine, in the entire course of our lives, anywhere within the immeasurably massive realm of saṃsāra—which constitutes the entirety of physical and mental space—has come into being on account of its own emptiness. Emptiness gives rise to existence. Emptiness, as the truth of how things exist, pervades and unifies all.

The logic of emptiness extends even to the very ideas of "true" and "false." We deem something false because it does not appear to be true, and deem something true because it does not appear to be false. The very notions of "true" and "false" exist only in relation to one another. Rather than being opposites, true and false are facets of a greater unity. The fact that this may seem paradoxical to us does not make it any less true, but rather reveals the profound limitations of our conventional, saṃsāric ways of thinking.

The ultimate view transcends even this. To call a phenomenon "false," "illusion-like," or even "empty" is to suggest that the phenomenon is ontologically distinct. But because of its empty nature, there is in fact no ontologically distinct phenomenon to which any label can be applied—not even the label of "emptiness." What's more, there would be no emptiness if there were no empty things, and emptiness cannot be established as independent of the consciousness that perceives it. Therefore, emptiness cannot be said to itself exist, independently, as its own phenomenon. Emptiness is just as empty as everything else. This leaves us with no fixed point of reference from which a reality can be determined.

In the Mahāyāna Buddhism of Tibet, the emptiness of the phenomena that sentient beings encounter is often described via analogies of their illusoriness (*sgyu ma'i dpe*). Things as we know them are like a dream, like a mirage, like a reflection in a mirror, like an optical illusion, like a trick performed by a magician, like the moon reflected on the surface of a body of water. Things are like bubbles in the way they are formed, then just as readily disappear without a trace. Things are like the towns inhabited by the *gandharvas* of Indian mythology, bodiless spirits who wander throughout existence (in Tibetan they are *dri za*, "smell eaters"): although we may glimpse one of their cities in the sky, we can never actually arrive there.

As an individual internalizes this understanding of the utter insubstantiality of all phenomena, he or she is expected to become less concerned with and attached to the affairs of the human world. In Tibet, this is often described through the rubric of abandoning the "eight worldly concerns" (*'jig rten chos brgyad*). Once one has become indifferent to profit or loss, pleasure or pain, praise or blame, fame or infamy, only then can the process of genuine religious transformation begin.

An individual's karmic and realizational progress toward the ultimate goal of total liberation was traditionally described using the interrelated rubrics of the ten Stages (Sanskrit, *bhūmi*; Tibetan, *sa*—literally, "grounds") of spiritual accomplishment (often called the *bodhisattvabhūmi, byang chub sems pa'i sa*) and the five Paths (*mārga, lam*) to which they are related. These "paths" (which are themselves like stages) are typically enumerated as the Path of Accumulation (which one steps onto when first one first develops compassionate *bodhicitta*, to be described shortly), the Path of Connection, the Path of Seeing, the Path of Meditation, and, lastly, what is known as the Path of No More Learning, or the Path of Perfection—in other words, perfect buddhahood. The Madman of Ü is described as progressing through all the Stages and Paths, but also as skipping right over them. With the right teachings and motivation, it is believed that certain rare individuals can achieve spiritual perfection very quickly. What's more, in light of the emptiness of all phenomena, conceptual categories like these lack any true basis in external reality.

As elites of Mahāyāna Buddhism in India explored the implications of *śūnyatā*, they arrived at a radical and mind-bending conclusion: that the so-called states of saṃsāra and nirvāṇa exist only in relation to one another, on the same model as conceptions of "true" and "false." If saṃsāra is "that which is not nirvāṇa," and nirvāṇa is "that which is not saṃsāra," neither can be defined independently of the other. Therefore, saṃsāra and nirvāṇa are not two separate, incompatible states, but actually exist coterminously with one another. For some elite Mahāyāna Buddhists, saṃsāra and nirvāṇa were no longer understood as being two separate realms, but as constituted by different ways of viewing existence. Saṃsāra is pursuing the misleading way things appear to us; nirvāṇa is seeing the truth of how things really are. As will be expanded upon later, the Madman of Ü's Kagyü tradition further specifies that to understand how things exist is actually to understand the true nature of the mind, and vice versa.

In the *Life of the Madman of Ü*, the saṃsāric and nirvāṇic states are referred to as *'khor 'das*—"saṃsāra and the beyond"—or as *srid zhi*, which I translate as "existence and the tranquil [beyond]." While this "tranquil beyond" refers to a state (or a non-state) that enlightened beings may enter when they die and pass forever from this realm of rebirth, it also refers to the way enlightened beings can live within saṃsāra while not being subject to its laws. Although these highly realized beings may still appear to inhabit the realm of suffeing and rebirth, their experience of existence is completely different from ours. The rare individual who possesses an understanding of the utter emptiness of everything is no longer bound or limited in any way. He can engage playfully with existence, while the rest of us experience it as a burden. In his wisdom, he constitutes a stable axis around which saṃsāra, in all its multiplicity, revolves.

Gaining some familiarity with the idea of emptiness is one thing; fully internalizing it is another. According to the Mahāyāna Buddhist tradition, it is not enough to have only a conceptual understanding of these truths, arrived at by being told of them. Instead, one must spend years meditating formally on these matters, to see their truth from within, rather than without. Realization (in Tibetan, *rtogs pa*) can only come from direct personal "experience" (*nyams myong*) of the truth.

Of more immediate consequence to many Buddhists' lives, the idea of emptiness applies to directives about right and wrong ways to act. For instance, how can the taking of life be definitively classified as a wrong, immoral thing to do when in fact there can arise situations in which killing a person would actually *mitigate* wrongdoing and bring some benefit to the individuals involved? An example of this would be eliminating a murderer before he can hurt others and thereby create negative karma for himself. In this system, morality cannot be based on lists of absolute dos and do-nots. Instead, Mahāyāna Buddhism maintains that a proper moral compass can be established in pursuing the ideal of the *bodhisattva*—one who has compassionately committed himself, above all else, to relieving the suffering of other sentient beings. The bodhisattva vows to remain in saṃsāra lifetime after lifetime in order to help relieve the suffering of other sentient beings, for as long as there are beings subject to the trials of existence. A practitioner will regularly recite a prayer in which he restates his commitment to this ideal. This selfless motivation is referred to as *bodhicitta* (in Tibetan, *byang chub kyi sems*), which translates literally as the "mind of enlightenment." In other contexts, *bodhicitta* can refer to full enlightenment itself. In the Mahāyāna Buddhism of Tibet, enlightenment and the compassionate motivation to help others become folded into one.

Individuals pursuing the bodhisattva ideal improve themselves by developing what are known as the Six Perfections or *pāramitās*: generosity, ethics, patience, diligence, meditation, and wisdom about the emptiness of things—the *prajñāpāramitā*, here translated as "the Perfection of Wisdom." The bodhisattva lives in such a way that the strength of her compassion and her understanding of the emptiness of phenomena actually reinforce one another. Although the sufferings people experience may not exist as objective fact, on the conventional level they are real enough to warrant the bodhisattva's compassion; knowing appearances to be illusory, there are no limitations to how the bodhisattva might act in the course of selflessly assisting others. One should pursue the "two aims" (*don gnyis*), personal enlightenment and compassionate benefit to others, simultaneously and equally.

The expanded application of the idea of emptiness and the rise of the ideal of the bodhisattva are only two among many important developments that took place between the lifetime of the Buddha and the Dharma's eventual arrival in Tibet. In the centuries after his death, stories had developed telling not only of our Buddha, but of buddhas who came long ago, and others who would come in the future. There was now talk of semi-divine bodhisattvas, like Avalokiteśvara, the purest embodiment of compassion, and Mañjuśrī, the embodiment of wisdom. These enlightened beings travel throughout a universe much more expansive than the one the Buddha originally spoke of. Rather than there being only one world, it was now believed that there were uncountable world systems, all existing simultaneously. At any given moment in time, some of these world systems are blessed with the presence of a buddha's teachings, while others remain in the darkness of ignorance.

As this expanded mythology developed over time, Mahāyāna Buddhists came to think of the Buddha in dramatically new ways. In the early years of Buddhism, people typically conceived of Siddhartha Gautama as an ordinary human who was born on earth, then managed to achieve something extraordinary. Over time, however, the story of our Buddha was expanded upon. Now the events of his final life, as Siddhartha, were viewed as the culmination of a long course of spiritual development taking many thousands of lifetimes. What's more, Śākyamūṇi was no longer *the* Buddha, but *a* buddha—one among the many who have ever existed throughout the countless worlds. All of these buddhas possess and teach the same wisdom, which means that they together constitute a unified force of truth. Buddhahood therefore exists outside time and space.

This led Mahāyāna Buddhists to assert that buddhahood can come in three potential forms, on three different levels of manifestation. These are the three "bodies" (in Sanskrit, *kāya;* in Tibetan, *sku,* which is the honorific, respectful word for "body") of buddhahood. Buddhahood may become manifest within the physical world in the form of a living individual, as in the case of Siddhartha Gautama. These embodiments of enlightenment are said to constitute the *nirmāṇakāya,* or Emanation Body, of buddhahood. Meanwhile, the enlightened deities that one encounters in the visionary world, the world entered into via tantric meditation, are also embodiments of buddhahood, although they do not have saṃsārically manifested physical forms. They are said to be of the *saṃbhogakāya,* or Enjoyment Body, of buddhahood. Here the word *saṃbhoga* (in Tibetan, *longs spyod rdzogs pa*) suggests the heavenly enjoyments of divine beings. The Enjoyment Body can serve as an intermediary, facilitating communication and interaction between the enlightened and the unenlightened realms.

At the same time there is a general, all-pervading force of buddhahood that is referred to as the *dharmakāya,* the Dharma Body. Over the many world ages, the buddhas have been the source of all true wisdom. By the same token, pure wisdom constitutes this "body" of buddhahood.

In the *Life of the Madman of Ü*, Nyukla Peṇchen glosses the term Dharma Body as referring to "completely non-conceptual wisdom" (75). One's own mind—the source of one's understanding and one's reality, defined by its innate potential for awareness—is, properly understood, inseparable from the Dharma Body.

The relationship between the three "bodies" of buddhahood is sometimes described by way of an analogy. The Dharma Body is like open physical space; the Enjoyment Body is like the moon; and the Emanation Body is like the reflection of the moon on the surface of a body of water. The three are interdependent and inseparable; none can exist without the other two. The three "bodies" comprise the totality of buddhahood, which is both unitary and multiple, all-encompasing and specific—serene, as an unchanging source of potentiality, and active, as the unenlightened engage with it.

Further, because all things in the mental, the metaphysical, and the physical dimensions exist only as they are perceived and constructed by individual beings (emptiness negates the possibility of an objective external reality), *everything* that may ever exist within saṃsāra has been brought about by *awareness* of it. All awareness has a luminous, buddha-like quality. Therefore buddhahood, as basic awareness, actually pervades and proves coterminous with all things. Some translators thus render the term *dharmakāya* as the "truth" or "reality body." This understanding of the *dharmakāya* entails a major problem for the tradition, however: if everything is pervaded by the *dharmakāya*, it follows that our discursive thoughts or delusory ideations (*rnam rtog*) are also of the *dharmakāya*—a view that many Buddhists find anathema. The Madman of Ü addresses this paradox in a conversation with his disciples (165–6).

Another major development between the early days of Buddhism and the time when it was finally brought over the Himalayas to the Land of Snows was the rise of Buddhist tantra, which will be addressed separately later in this Introduction.

The Religion of Tibet

In Indian and Tibetan Buddhism, karma is a central concern. People commit sins (*sdig*) and negative actions, which creates *karma* (in Tibetan, *las*) that will continue to bind them to existence in the future. We may also commit acts of virtue (*dge ba*) and generate religious merit (*bsod nams*), which can improve our individual situations. Thus one's own personal balance of karma and merit matters a great deal, determining what we experience in life. But once one achieves enlightenment, the question of one's karma or merit becomes irrelevant, since they are ultimately just as illusory as anything else.

But as it took root in Tibet, the system formulated by the Lord of Sages became intertwined with other ways of understanding the world. Thus Tibetan Buddhists traditionally believed that there are other important factors, unrelated to issues of karma, that can also shape the outcomes of our lives.

Perhaps most important, many Tibetans believed in the existence of various classes of disembodied spirit beings. Although demons were rarely seen, everyone knew of their handy work. Their interventions might be perceived in cases of illness or other acute misfortune. Demons were also known for harassing and distracting meditators staying in retreat. Traditionally, demons were conceived of as autonomous, external spirit beings, but also as being anything that might stand in the way of spiritual perfection. One of the "demons" that must be defeated is personal pride.

Bodies of water were believed to conceal the secret world of the serpent spirits or *nāgas* (Tibetan, *klu*). Based on the mythology of India, the *nāgas* are said to serve as protectors of Buddhism as they live in a society that uncannily mirrors that of humans. At the same time, drawing from a more indigenous Tibetan mythology, *nāgas* are also associated with certain negative forces, such as leprosy or drought.

Traditionally, Tibetans also believed in the existence of some constellation of low-level gods and goddesses, each with his or her own backstory. These unseen spirit beings of limited power tend to be associated with specific geographic features of the varied landscape, from ethereal mountain peaks to smaller formations of more local significance. Any usable piece of land is likely to fall within the domain of an individual earth spirit, with whom one has to maintain good relations. There are deities particular to a clan or even a household, who function as a vital means of memorializing their histories and values. Deities associated with fertility and increase are universally popular. Jambhala or Vaiśravaṇa, the god of the North, is associated with wealth. He is depicted as holding a mongoose that magically disgorges precious jewels.

Some of these spirit beings are regarded as "Dharma protectors" (*chos skyong*). The protector uses his capacities to prevent misfortune from befalling a Buddhist community. For this reason, much of what the protector does to aid the lineage must necessarily remain invisible and unknowable to us. The very existence of the lineage, across so many generations, is sufficient proof of the protector's efficacy. The "four-armed wisdom protector" Mahākāla is of concern to the Madman of Ü throughout his spiritual life.

Topping the hierarchy of spirit beings are the *yidam* (*yi dam*), which I translate as "tutelary" deities. These supreme tantric deities, like Cakrasaṃvara and Kālacakra, are seen as embodiments of highest enlightenment. These buddhas are believed to reside in the more impressive peaks of the Himalayan range, while also existing everywhere and nowhere at once. Cakrasaṃvara is blue, dressed in skulls and ornaments made of bone, and can be seen as having either two or twelve arms, in which he holds various weapons and tantric implements. He remains in perpetual union with his consort, the red goddess Vajravārāhī. Together they trample on the bodies of lesser, non-Buddhist deities.

There are also less individualized and less powerful tantric gods and goddesses, known as "heroes" (in Sanskrit, *vīra*; Tibetan, *dpa' bo*) and *ḍākiṇīs*. They are said to swarm around and provide guidance to meditators who have achieved sufficient greatness. A number of different types of *ḍākiṇī* are mentioned within the *Life*: there are *ḍākiṇīs* of the body, of speech, of the mind; *ḍākiṇīs* associated with karma, wisdom, enlightened activity; and more. These beings can take many different forms, existing on many different levels of embodiment and reality, as invisible spirits or as human women.

Tibetans had—and continue to have—many different ways of interacting with these various spirit beings. They make offerings in the form of food, water, alcohol, pleasant odors, and melodies. Prayers and incantations can be addressed to these different beings. *Tormas* (*gtor ma*), conical ritual cakes typically made from flour and butter, are a key means of interaction with many classes of deities, whether friend or foe. Good intentions and tidings can be concentrated into the *torma*, then humbly offered to the deity. Alternatively, negative forces can be concentrated within the *torma*, then destroyed. Ritual specialists performed divinations in which gods of local, regional, or even national significance were asked to provide answers to questions of whether a particular decision will have a positive outcome, how to best deal with a case of illness, or on what day to begin an important undertaking. While a small percentage of religious elites interact with the supreme Buddhist deities during their journey toward enlightenment, most everyone has dealings with the lesser entities in the spiritual hierarchy, in hopes of meeting with success, ensuring stability, or at least to head off calamity,

Many Tibetans have put great stock in astrology, believing that endeavors are more likely to succeed or fail based on the alignment of the celestial bodies at the time when they are undertaken, and that certain facts of life (like who will make a sustainable marriage match for one another) are to some extent determined by the timing of one's birth.

In addition to and simultaneously with what has already been described, many Tibetans have also held a more "superstitious" understanding of things, based on a belief in *rten 'brel*. This is the mysterious system of "dependent connections" between occurrences, which relies on an underlying faith in the significance of resemblances. Certain actions or events were seen as resonating into the future or as foretelling it. Seeming coincidences were sometimes interpreted as signs. As described in the *Life*, the Madman of Ü used to pay close attention to the things that happened around him and to what appeared to him during his meditation, looking for indications of what he should do and what the consequences of certain actions might be. Individuals often requested a short teaching from a Buddhist master in hope that this would create a positive link (*rten 'brel*), ensuring that they would learn a good deal more from him at a later time, whether in this lifetime or a future one. People also sometimes asked the Madman of Ü to create "dependent connections" that would enable them to become wealthly in sons or material things. In 1511, when one of the Madman of Ü's disciples handed an empty skull cup to him (rather than one filled with drink), this was interpreted as indicating, or perhaps even causing, the disruption of the proper relationship (*rten 'brel*) between student and teacher. The disciple died soon thereafter (154). Although we may catch glimpses of the effects of this system, its internal workings will always remain mysterious and obscure to unenlightened beings like ourselves.[2]

The Life of the Madman of Ü makes frequent mention of "prophetic assurances" (*dbugs dbyung*). From a Western perspective, this may be considered a combination of a command and a foretelling of future happenings, and can be issued by one's lama, a buddha, or a lesser divine being.

In addition to all of these concerns, most Tibetans traditionally believed in a general factor of relative auspiciousness (*bkra shis*), similar to luck, which could be cultivated or lost. Many people wore special amulets, which they believed would foster auspiciousness and ward off evil. There were rituals and other means of combating the effects of these different types of causality.

Thus by the fifteenth century, the main religious system of Tibet incorporated various models of causality—some of which were derived from the teachings of the Victor, some of which were not. People believed that outcomes in life could be determined by the workings of karma, as dictated by basic Buddhism—but also that there were invisible spirit entities, forces of auspiciousness and negativity, the workings of "dependent connections," and even pure chance. Others, taking the view of emptiness, believed that they saw straight through all of these concerns. This was a highly heterogeneous tradition containing many beliefs which to an outsider may appear to be in contradiction, but which to an insider combined neatly to describe the mysterious ways in which life seemed to work. The system is perfect in its imperfection, characterized by contradictions, uncertainties, and ironies, the likes of which our lives, beliefs, and cultures always seem to entail.

Tantra

For the past millennium and a half, tantra—also known as Secret Mantra, Vajrayāna, or "esoteric" Buddhism—has existed as a subcurrent within many traditions of Buddhism, first in India, then in other places across Asia. Defined always in contrast with exoteric or sūtric Buddhism, tantra presents itself as the most potentially powerful form of Buddhism, since it offers the possibility of achieving enlightenment in the course of only a single lifetime. The central-most symbol in tantra is the small scepter-like implement known as the *vajra* (in Tibetan, *dorjé*, spelled *rdo rje*, meaning "the lord of stones"), which is conceived of as indestructible. While powerful, tantra is also considered to be dangerous, and those who misuse or mistreat it will find themselves spending an impossibly long time in Vajra Hell. Tibet's Buddhism is the most thoroughly tantric in all of Asia. Tibet's Buddhism is also the most highly monasticized. Much of the history of Buddhism in Tibet has been driven by the inherent tension between, on the one hand, the potentially transgressive dictates of the holy tantras and, on the other, the structured and rule-driven monastic life.

Many of the ritual actions of tantra are intended to enable the practitioner to tap into various sources of power that exist in the universe, most important among them being enlightened deities with whom the meditator enters into a deep and all-pervading relationship. The mental and physical alchemy of the Vajrayāna involves directed visualization, the repetition of *mantras*, tactile rituals, the cultivation of specific perceptions and mental states—feelings, emotions, experiences—and much more. Tantric practices often involve the use of a maṇḍala, which is a symmetrical configuration of deities (usually in the form of a central supreme divinity surrounded by its retinue of subordinates) representing the totality of an enlightened realm. The maṇḍala can be represented by a two-dimensional diagram or a three-dimensional palace. Meanwhile, a *mudrā* involves manipulating the physical body in a meaningful, symbolic way, often serving as a means to equate the practitioner with the deity.

After running away to the holy mountain of Tsari—one of the "abodes" (*gnas*) of the *yidam* Cakrasaṃvara—and becoming a monk, Künga Zangpo apprenticed himself to his first guru, Künga Namgyel, from Chuwori. The first tantric initiation ceremony Chuworipa ("the one from Chuwori") blessed the young man with pertained to the goddess Vajravārāhī, Cakrasaṃvara's other half. This would be followed in time by a great many more initiations. Such an empowerment, in which the guru reveals the maṇḍala and imparts a secret transmission to the disciple, was said to "ripen" the disciple's mental continuum, transforming the initiate into a different kind of being in the world.

Before he could study or make use of a tantric text of great significance, a disciple would need to receive a "reading transmission" (*lung*), in which the guru reads the text (often very quickly) to him. This empowers the initiate to then read and understand the text for himself. The reading transmission would often be accompanied by oral instructions (*khrid*) concerning the ideas or practices described therein.

After undergoing each ritual empowerment that opened him up to a new deity, Künga Zangpo was expected to maintain a series of vows and commitments (*samaya, dam tshig*) that he had made to the enlightened being, such as promising to do meditations on and to repeat the mantras of the deity. He would also perform deity yoga, in which he visualized himself as the deity, in sexual union with his consort, at the center of his maṇḍala palace. The union of the male and the female *yidam* deities is often said to represent the bringing together of *thabs* and *shes rab*, "skillful means and discernment": an understanding of practical applications, and discriminating wisdom. These two qualities are also represented by the complementary ritual implements of the (phallic) *vajra* and the (yonic) bell.

In time, these practices are meant to result in the meditator's achieving full self-identification with the deity. By becoming the deity, one gains all of his or her excellent qualities, including enlightenment itself.

Künga Zangpo had this kind of relationship with a number of beings that fall under the category of *yidam*, or "tutelary deities," but his chief concern was to achieve union with Cakrasaṃvara. Much of Künga Zangpo's practice and lifestyle was based ultimately on the *Laghusaṃvara Tantra* (which I refer to as the *Cakrasaṃvara Tantra*) and the *Hevajra Tantra*. (Throughout the *Life*, the *Hevajra Tantra* is referred to by the more common name of *brtag gnyis*, the *Two-Parted*.) The deities Hevajra and

Cakrasaṃvara, whose identities are not always kept strictly separated, are both referred to as "Heruka."

The tutelary deity's perfect understanding of the emptiness of all phenomena has the corrolary of a perpetual feeling of bliss (*bde ba*). Thus one of the indications of progress in achieving self-identification with the deity is feeling bliss oneself. When one reaches the highest state, this becomes the great bliss (*bde ba chen po*). The sought-for knowledge is often referred to as "great bliss wisdom" (*bde chen ye shes*), for the two are inseparable.

Many advanced tantric practices deal with the movements of the psychophysical "winds" (*prāṇa* in Sanskrit, *rlung* in Tibetan) and "drops" (*bindu, thig le*) that circulate within the yogic body, a system of channels (*nāḍī, rtsa*) that run throughout the physical frame. This "subtle" body, sometimes called the "*vajra* body" (*rdo rje lus*), cannot be seen with the eye, but it is known by meditators who can visualize it inside themselves. This circulatory system is composed of the central channel running from the top of the head down to the tip of the sex organ; the left and right channels (*rasanā* and *lalanā*), which crisscross the central one (*avadhūti*); the lesser channels that branch out from the four or more *cakra*s or "wheels" (in Tibetan, *'khor lo*) located at the points where the three main channels meet; and the thousands of lesser channels that branch out into the body from those. The "winds" that move through this network like currents are the means of our most essential physical processes, including movement and respiration. But the winds are also the means of our mental processes, and thus the practitioner who can manipulate and control his winds will gain perfect control over his own mind. There are different types of winds, both coarse and subtle, associated with karma, wisdom, and other matters. The "downward-voiding" wind, for example, controls the discharge and retention of bodily wastes. The practitioner must force the primary winds into the central channel (*rtsa dbu ma*), which connotes the Buddhist ideals of perfect focus, equanimity, and even seeing the truth of emptiness. Achieving mastery over the winds can thus bring health, longevity, miraculous abilities, and eventually full enlightenment. In the course of the two parts of the *Life*, the Madman of Ü is attributed with being able to lift boulders, to heal himself, and to disappear—all on account of his control of his psychophysical winds.

In order to keep the subtle, yogic body functioning optimally, a tantrika needed to perform the "yogic exercises" (*yantra, 'khrul 'khor*), which are a series of bodily poses and stretches combined with visualization and controlled breathing. These exercises have the power to undo any knots or constrictions in the channels and *cakra*s, ensuring the healthy circulation of the winds. The drawings in figures 1 through 6 depict some of these exercises.

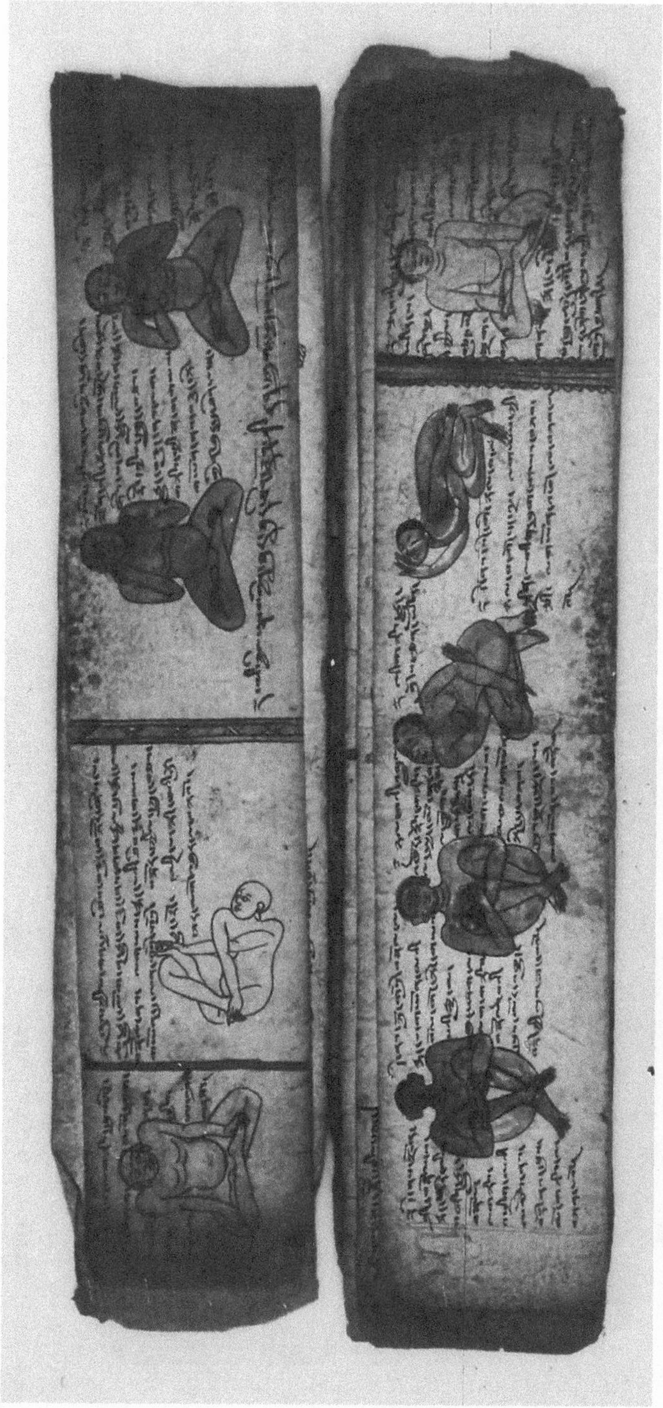

FIGURES 1 THROUGH 6 Yogic exercises (*yantra, 'khrul 'khor*) pertaining to the Six Dharmas of Nāropa

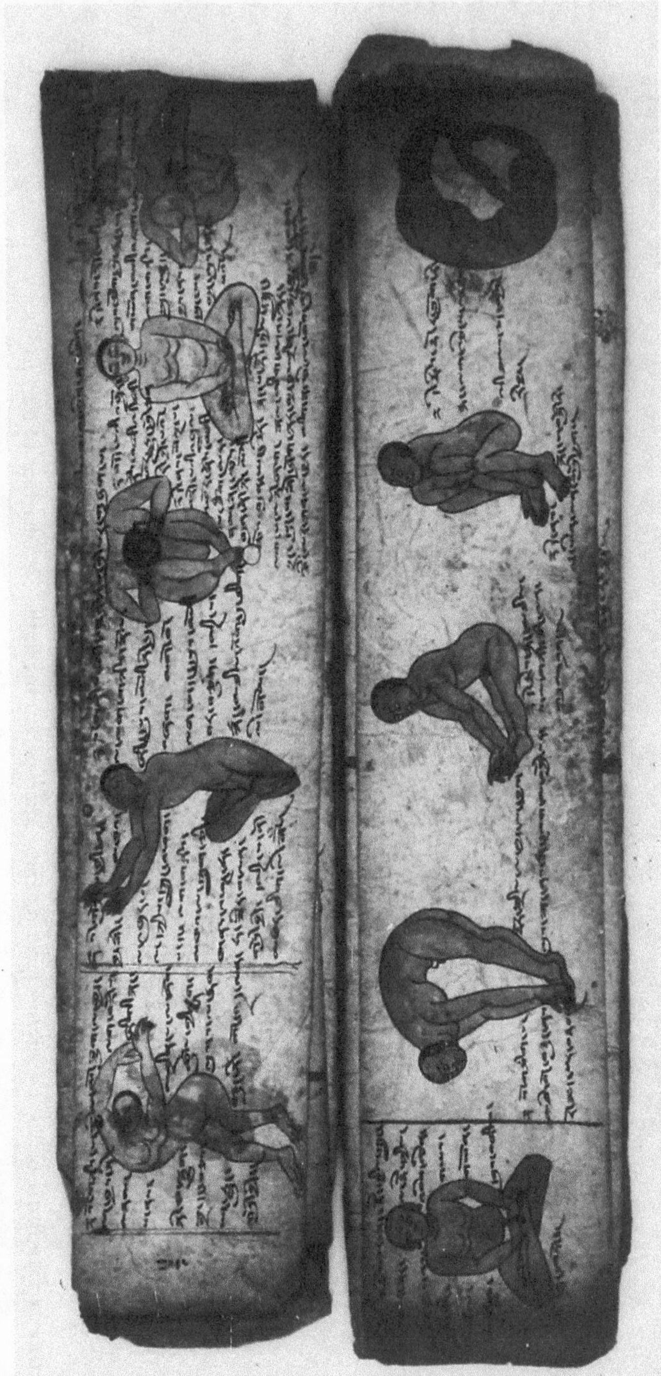

FIGURES 1 THROUGH 6 Continued

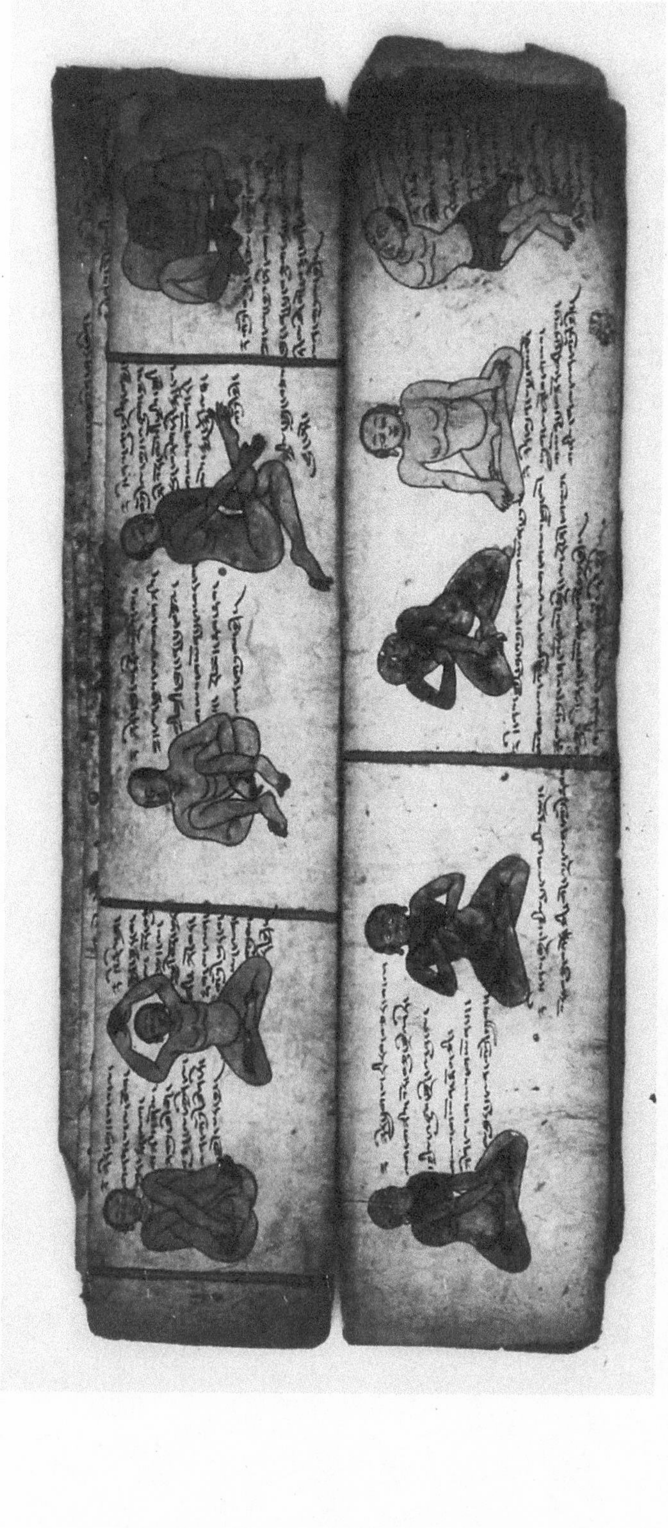

FIGURES 1 THROUGH 6 Continued

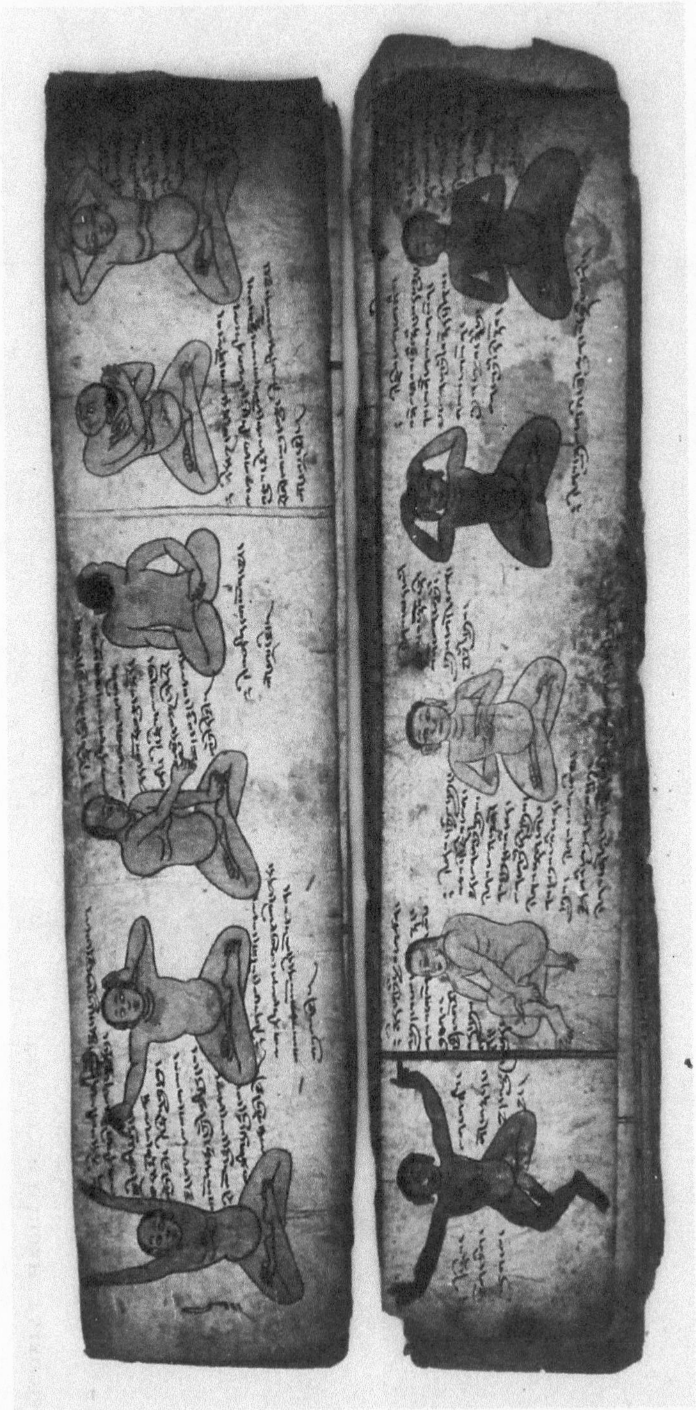

FIGURES 1 THROUGH 6 Continued

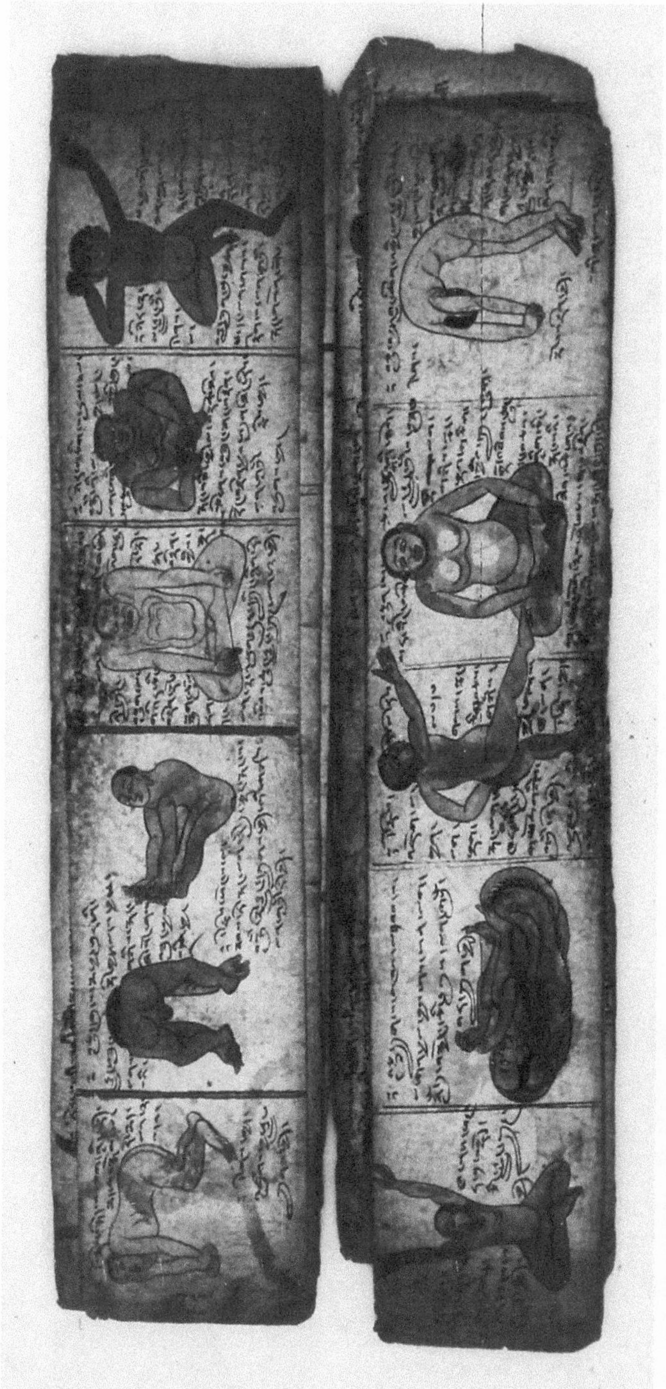

FIGURES 1 THROUGH 6 Continued

FIGURES 1 THROUGH 6 Continued

There are places in the yogic body that are said to correspond to twenty-four tantric Buddhist holy sites in India. As mentioned in the *Life,* the very top of the practitioner's head corresponds to and remains mystically connected with Puliramalaya; the crown of his head corresponds to Jālandhara; and so on (96). Tantra frequently plays with the interrelations between the internal and the external, since microcosm and macrocosm together encompass a single reality. This connects the individual practitioner—bodily and theoretically—with concerns of much greater scope than his own self.

We can gain some sense of how these associations played out by considering the way the *Life of the Madman of Ü* portrays the holy mountain of Tsari (*tsa ri* or *tsA ri*). To an unenlightened person, it may look like an ordinary, earth-and-rock mountain. But this is to take in only the most superficial level of reality. Tsari is one of the "abodes" of Cakrasaṃvara; his subordinate deities inhabit the lesser mountains around it. This means that the entire area is in fact a maṇḍala. Tsari is also said to be the equivalent of the divine realm of Khecara (*mkha' spyod*), home of the *ḍākiṇīs*—a slice of heaven on earth. Further, the *Life* states that Tsari corresponds to the Indian holy place called Cāritra (in Tibetan, *tsa ri tra* or *tsA ri tra*). The name Tsari is also sometimes said to mean "channel mountain" (*rtsa ri*)—as in, the mountain *is* a working subtle body, that of Cakrasaṃvara. Tsari is also said to be a *stūpa* or a *caitya*—a Buddhist reliquary monument. For many pilgrims, simply visiting holy Tsari was understood to be a potentially powerful and transformative experience. For committed adepts of tantra, doing deity yoga or subtle body meditation in such an empowered place was believed to yield dramatic results.

In the course of the *Life,* its authors refer to all of these understandings of Tsari as a holy place, piling all of these layers of meaning on top of one another. The authors play with the name Tsari itself, spelling and transforming it in ways that suggest the different conceptions of the place. For those whose perceptions have not been purified, Tsari will continue to appear like an ordinary mountain. But for those capable of seeing the truth, Tsari is all of these special things at once. The Madman of Ü is said to have fully perceived this more perfected reality in the area surrounding Tsari: while staying there, it is said that the yogin was taken up with "connecting what is external, what is internal, and what is secret" (94).

In tantra, sexual intercourse can be used to catalyze the yogic processes within, ultimately toward arousing the forces of enlightenment that already exist inside oneself. During intercourse, the practitioner's yogic winds become amplified. If the practitioner can force the invigorated winds into the central channel, they will stimulate the flow of *bodhicitta*, which originates from the syllable *haṃ* that rests near the top of the subtle body, inside the practitioner's head. As the *haṃ* is warmed by internal yogic processes, *bodhicitta* begins to drip from it. This *bodhicitta*, in the form of a white fluid, travels down the central channel, and as it passes through the *cakras* at the throat, the heart, the solar plexus, and the sex organ, one experiences the "joys of descent" (*yas babs kyi dga' ba*). If the practitioner can then force the accumulated *bodhicitta* back up his central channel, to be stored in his brain, he will also experience the "joys of ascent" (*mas brten gyi dga' ba*).

This *bodhicitta* is understood as the very stuff of enlightenment, in the form of drops of white fluid. These drops represent—and are considered to be—religious potential. (The syllable *haṃ* from which they descend is said to be the supreme being Cakrasaṃvara himself.) Like the drops, such achievement already exists inside each of us, but can only be actuated through a good deal of concerted effort in yoga. In this way the semen generated by the ritual of tantric sex is referred to and understood as *bodhicitta*, the "mind of enlightenment." Reaching the point of orgasm constitutes the fruition of some of these key internal processes. Orgasm can also offer a sense of what enlightenment is like, as a state of non-conceptuality and bliss. But it is important that the practitioner avoid the degrading reflex of ejaculation, which would mean losing the spiritual energy that has been generated by the practice.

The biography states that the Madman of Ü achieved "the *siddhi* of 'not transferring the yogic drop'" (98), which refers to the ability to have an orgasm without ejaculating (which is indeed physically possible). The biography also states that he mastered the teachings on the "action seal" (*karmamudrā, las kyi phyag rgya*) or sexual consort (68). Thus there are indications that Künga Zangpo most likely had intercourse as part of his tantric practice, although we are told nothing specific about his sexual history, or the women who necessarily played an indispensable part in it.

Relationships under tantric subculture replicate those of the lay, biological family. The guru is the disciple's spiritual father; the guru's consort is his spiritual mother; the disciple's fellow initiates are his Dharma brothers and sisters. In time, he may have a consort, disciples, and eventually grand-disciples of his own. The ritual by which the supplicant gets initiated into this new family is based on the physiology of human procreation. In some circles, the ritual was performed in such a way that at its climax, the master would have intercourse with his consort. The resulting mixture of ejaculate—*bodhicitta*—and vaginal fluid would then be dabbed onto the tongue of the disciple. At the moment of tasting this empowered nectar, the newly reconceived disciple is meant to achieve an understanding of the emptiness of all phenomena, combined with a corporeal bliss. He will enter into his new life with an altogether different understanding of the world. This type of ritual was only one of the many avenues by which the theme of sex became an important element of tantric culture. It is unclear whether or not sex was used in this way during the tantric initiations Künga Zangpo underwent or gave to his own disciples. In Tibet, the ritual was often performed in a modified form, with the intercourse visualized in meditation rather than literally enacted, and a substitute used in place of actual semen.

All of the preceding was practiced behind a veil of secrecy (often a porous one, in spite of the tradition's rhetoric), by which the separation between the initiated and the uninitiated was maintained. Those who had not received the secret instructions would be unable to decode the sacred tantric scriptures. Those who had not been empowered would find their deity yoga to be fruitless.

The world of tantra is a vast one, including within it a broad range of practices. Tantric rituals can involve the consumption of substances considered impure in traditional Indian culture, like alcohol, human waste, and the flesh of various animals. Rather than avoid such things, the practitioner is to revel in them, thus transmuting them from a source of pollution into a source of power. The ultimate source of all such pollution is death itself. The tantric practitioner is to embrace the all-powerful force that is death by performing the cult of the macabre. Tantric imagery is rife with skulls, violence, and the charnel grounds where corpses are disposed of. Tantric practitioners may invoke ugly, nightmarish forces through the recitation of incantations and the fabrication of mystical diagrams. Some practitioners of tantra prepared exotic potions through elaborate rituals. Their accompanying incantations transformed them into substances that could grant superhuman capabilities. Much of what serious tantrikas did would have been considered witchcraft if it had been performed in European society at the time.

Tantric meditations are often grouped under the categories of the Generation Stage (*bskyed rim*) and the more advanced Perfection Stage (*rdzogs rim*). (These terms can also be translated as Development Stage and Completion Stage.) Generation Stage meditations are typically said to be those that involve the practitioner's visualizing the deity, as well as visualizing himself *as* the deity. Perfection Stage practices are said to be of two types: those "with" and those "without elaborative elements" (*spros bcas, spros med*). The former include practices involving the subtle, yogic body, while the latter are more abstract explorations of the profound.

Through these and other types of meditation and ritual, practitioners of tantra hope ultimately to achieve the "supreme *siddhi*" (*mchog gi dngos grub*), meaning total enlightenment. It is believed that in the process they would achieve "mundane *siddhis*" (*thun mong gi dngos grub*), which are typically listed as eight superhuman abilities: to make magical pills, to heal peoples' eyes, to locate valuables buried underground, to prove impervious to attacks with weapons, to fly, to become invisible, to go unaffected by illness, and to live for as long as one likes. Although possessing these *siddhi*s may empower one to perform impressive and awe-inspiring feats, they should never be allowed to distract from the pursuit of enlightenment.

The achievement of *siddhi*s made one a *siddha*, which can be thought of as a tantric saint. One proved one's *siddha*hood by making "indications of one's *siddhis*" (*grub rtags*). These are miraculous feats, such as flying, leaving footprints in solid rock, and emerging unhurt from bodily harm. Such miracles could be understood as resulting from the achievement of the mundane *siddhi*s, or could be understood as indicating one's having a fully integrated understanding of the emptiness of phenomena. While ordinary people are subject to the elements of the physical world, the enlightened *siddha* has mastery over them. When the Madman of Ü effortlessly makes a handprint on the surface of a boulder, Lhatong Lotsāwa describes the rock as "seen as symbolizing the solidified mass of ideation accumulated since beginningless time, having been hacked at by the pickaxe of wisdom" (151).

One way to indicate great spiritual accomplishment is to make one's own body disappear at the moment of death, which is known as attaining the "rainbow body" (*'ja' lus*). The *Life* states that the Madman of Ü could have shown the miracle of the rainbow body when he died, but instead chose to leave bodily relics behind, for the sake of his faithful followers.

In the course of their religious careers, some Tibetan Buddhists concurrently pursued the three goals of becoming a *siddha*, living as a true a bodhisattva, and striving to achieve full buddhahood. They thus cultivated, simultaneously, supernatural powers, compassion, and the enlightenment that entails an escape from all of existence. In the circles within which the Madman of Ü moved, great spiritual accomplishment was often referred to as achieving the state of a *vajradhara* (*rdo rje 'chang*), a "holder of the vajra." In the Kagyü tradition, Vajradhara is also the name of the primordial buddha. In Tibet, the spiritual accomplishments of some individuals are alluded to by the label of *mkhas grub*, which means being very learned, and also greatly accomplished in meditation.

Although the highest state of realization that Vajrayāna practice is meant to engender may strike the reader as being something free-form, it was described and determined beforehand. Each of the sects of Tibetan Buddhism has developed its own categories and terminology for describing the realization of the ultimate emptiness of all phenomena, breaking down the abstract into identifiable parts. The various states and forces of tantra are in this way quantified and commodified. Thus at the same time that it undermines the validity of all the conceptual categories of mundane, worldly thought, tantra offers countless categories of its own. In spite of its rhetoric of fluidity and freedom, tantra must be thought of as constituting a complex and coherent system in its own right.

Throughout his career, Künga Zangpo was also engaged with aspects of Buddhism that were not tantric in nature. He studied some of sūtric Buddhism's texts and practices as a foundation for his training in tantra. He also developed the abilities to slip into specific states of concentration, called *samādhis*, which had been long since codified by the sūtric Buddhist tradition. The term *samādhi* (in Tibetan, *ting nge 'dzin*) is often translated as "meditative absorbtion" or "meditative stabilization." These include the states of mind referred to as the "Going Heroically," "*Vajra*-Like," and "Overwhelming All of Phenomenal Existence, Saṃsāra and Nirvāṇa, with Glory" *samādhis*. The biography describes how remaining within these non-tantric meditative states at certain times allowed the Madman of Ü to do miraculous things.

The Kagyü

Kyepo Dar did not wade directionlessly into the expansive waters of Tibetan religion, but from the very beginning pursued the system of training offered by the Kagyü sect. He would remain dedicated to the Kagyü to the very end of his life.

The mythology of the Kagyü maintains that it was established, as a unique tradition within Buddhism, when the buddha Vajradhara appeared before Tilopa in the holy land of Oḍḍiyāṇa (often said to be located in northwestern India) to impart to him some special teachings. Tilopa entrusted these teachings to his disciple Nāropa, who had been a famous scholar at Nālandā monastery before he departed to follow the tantric path. The Tibetan Marpa Chökyi Lodrö (1012–1097) traveled to India, trained under Nāropa, then brought the teachings back to his homeland, where he gave them to Milarepa (1028/40/52–1111/23), the foremost saint of the Kagyü in Tibet. In his youth, the boy who would later become known as Milarepa experienced grave personal injustices, then exacted murderous revenge by way of black magic. Feeling remorse for what he had done, Milarepa turned to Buddhism, toiling extensively in order to ingratiate himself to the guru Marpa. Eventually Marpa accepted Milarepa as a student and gave him initiations and teachings. Then, after years of meditation and extreme asceticism in the mountains along the modern Tibet–Nepal border, Milarepa achieved highest enlightenment. Milarepa is often referred to as Laughing Vajra, the name said to have been given to him by the *ḍākiṇīs* who appeared above the maṇḍala by which Marpa initiated him into his relationship with Cakrasaṃvara. Milarepa passed the teachings on to his disciples, including Gampopa (1079–1153) and Rechungpa (1083/84–1161).

In the first few generations after Milarepa, a variety of subsects, traditions, and lineages were established within the broader Kagyü, all of which connect back to their shared original mythology through direct master–student relationships. The Drukpa, Pakmodrupa, Drikung, Shangpa, Taklung, Karma, and other subsects each had their own monastic institutions, favored teachings, and eminent hierarchs. The foremost disciple of Gampopa, Düsum Khyenpa (1110–1193), would be considered the first in the Karmapa reincarnation lineage, which is central to the Karma Kagyü. The Madman of Ü lived during the time of the Seventh and Eighth Karmapas, Chödrak Gyatso (1454–1506) and Mikyö Dorjé (1507–1554). There were other important incarnations with whom Künga Zangpo had dealings, based at Drikung, Taklung, and other places in central Tibet.

One touchstone for the culture of the Kagyü were the *dohās*. These are songs expressing supreme tantric insights, attributed to the famous Buddhist *siddhas* of India (the greatest of whom are referred to as *mahāsiddhas*, often enumerated as eighty or eighty-four), read in their Tibetan translation. The foremost among them were the three cycles of *dohās* by Saraha, which are mentioned repeatedly in the *Life of the Madman of Ü*. Often when the *Life* simply states that the yogin received or taught "the *dohās*," it is Saraha's songs specifically that are meant.

In some ways, the Kagyü can be said to value meditation and direct experience over study and reasoning oneself to the truth. Some have even taken to referring to the Kagyü itself as "the Meditation Tradition" (*sgrub brgyud*).

The Mahāmudrā and the Six Dharmas of Nāropa

In the Kagyü tradition, the highest realizational goal is described using the rhetoric of the Mahāmudrā or "Great Seal" (in Tibetan, *phyag rgya chen po*). Achieving the Mahāmudrā *is* enlightenment, and thus it constitutes the "supreme *siddhi*." Within the *Life*, Nyukla Peṇchen describes the Mahāmudrā as "an understanding of reality in which phenomena are neither superimposed upon nor negated by conceptions of existence or emptiness" (82). The Mahāmudrā is a fully internalized understanding of the emptiness of everything, including both external phenomena and an individual's perceptions. Everything is "sealed" with the fact of its true nature, likened to the way a stamp is pressed into the wax seal on an official decree.

Part of Mahāmudrā practice involves examining the ordinary perceiving mind, in order to understand the nature of awareness. Thoughts arise out of nowhere and dissolve into nothing. But the natural state of mind is not blankness, but a clear awareness. Although we may experience all sorts of pleasant and unpleasant things, the fact of experiencing remains the same. This is indicative of a subtler and universal kind of awareness, which remains throughout one's life and which is passed on after death. This basic awareness, the true nature of the mind, is the universal seed of enlightenment. This basic capacity for awareness exists in all sentient beings, and has nothing to do with accumulated knowledge or intellectual ability. All thoughts and perceptions, all conditioned phenomena, can only come into being if there is a mind, which is unconditioned, to reflect and support them. Knowing this is the key to cutting the very root of saṃsāric ignorance. This understanding must necessarily not be dualistic in nature, but self- or reflexively aware (*rang rig*).

When assuming the view of the Mahāmudrā, there is no referenece point, internal or external, from which to determine a truth or undertake an action. Because a perceiver and its perceived object cannot exist except in dependence upon one another, both mental formations and what *seem* to be external appearances are in fact of precisely the same nature. Kagyüpas maintain that one's entire experience of existence is filtered through an individual's subjective perspective, and thus to understand the nature of the mind is to understand the nature of everything. (To understand the nature of the mind is also to gain perfect control over it, and everything else.) One's relationship to one's thoughts determines the texture of one's reality, which is discovered to be pliant and varied.

A key concept in this system is that of *lhan cig skyes pa* (in Sanskrit, *sahajā*), which I translate as "co-emergence." The term is frequently used in the Mahāmudrā tradition to indicate the nature of things: all phenomena are generated by, or "co-emerge with," the mind. Paradoxically, things are knowable because they are empty projections, and all that can be known must necessarily be empty. Anything that you see or experience, anything that you might feel or think—whether pleasant or unpleasant, whether seemingly positive or negative—is of the *dharmakāya*, the Dharma Body, the mind as the generator of all reality. Everything is co-emergent with the mind itself. When one recognizes that faults, experiences, and feelings arise in this way, they are in fact "self-liberated." One does not need to do anything in order to unmake them: they simply never really were. Delusion is self-dispelled. What's more, with no way of determining where one's mental projections end and external reality begins, the two categories themselves must be done away with. The "wisdom of co-emergence" (*lhan cig skyes pa'i ye shes*) refers to a nondualistic understanding in which phenomena are seen as inseparable from the mind. One cultivates this understanding through the teachings and the practices of the Mahāmudrā of Co-emergent Union, as famously described by *chennga* Sönam Gyeltsen Pel (1386–1434)—the twelfth abbot of Densa Til monastery, who is also known as Lazik Repa, or Nyernyipa, "the one who died on the twenty-second [day of the month]"—in the text titled *Dispelling the Darkness of Ignorance*. (The abbots of Densa Til are referred to by the title of *chennga*, spelled *spyan snga*, meaning "in the presence of.") There are other systems of approaching the Mahāmudrā, including the Five-Parted Mahāmudrā, the Amulet-box Mahāmudrā, and the Pebble Cycle of teachings.

Another key concept in the Mahāmudrā tradition is the "Equalization of Taste" (*ro snyoms*). This refers to the goal of achieving an attitude of sameness with respect to all the phenomena of saṃsāra, a state of complete and utter equanimity.

Getting to the goal of realizing the Mahāmudrā—at which point one transcends the forces of karma and ignorance and unlocks the potential for total compassion—requires many years of ordered religious practice and hard work. For many Kagyüpas, this means performing a set of advanced tantric practices known as the Six Dharmas of Nāropa (*nA ro chos drug*, often referred to in English as the Six Yogas of Nāropa). References to these instructions are ubiquitous throughout Künga Zangpo's training, meditation practice, and teaching career. In the following paragraphs I will give brief descriptions of each of the six practices: *tummo*, illusory body, dream yoga, luminosity, ejecting one's consciousness at the moment of death, and controlling the between-lives process.

It is often said that the most important of the Six Dharmas, the indispensable foundation for all the others, is *tummo* (*gtum mo*), or inner-fire meditation (also commonly referred to as "yogic heat"). In this practice, the meditator visualizes a red-hot syllable *a* (ཨ) inside his subtle body, located at the *cakra* seated at the base of the spine. When stoked by the yogic winds, fire blazes forth from it. The tongue of fire snakes its way up the central channel to just under the fount of enlightenment, the white syllable *haṃ*, located in the head, which melts into drops of *bodhicitta*. Sexual intercourse could be used to catalyze this process. *Tummo* is derived from Indian meditation traditions that concern themselves with the goddess Caṇḍalī—"Fiery One," *gtum mo* in Tibetan—who resides coiled at the base of one's spine. In tantric Buddhism, the fiery syllable *a* is said to be the goddess Vajravārāhī, while the syllable *haṃ* represents Cakrasaṃvara. Through the complementary processes of blazing and melting, the two become joined, reunified, as is their natural state.

A byproduct of this practice is that it can actually raise the meditator's internal body temperature significantly, enabling yogins to survive Tibetan winters wearing nothing more than a simple cotton cloth. Yogins successful in this practice would on occasion make displays of their remarkable ability to their community, or even the broader public. In the *Life of the Madman of Ü*, it is mentioned that his disciples performed what was called "the Presentation of a [Dried] Sheet" (*ras phud*). This was a formal rite in which the meditators would, while sitting in a cold, unheated place, each wrap themselves in a wet sheet. While this would put an ordinary person into shock, the meditators concentrate on their *tummo*, generate internal warmth, and dry the sheet. In recent decades, Western science has taken an interest in the remarkable and medically verifiable power of this practice.

The second of the Six Dharmas is called the illusory body (*sgyu lus*). This refers to taking control of the world of empty appearances in the course of one's waking experience and religious practice.

Dream yoga (referred to in Tibetan simply as dreaming, *rmi lam*) forms a pair with the practice of the illusory body. In dream yoga, the meditator attempts to seize control of his dreams, and to manipulate, expand, and clarify their contents. The time spent sleeping can thus become an opportunity to do further religious practice and good deeds, to meditate on the emptiness of experience, or to simply explore the vast universe we inhabit.

The practice of luminosity (*'od gsal*, often translated as "clear light") entails learning to recognize the immutability of the mind's most basic capacity for awareness. The "luminousness" of the mind is the fact that it takes in sensory perceptions. Since the mind is thus also the governor of our sense perceptions, mentation should not be thought of as existing only within ourselves, for it in fact pervades all that we perceive. All of experience is in fact nothing more than the play of luminosity. The cultivation of luminosity ideally leads to a complete transformation and purification of the practitioner's sense perceptions, resulting ultimately in clairvoyance, clairaudience, and the like.

Powa (*'pho ba*) or "transference [of consciousness]" refers to controlling the way one's sentience is ejected from the body after death. If the consciousness is simply allowed to depart from the body, it may pass out through one of the lower orifices, which is said to increase the likelihood of a bad rebirth. However, if one can force the consciousness to depart via the *cakra* at the top of the head—the "Brahmā aperture" or *brahmārandra*; *tshangs bug* in Tibetan—liberation is guaranteed. The initial training in this practice consists of the meditator's concentrating his consciousness into a single point, which he then practices moving up and down the central channel. Once he has become sufficiently adept at this, he will force his consciousness to smash through the top of his head and remain momentarily suspended above it. If the trainee is successful in this, a small, bloody hole should be detectable on the top of his head. Subsequently, if he should find himself about to die suddenly, before he has achieved enlightenment, he can quickly and safely eject his consciousness from the proper aperture. Skilled practitioners of *powa* are also believed to be able to enter into the body of a recently deceased person and force his or her consciousness out through the desired avenue.

The last of the Six Dharmas is the yoga of the intermediate or "in-between" state (*bardo*, spelled *bar do*), referring to the state between two successive lives. For most sentient beings, the period after death, when one's consciousness travels through a nightmare-like realm, is frightening and chaotic. However, those who have prepared for this experience through years of meditation can use the *bardo* to their advantage. After death, one's sensory and cogitative faculties are extinguished, meaning that there are no more sources of potential distraction. This gives adept meditators a brief window of opportunity during which enlightenment is not difficult to obtain. If a meditator does not bypass the saṃsāric process, he or she may be able to exercise choice in which life to inhabit next, among all the six realms of cyclic existence.

The first four of the Six Dharmas, as listed here, are often said to be significantly more important than the last two. The *powa* and *bardo* yogas must always necessarily be regarded as backup plans to one's foremost stated intention: to break the ties of existence in the course of one's practice in the present life, for the benefit of all beings.

There are other practices sometimes counted among the Six Dharmas, or as comprising an expanded list of prized yogas. One of these is the "action seal" (*las rgya, karmamudrā*), which refers to sexual yoga performed with a consort. The yoga of "entering the dead" (*grong 'jug*) enables a meditator to implant his consciousness within the dead body of another sentient being. Existing in parallel to and overlapping with the Six Dharmas of Nāropa are the Six Dharmas of Niguma, who was storied to have been Nāropa's sister. The Six Dharmas of Niguma were long a specialty of the Shangpa subsect of the Kagyü.

The Six Dharmas of Nāropa are of central importance in the life of the Madman of Ü. Nevertheless, they always remain a means to the ultimate end of realizing the Mahāmudrā, which ultimately both trumps and undermines them completely.

Fifteenth-Century Tibet

In the course of his life, the Madman of Ü dealt not only with tantric yogins and Kagyüpas, but with members of many different groups within society, both clerical and lay. He had a number of unpleasant confrontations with *geshés* (*dge bshes*), well-educated monks who represent institutional, "book" learning in Buddhism. He is also described as once having an altercation with some *mantrikas* (*sngags pa*) of the Nyingma sect, the oldest Buddhist tradition in Tibet. Some of the religious figures Künga Zangpo encountered and studied under were considered *tülkus* (*sprul sku*)—reincarnations of past masters. Each of these different religious identities entailed its own configuration of relationships with Tibetan society's power structures. While some individuals were born into religious significance and notoriety, others, like Künga Zangpo, achieved prominence entirely through their own efforts in the present life.

Künga Zangpo lived during the time of the First and Second Dalai Lamas, although neither was known by that title during his time. (After the "Third" Dalai Lama was given the praiseful epithet of "Ocean Lama" by the Mongolian warlord Altan Khan in 1578, it was applied to the first two posthumously.) The Dalai Lamas were a new reincarnation lineage of only middling importance at the time; it by no means appeared destined that they and their Geluk sect would rise to political and religious dominance, as they would in the first half of the seventeenth century. Although in the fifteenth century the Geluk sect was still in its adolescence, it nevertheless constituted a significant disruptive force in the Buddhist culture of Tibet.

While the vast majority of Tibetan laymen were struggling to eke out a living through subsistence agriculture, there was a stratum of elites, comprising a tiny percentage of the population, who dominated central Tibetan society. Land was the foremost commodity, and ownership of plots of usable land was the foundation of all power. Tibet's rocky and uneven terrain strictly limited the amount of land that could be cultivated. What's more, at this high altitude, and in the rain shadow of the Himalayas, crop yields were rarely better than marginal. These factors combined to make productive agricultural lands all the more precious. Individual lords inherited, were gifted, or forcibly seized control over plots of land, which were farmed by the peasantry. The produce of these lands was the main currency of this economy.

At the peak of official governmental power in central Tibet during this time was the *gongma* (*gong ma*), which means something like "superior one," understood similarly to the way we would take the title of "emperor." With its official seat at Nedong, not far from Künga Zangpo's home village, this position was passed down through the men of one wealthy and powerful family of noblemen. But the *gongma*'s power was often rather precarious and limited. He had to rely on other nobles to faithfully serve as the local administrators of his government. Their primary responsibility in this capacity would have been to oversee the collection of taxes. Across generations, it was through these noble families that state power was exercised.

But these nobles, often from families that were in direct competition with the *gongma*'s own, had their own agendas, and Tibetan political affairs were dominated by the ever-shifting relationships between these families. Some of these families had extensive landholdings, allowing them to dominate the affairs of a particular area for long stretches of time. Although these positions of power were in some cases held by the same family for generations, those who ran afoul of or betrayed the central government could be stripped of their official holdings and forced into retirement from politics. But nobles had their own private armies to do their bidding (often composed of conscripts) and did not always capitulate without a fight. The central government therefore had to make its political appointments based on the existing map of power. Tibet's aristocrats were often major patrons of Buddhism. Many of the seats of ecclesiastical power were held by sons of these elites.

The Madman of Ü lived during a period of civil war. The *gongmas* of the Pakmodru regime had tentatively ruled central Tibet since the middle of the fourteenth century. But starting in the 1430s, they faced a rebellion led by the Rinpungpa family, based in Tsang. Although the Rinpungpas and their allies at times fought openly with the Pakmodru regime, they nevertheless continued to occupy official positions within its government. Such were the politics of the day. The members of the Rinpungpa family were among Künga Zangpo's primary patrons. He met at various times with the ruling head of the family, the famous warlord Dönyö Dorjé (1463–1512), as well as with Dönyö Dorjé's uncle, his father, and his brother. Another major supporter and patron of the Madman of Ü was Tashi Dargyé (died in 1499), a powerful ruler based in Ja, who was an ally of the Rinpungpas and an occasional antagonist of the Pakmodru regime.

The Madman of Ü

Among the many remarkable yogins and yoginīs of Tibetan Buddhism over the last thousand years (not to speak of the uncountable Buddhist ascetics of other places in Asia during the past two and a half millennia), Künga Zangpo is notable, even notorious, for three main reasons.

First, he is one of a myriad of Tibetan Buddhist ascetics who have taken on strict, long-term meditative retreat. Künga Zangpo spent these periods of a year, three years, or more, living in particular caves or monastic retreats. While attempting to live in such a manner that he was effectively cut off from the world, the meditator would perform specific visualizations and other types of practice, day in and day out, until signs of accomplishment arose, and beyond. These heroic individuals have made careers out of their religious practice.

Second, the subject of this biography is among scores of Tibetan Buddhists over the past millennium who have become renowned as "holy madmen" (*smyon pa*)—in some cases referred to as "mad *siddhas*" (*grub thob smyon pa*), "mad *lamas*" (*bla ma smyon pa*), or "mad yogins" (*rnal 'byor smyon pa*). The holy madmen and madwomen of Tibetan Buddhism have lived and traveled in every region of the Tibetan cultural world. Their lives and careers have followed many different trajectories, imbuing their "madness" with different nuances of meaning. Many were extremely dedicated Kagyüpa ascetics who, through their rhetoric and behavior, toyed with the idea of madness-as-enlightenment. Other "mad" Tibetan ascetics were members of the Cutting (*gcod*) tradition. Some of these individuals lived in manners that were by no means unconventional, but nevertheless signed their writings using "madman" as a pen name or a pseudonym. As individuals have achieved enduring reputations as "madmen," they have always done so with the assent, participation, and input of Tibetan society at large. Some madmen were particularly controversial and divisive figures, about whom having strong and widely varying opinions was natural. The career of the Madman of Ü is only one example of how the rhetoric of religious madness can be employed.

Third, Künga Zangpo is among a small number of Tibetan yogins—perhaps a few dozen in total—who sought to establish themselves as foremost upholders of the tantric tradition by enacting a literalist reading of the Unexcelled Yoga tantras (*rnal 'byor bla na med pa'i rgyud, *anuttarayogatantra*)—the most transgressive of the Buddhist tantras, written in late first-millennium India. Sangyé Gyeltsen, "the Madman of Tsang," was also a member of this group, although it was by no means the case that all of these figures became renowned as "madmen." They focused in particular on the parts of the Unexcelled Yoga tantras that describe the yogic training variously referred to as the Practice (*caryā* in Sanskrit, *spyod pa* in Tibetan), the Observance (*vrata, brtul zhugs*), the Practice of the Observance (*caryāvrata, vratacaryā, brtul zhugs spyod pa*), and so on. (The Secret Practice, *gsang spyod*, was considered part of or perhaps an alternative way of referring to the Practice; Künga Zangpo declares that the Secret Practice is "the essence of all the Teachings and all the treatises"; 176.) The Observance, or the Practice, was a prescribed period of ascetic wandering during which the trainee was meant to submit himself to experiences that challenged him to make manifest his understanding of emptiness. He was to pay no heed to where he went or slept, nor to what he ate or drank. He was to submit himself to jarring and frightening experiences, like those cultivated by the Madman of Ü when he consumed disgusting things or provoked people to attack him. The practitioner is also instructed to dress in a set of six ornaments made from human bone, including a head ornament, earrings, a necklace, a Sacred Thread, bangles on the wrists, and bangles on the ankles. The directions often specify smearing one's body with the ashes of a corpse.

To dress in this way was to assume the same costume as the Herukas—the fearsome, wrathful deities featured in certain Buddhist tantras, who are representatives of supreme enlightenment and all of reality itself. The tantric literalism of the Madman of Ü and the Madman of Tsang amounted

FIGURE 7 "Homage to Künga Zangpo, the Madman of Ü."

in many ways to a sort of lived deity yoga, in which they collapsed their identity with that of the Heruka within ordinary, waking, public life—not just during formal seated meditation. Both emulated the deity so completely that many people referred to them as Herukas.

Figure 7 shows the Madman of Ü in his tantric, Heruka garb. Künga Zangpo is here depicted with a meditation belt or strap (*sgom thag* or *pus 'khyud*) draped over his shoulder like a sash, which is typical for dedicated meditators. While seated in actual meditation, the strap is worn around the lower back and beneath the knees, giving stability and support. Also clearly discernable, and more characteristic of Künga Zangpo's unique lifestyle, are earrings, bangles on his wrists, upper arms, and ankles, and a Sacred Thread (*mchod phyir thogs*), which is a set of interconnected garlands of bone worn over the torse. In this picture the yogin holds a cup fashioned from a human skull, while his richly ornamented *khaṭvāṅga* staff stands next to him. The reasoning behind Künga Zangpo's decision to give up his monkhood and take on this super-tantric lifestyle is described in detail by Nyukla Peṇchen (85). Künga Zangpo's enacting what can be called a fundamentalist reading of tantra evoked a wide range of highly polarized opinions. This lifestyle struck many of his Tibetan contemporaries as being anachronistic, a relic from a form of Buddhism that no longer existed in the world. Others denounced it as downright un-Buddhist. Many others, meanwhile, understood this lifestyle to represent that of an unquestionably enlightened being. Much more is said about all of these matters in *The Holy Madmen of Tibet*.

For many decades of his life, Künga Zangpo was an itinerant wanderer, ranging from the monasteries of central Tibet to particular holy mountains, to the six or twelve "fortresses" where Milarepa was believed to have meditated, to Kathmandu—and even, according to the biography, all the way to India's Bodhgaya, where the Buddha is believed to have achieved his enlightenment. In 1502, however, Künga Zangpo founded and settled at his own monastery, called Tsimar Pel, in the area of Penyül, just northeast of Lhasa. The abbotship of the monastery and the responsibility of continuing the Madman of Ü's spiritual work were passed on to a boy described as his nephew (*dbon sras*), whom he named Künzang Nyida Pembar.[3] This nephew was most likely the offspring of one of Künga Zangpo's brothers, with one of their shared wives. If he had not renounced his inheritance and become a monk, the child would have been, in effect, his own son. Thanks to the spiritual prominence attained by the Madman of Ü, the economic unit of his family gained access to significant new lines of wealth. By establishing this monastery in the last decades of his life, the charisma generated through the yogin's wandering and provacitve asceticism was concentrated in one place. Tsimar Pel, its community, and the yogin's nephew would become the treasuries of his holiness after his death.

Thus in the course of his life, Künga Zangpo was many things in addition to being a "madman." He was a son, a sibling, an uncle, a student, a meditator, a teacher, a tantric figurehead, a disruptive presence, and the founder of a religious community.

The Biography and Its Authors

The biography translated here was written in two parts, by two primary authors. The first part (177 folio sides in the 1972 edition) was composed by

FIGURE 8 "Homage to Ngawang Drakpa, the great *paṇḍita*."

Ngawang Drakpa (1458–1515; figure 8), a monk known as Nyukla Peṇchen, or "the great Paṇḍita of Nyukla." As is mentioned in the *Life*, Nyukla Peṇchen first encountered the Madman of Ü around 1490, when the yogin arrived at the village of Nyukla wearing his strange costume. The people harbored such skepticism about the odd yogin that they were moved to attack him ferociously. After he miraculously survived, the yogin was invited to stay at Nyukla for a while, during which time Ngawang Drakpa got to know him well. In the fourth chapter, Nyukla Peṇchen relates the proceedings of a conversation that took place between them during this time. Just a few years later, in 1494, he would write the first part of the biography. The bulk of Künga Zangpo's biography was in circulation throughout the second half of his life, from the age of about thirty-six onward. This makes the Madman of Ü a rather unique case in the history of saintly figures, since they are typically not immortalized hagiographically until after their deaths.

Nyukla Peṇchen may have been a cousin of the most powerful and infamous Tibetan layman of the day, Dönyö Dorjé of the Rinpungpa family.

The text's printing in 1494 was sponsored by a lord named Tamdrin Tseten, who was most likely a member of Nyukla Peṇchen's family. A woman who served as a key patron of the Madman of Ü during this time was likely Nyukla Peṇchen's mother.

A biographical sketch of Nyukla Peṇchen is given in the *Scholar's Feast*, a Kagyü-centric history of Tibet written in 1545 by Tsuklak Trengwa (1504–1564/66), the second in the Pawo incarnation lineage. (The young Tsuklak Trengwa came to visit Künga Zangpo at his monastery in the mid-1520s, as described in chapter 8; 172.) This brief account of Nyukla Peṇchen's life is contained in the section relating the lives of the contemporaries and disciples of the Eighth Karmapa.[4]

The biography states that the intelligent and virtuous Ngawang Drakpa was at first a follower of the Kadampa sect—it even being renowned that he was a reincarnation of the famous eleventh-century Kadampa master, Chennga Tsültrim Bar. But after encountering the Madman of Ü, the monk came into the fold of the Kagyü. After studying under many eminent masters, Nyukla Peṇchen quickly rose to prominence, his teachings sought out by many. The biography mentions that Nyukla Peṇchen sometimes had responsibilities pertaining to political matters (inherited from his highly placed mother and father), but he was able to dispatch trusted stewards to handle his affairs, and thus keep his attention focused on religion. He was always generous with the means at his disposal, remaining untainted by his family's wealth until the end.

Another source of information about Nyukla Peṇchen is the record of his correspondence with Drukpa Künlé, Madman of the Drukpa, which is contained in the first and third volumes of the latter's *Miscellaneous Writings*. One passage records a moving and heartfelt prayer Drukpa Künlé wrote with the intention of helping to prolong the life of his ailing friend.[5]

The second part of the *Life* was written in 1537, five years after the yogin's death, by Lhatong Lotsāwa Shényen Namgyel (100 folio sides in the 1972 edition). Little is known about him beyond the fact that he was born in 1512. He refers to himself as *lha ris kyi bstun pa*, translated as "a monk of noble descent," which likely denotes a royal heritage (183). According to its colophon, the second part of the *Life* was composed based on records maintained by the Madman of Ü's nephew and spiritual successor, Künzang Nyida Pembar. All of these authors drew from stories told to them verbally by others (some by the Madman of Ü himself), making their true authorship in each case a collaborative effort. The second part was printed again thanks to offerings made by Tamdrin Tseten.

The Life of the Madman of Ü tells the story of Künga Zangpo's life in the straightforward, chronological manner that is typical of Tibetan religious biographies. The authors were consistent in the way they formulated the nine chapters of the biography, creating a single, continuous narrative. The two parts of the *Life* are written in a functional Tibetan, and are of middling literary quality. When referring to the Madman of Ü and other eminent figures, both clerics and laymen, the biography uses honorific forms of certain nouns and verbs, as is traditional in the central Tibetan dialect. The biography uses the auxiliary verbs *yin, 'byung,* and *'dug,* but not *red* or *yod red.* Each author has his own predilections for certain sentence structures.

One place where the text's two primary authors shine is in their flare for analogies and similes. Many of the similes employed in the biography are common in Tibetan literature and Buddhist lore. Realization is often described as being "sky-like," which evokes the qualities of being untainted, unchanging, unobscured, undelimited. The biography frequently describes someone as making "heaps [literally, clouds] of offerings like Samantabhadra" (*kun tu bzang po'i mchod sprin*). This refers to imagining the celestial bodhisattva or primordial buddha Samantabhadra emanating forth countless precious things—which is said to have the same beneficial effect as actually physically offering such things. Other similes appearing in the biography are more unique, such as when Nyukla Peṇchen describes people and gods as "obeying [the Madman of Ü] as if they were serfs" (*bran bzhin du nyan,* 93). When something miraculously goes unharmed, it is likened to a rainbow that someone has misguidedly tried to hit with a sword. The yogin runs off "like a hero charging into battle" (117). A rocky defile is described as "so narrow that it was like passing through the birth canal all over again" (140).

Poetic verses appear at the openings of both parts of the text, at the end of each chapter, and a handful of places in between. These typically pause to wonder at the accomplishments of the great yogin or to restate the most important events covered in each chapter's narrative. These verses are written in a high style that strives to emulate Sanskrit's ornate *kāvya* poetry. All of the verses are written with nine syllables per line, save for two, which have eleven and fifteen per line. The majority of these compositions use the universally appealing poetic form of the quatrain.

These verses draw heavily from classical Indian lore, much of it non-Buddhist. Although Hinduism itself was never transmitted to Tibet, the mythology of its more popular gods certainly was, and constituted one means by which a Tibetan author might make a display of the breadth of his knowledge of classical Sanskrit literature (usually by way of Tibetan translations).

Throughout these verses, the Madman of Ü is persistently made analogous to the moon: a light in the darkness, beautiful to behold; an unfailing bastion of enlightenment that is high above this world, but still shines lovingly upon it. His disciples are likened to water lilies, which, when the moon acts as a second sun, open at night to soak in its cool rays. Another trope consistently employed in these verses to characterize the yogin's spiritual training—by which he became possessed of the holy Dharma, the most valuable thing of all—is that of traveling to the land of the *nāgas* to snatch the crown jewel from their king. This is a magical, wish-granting jewel. In the poetic verse that closes chapter 3, it is imaginatively described how Künga Zangpo arrived at this distant land by crossing the great ocean of learning both the *sūtra* and mantra systems in the ship of his body, speech, and mind—impelled by the wind of his perseverence, which filled the sail constituted by his great fortitude.

One distinguishing feature the *Life of the Madman of Ü* is the way its authors frequently end a passage with a phrase like "so it is renowned" (*zhes gleng so*, etc.). This would seem to indicate that these tales were in circulation in the oral traditions of late fifteenth- and early sixteenth-century Tibet; the authors portray themselves as simply recording these stories on paper. Some passages are punctuated with a phrase like "so he has said" (*zhes gsung ngo*, etc.), which seems to indicate that it relates something told to the author by the Madman of Ü himself. The contents of the *Life* are cobbled together from stories being told and heard in central Tibet at the time; from Künga Zangpo's own verbal description of his life; and from things told to the authors by other followers and acquaintances of the yogin—all structured and connected by passages composed by the primary authors. The authors refer to the actual life lived by the Madman of Ü as being a sort of urtext: their biography, no matter how detailed, could only ever give a pale reflection of the facts of the historical reality that transpired.

The Translation

In making this translation I drew from three different versions of the Tibetan text: a print of the first half of the *Life* made from the original 1494 woodblocks (the print is now preserved on microfilm by the National Archives of Nepal, thanks to the efforts of the Nepal–German Manuscript Preservation Project; figure 9); an undated handwritten manuscript of the complete biography (also on microfilm; figure 10); and the 1972 edition of the complete biography printed by the Sungrab Nyamso Gyunphel

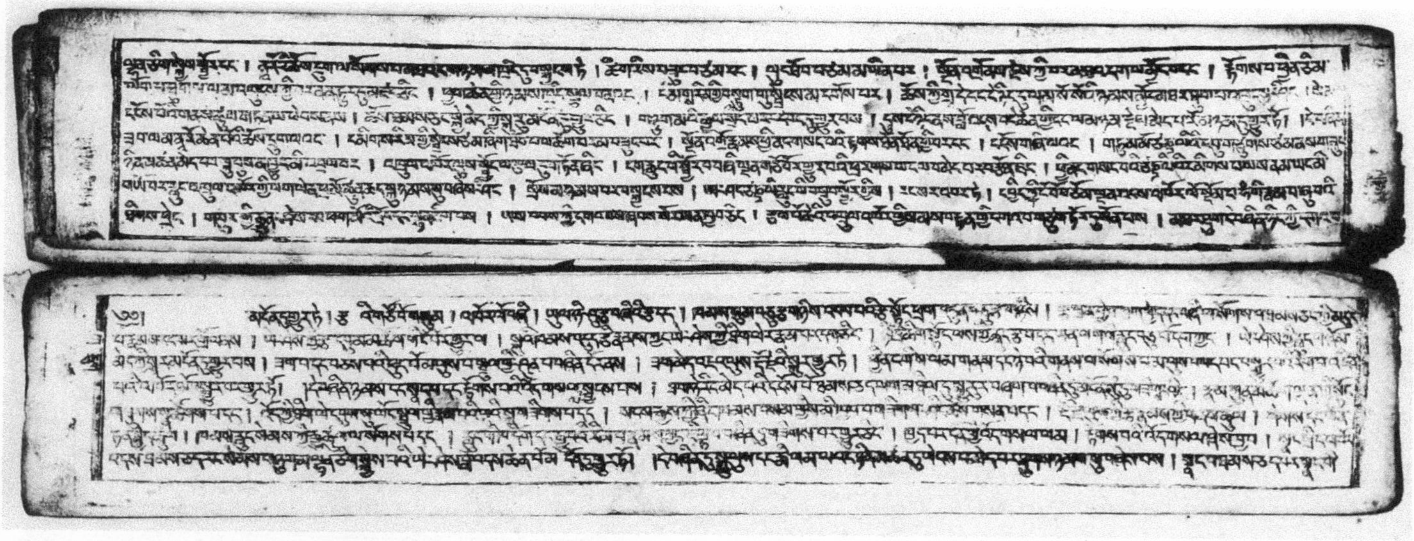

FIGURE 9 Pages from Part I of the *Life*, 1494

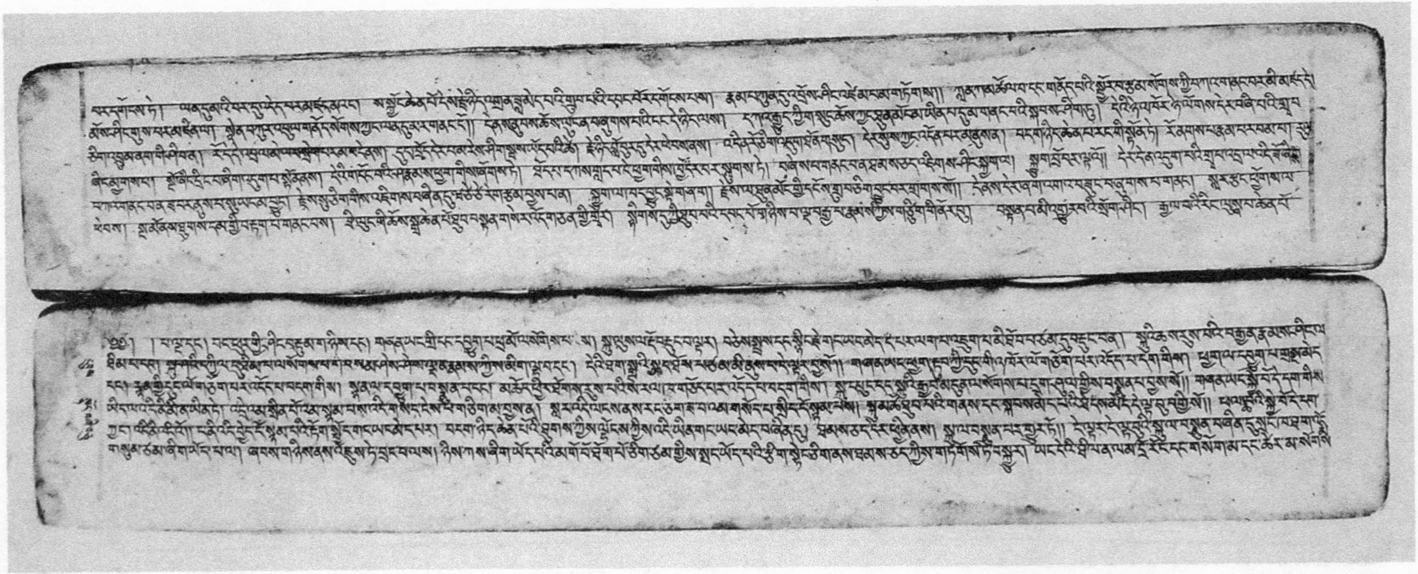

FIGURE 10 Pages from an undated manuscript copy of the *Life*

Parkhang in Palampur, Himachal Pradesh, India. A scan of the 1972 edition can be acquired from the Tibetan Buddhist Resource Center.

Readers who know literary Tibetan may desire a more fine-grained understanding of the original text than my translation can offer. To facilitate further exploration of the Tibetan, throughout my translation I have indicated the corresponding page numbers from the 1972 edition using {curly brackets}. A syllable-by-syllable comparison shows that there are 160 places where the text of Part I of the 1972 edition diverges from the 1494 original. However, the differences are quite small—confined almost entirely to alternate or incorrect spellings and usage of grammatical particles, or the occasional missing word. Considering how frequently scribal errors tend to appear in Tibetan texts, the 1972 edition is remarkably faithful to the original.[6] The few places where my translation diverges noticeably from the 1972 edition are indicated in the endnotes.

The process through which this translation was made is as follows. Between 2008 and 2009, I read and made a rough translation of the biography. I also typed out the entire 1972 edition, in order to create a searchable version of the text. Then while doing dissertation fieldwork in India in 2009, I sought out learned Tibetans with whom I could refine my understanding of the text. With them I discussed (either mostly or exclusively in Tibetan, depending on the case) all of the parts of the text that posed challenges: sentences whose grammar I did not understand; regionalisms and words that could not be found in dictionaries; references to classical Indian lore; certain intricacies of Buddhist thought and practice; and so on. The two individuals who contributed most to my understanding of the text are Sangye Tendar Naga and Khenpo Tsülnam Rinpoché, who are mentioned in the acknowledgments. I also discussed parts of the text with other Kagyüpas in India, as well as with some learned Tibetans residing in the United States. In this way I solicited a second, third, and sometimes fourth opinion on all the points of the text about which I felt unsure. In the years since 2009 I have worked through the text a few more times. The handful of passages about which I remain uncertain are discussed in the notes. Any deficiencies or mistakes in the translation are attributable to me alone.

A Tibetan scholar has written a brief summary of the *Life of the Madman of Ü*, which has been published in English and Chinese. Franz-Karl Ehrhard has published an article that gives a thoroughly annotated summary of the *Life*, against which I was able to check many of my facts.[7]

My aim has been to create a highly accessible translation, which will invite new readers into the world of Tibetan literature. I have prioritized readability in English over literal faithfulness to the Tibetan text, while trying nevertheless to maintain some of the texture and feel of the original Tibetan. I have purposefully kept to a minimum my use of notes and editorial insertions using [square brackets].

Literary Tibetan is a highly telegraphic language, in the sense that the subject or object of a sentence is often left unstated, it being expected that the reader will know to supply the necessary information from context. In the *Life*, there are many sentences that take the form of something like, "Then departed for Tsang." This is a perfectly normal Tibetan sentence, but would be grammatically unacceptable in English. Throughout my translation, I have had to insert words to make sentences like these grammatically complete. Most typically it is the doer of the sentence that must be supplied, which is usually our protagonist, the Madman of Ü. If I were to make this a more technical translation and adhere to the convention of indicating each of these insertions with square brackets, the text of the translation would be completely overwhelmed by them.

What's more, there are places in the translation where I insert small pieces of information that would be known by a Tibetan reader but which are not made explicit in the text itself. For example, although some readers of this translation may not know that "the *ācārya* from Oḍḍiyāṇa" refers to the famous tantric saint Padmasambhava, any reader of the Tibetan text would immediately make this association. When the biography mentions the *dus gsum*—literally, "the three times"—I render this as "the past, present, and future," which is what Tibetans understand the term as meaning. Where the original Tibetan mentions the "three doors" (*sgo gsum*)—the three avenues through individuals have intercourse with the world—I translate this as the "body, speech, and mind." In places such as these, rather than rendering the Tibetan term with its most literal English equivalent (which would require an explanatory note), my translation reflects what readers of the Tibetan text would understand the term as *referring to*. In these ways, my translation does not in all places reflect literally what the Tibetan says, but reflects the meaning expressed by it.

The authors of the biography refer to Künga Zangpo in a handful of different ways. Most often he is simply referred to as *rje*, meaning "the master" or "the lord." In the biography, I render this as "the Master." He is also referred to as *rje btsun*, "the Noble One," and as *bdag nyid chen po*, "the Great One," which is the equivalent of the Sanskrit title *mahātma*. He is also called *rigs bdag*—literally, "lord of the family." After the rise of tantra, buddhas and other divine beings were conceived of as existing in terms of five separate "families." To refer to Künga Zangpo as the lord of these combined families is an expression of hyperbolic respect for his personal degree of religious accomplishment.

Within the body of the biography I have chosen to capitalize the word Dharma (in Tibetan, *chos*), to reflect the respectful attitude the authors of the biography maintain toward their religion (just as Christians in the West would capitalize the Word). I capitalize the word Teachings (*bstan pa*) when from context it is not obvious that this means the teachings of the Buddha. The term "buddha" is not capitalized unless it is being used to refer to Śākyamūṇi, the buddha of our world age. However, other terms, like Victor, Victorious Lord, and Sugata ("the well-gone one"), which can refer to our buddha or to others, are capitalized throughout.

For better or for worse, English-language translators of Tibetan literature have often back-translated certain terms into Sanskrit. For example, early in the process of bringing Buddhism to Tibet, it was decided that the Sanskrit term for the realm of rebirth, saṃsāra, would be rendered in Tibetan as *'khor ba*, which is pronounced *korwa* and literally means "cycling" (as in, we are perpetually cycling through the realm of rebirth, until the point when we are able to escape). In the body of my translation, I could have chosen to translate *'khor ba* as "cycling," "cyclic existence," "life's round," or some other possibility that tries to capture the spirit of the Tibetan term. But readers might not recognize this as referring to the Buddhist idea of the realm of rebirth, so, for the sake of expedience, I have back-translated the term as saṃsāra. A handful of other commonly known Sanskrit terms are employed in the translation as well. There is a downside to this approach. Over the centuries, Tibetans have not simply imported Buddhism to their country, but have formulated their own responses to and understandings of elements of the religion. The creative act, long ago, of translating saṃsāra as *'khor ba* is a case in point. Back-translating into Sanskrit can have the effect of glossing over Tibetans' long history of creative engagement with Buddhism. This is but one of many areas where I had to make a decision between achieving accessibility for the majority of readers and satisfying the narrower interests and concerns of Tibetologists and Buddhologists.

Certain inconsistencies in the original text, which might cause confusion for some readers, have been smoothed over. Names have been standardized in some instances, so that while the names of Tilopa and Nāropa are spelled many different ways in the body of the text, they simply appear as Tilopa and Nāropa in my translation. In places, references to Gampo and Mila have been rendered as Gampopa and Milarepa. Where the original Tibetan text simply says "precious Dampa," I have given "precious Padampa Sangyé." There are places in my translation where I give "Drakar Taso" when the original only says "Taso." When the original mentions "Til" (*thel*), I have in places had to clarify whether this refers to Densa Til or Drikung Til. And so on.

I have in places provided translations glossing the meanings expressed by Tibetan place and personal names. For example, at the first reference to the place in Tsang called *rta nag*, I show that this name is pronounced "Tanak" and that it means "Black Horse." For Tibetans, *dag pa shel ri* is not just "Dakpa Shelri" but "the Pure Crystal Mountain." At one point the Madman of Ü encounters a particularly intractable hunter named *tshe mthar*, which is pronounced "Tsetar," and means, ironically, "lifesaver."

In some places, I have used quotation marks to indicate when the text is speaking in euphemism. *Nang mchod*, "inner offerings," refers to alcohol. *Gsang gnas*, "secret place," is one's sexual organ.

The chapter titles I have created are based on the brief distillations offered by the authors at the end of each chapter.

The first key at the end of the book reflects the spellings of personal and place names as they appear in the original Tibetan. However, corrected spellings have also been provided in a few cases. For example, the name of a famous cave in the Kathmandu region is spelled *yang le shel* in the biography. This is the cave more commonly known as "Yangleshö," spelled *yang le shod*. In order to help readers make the association, I have in my translation rendered the name of the place as Yangleshö, rather than maintain what may be a simple misspelling.

The second key gives the Tibetan spelling of the titles of all the texts referred to in the *Life*.

There are two areas of persistent ambiguity in the text, which can create challenges for the translator and the reader alike. One is attempting to discern whether many of the titles mentioned in the biography refer to bodies of teachings or to specific *texts*. Whereas in English prose, the titles of texts are typically capitalized and italicized, in Tibetan they remain unmarked in any way. The other challenge is in determining the identities of individuals who are mentioned, often laconically, by nicknames or titles of office. Some identifications still remain unresolved.

Tibetan Traditions

Finally, a few notes on Tibetan culture, to clarify some aspects of the biography that follows. The staple food for central Tibetans has traditionally been roasted barley ground into a flour, called *tsampa* (*tsam pa*). Black tea made savory with butter and salt was the national drink. Also almost universally appreciated was *chang*, a light alcoholic drink made from barley, similar to beer. The standard garment of clothing for the ordinary Tibetan, male or female, was the robe-like *chuba* (*chu ba*), which is typically made from wool, often lined with sheepskin for insulation. Noble men and women would have had other more refined, ceremonial outfits as well.

Arrivals, departures, and significant moments in between would be occasions for exchanging gifts, well wishes, and long strips of white silk or *khata* (*kha btags*). Although we commonly refer to these as "scarves," they were not worn for warmth or for fashion, remaining purely ceremonial. The whiteness of the silk is sometimes said to represent the purity of the giver's intentions. Charm boxes—wearable and portable holy objects—were appreciated by these often itinerant people. Horses were valuable and highly prized. Yaks were used for portage, while yak–cow crossbreeds, known as *dzo* (*mdzo*), were typically used for agricultural purposes like plowing and milking.

The calendrical system that Tibetans traditionally used was cyclical rather than fully linear. Each year was designated in terms of an element, an animal, and a gender. The five elements are earth, iron, water, wood, and fire. The twelve animals are the tiger, rabbit, dragon, snake, horse, sheep, monkey, bird, dog, pig, mouse, and ox. The element changes every other year; the gender of the year alternates; and the animal changes each year. The calendar runs on a continuous cycle, so that every sixty years there is a fire-female-ox year, followed by an earth-male-tiger year, followed by an earth-female-rabbit year, followed by an iron-male-dragon year. This ancient system has always proven somewhat cumbersome, with even the most careful of authors sometimes making mistakes in counting or in referring to particular years in history. Nyukla Peṇchen, author of the first part of the *Life*, refers to this as the Chinese calendrical system. He also knew of the traditional Indian method of counting years, which he employs when describing the year of the Madman of Ü's birth.

The passing of months was tied to the phases of the moon. The days on which the new and full moons fell were considered to be holiest. At this time in Tibet there was less than total agreement about what system to employ when referring to months. In the second part of the *Life*, Lhatong Lotsāwa in places employs three different systems for designating a month: one system derived from the *Kālacakra Tantra*, one imported from China, and another originating among the Hor, by which he means the itinerant peoples of Mongolia. Tibet has long been a crossroads of Asian cultures.

Tibetans traditionally calculated a person's age in a manner different from that predominantly used in the Euro-American world. The age of a newborn was not counted in terms of months; rather, one was said to be "one" year old once born (in effect, counting a person's age from the time of conception, rather than from birth). What's more, rather than remembering each person's individual birthday, everyone would be considered a year older at the beginning of each new year. Thus Kyepo Dar, born in 1458, would have turned "two" at the start of 1459. When he died in 1532, he was said to be seventy-five years old. The Western manner of determining a person's age will differ from his age in the Tibetan system by one or two years.

Traditionally, many Tibetans believed that every twelfth year of a person's life would be a challenging and unlucky one. One's twelfth, twenty-fourth, thirty-sixth, forty-eigth, and sixtieth years were expected to be times of great obstacles. The biography describes the trials the Madman of Ü experienced in his sixtieth year, when his monastery was attacked, as resulting from this. The years following these (when one was thirteen, twenty-five, and so on) were believed to be particularly good: one would see an uptick in one's fortunes when the troubled year was over, as the Madman of Ü did when he was sixty-one, when, instead of soldiers and thieves, offerings and honors poured into Tsimar Pel. Künga Zangpo's nephew came to Tsimar Pel monastery and was ordained as a monk in 1514, when he was thirteen years old, which was a favorable moment to make such a transition.

THE LIFE OF *the Madman of Ü* suggests many different ways of understanding the spiritual status that Künga Zangpo attained. The biography asserts that Künga Zangpo attained the state of non-reversion (*phyir mi ldog pa'i lam*), meaning that he became destined to achieve liberation (76). The *Life* also states that, in addition to many mundane *siddhi*s, he achieved the supreme *siddhi* of the Mahāmudrā. Although the Madman of Ü did not choose to manifest the miracle of dissolving into a "rainbow body" at the moment of death, the biography tells us that he could have done so. Instead, he chose to die in the traditional manner, which would leave a corpse behind, because he knew that this would be of greater benefit to his followers.

At the same time, the biography also suggests that Künga Zangpo had already been enlightened for many lifetimes before taking the form of Kyepo Dar. In places, the biography states that the religious training Künga Zangpo appeared to do in this life was only just for show, for the edification and religious benefit of those who are fortunate enough to know of him. The biography also mentions that Künga Zangpo had visions foretelling of his future lives, which suggests that when the Madman of Ü finally "laid down on the bed of the Truth of the Cessation of Suffering," this may not have marked the end of his gracious teaching activities.

Although I have spent countless hours reading and translating this biography over the past eight years, the man's life that it describes still remains wondrous and unfathomable to me. I remain humbled by the Great One's dedication, and I consider it an honor to be able to make his story available to a new audience of readers.

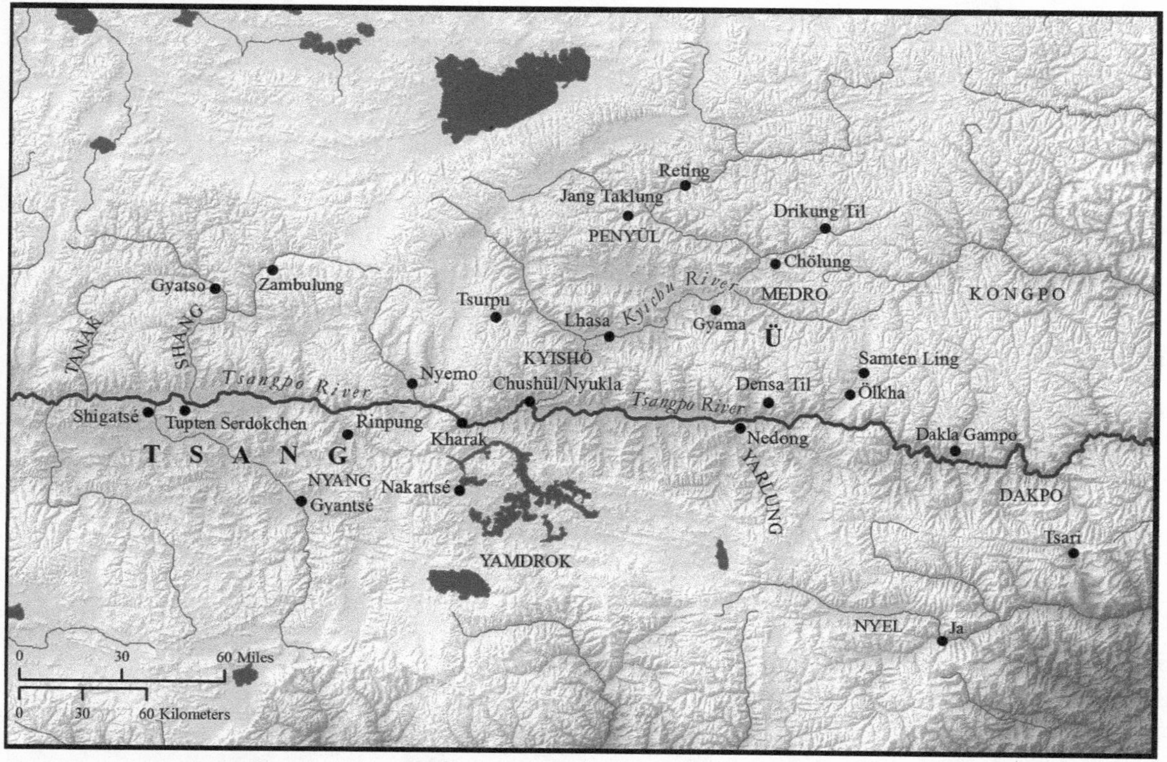

FIGURE 11 Central Tibet

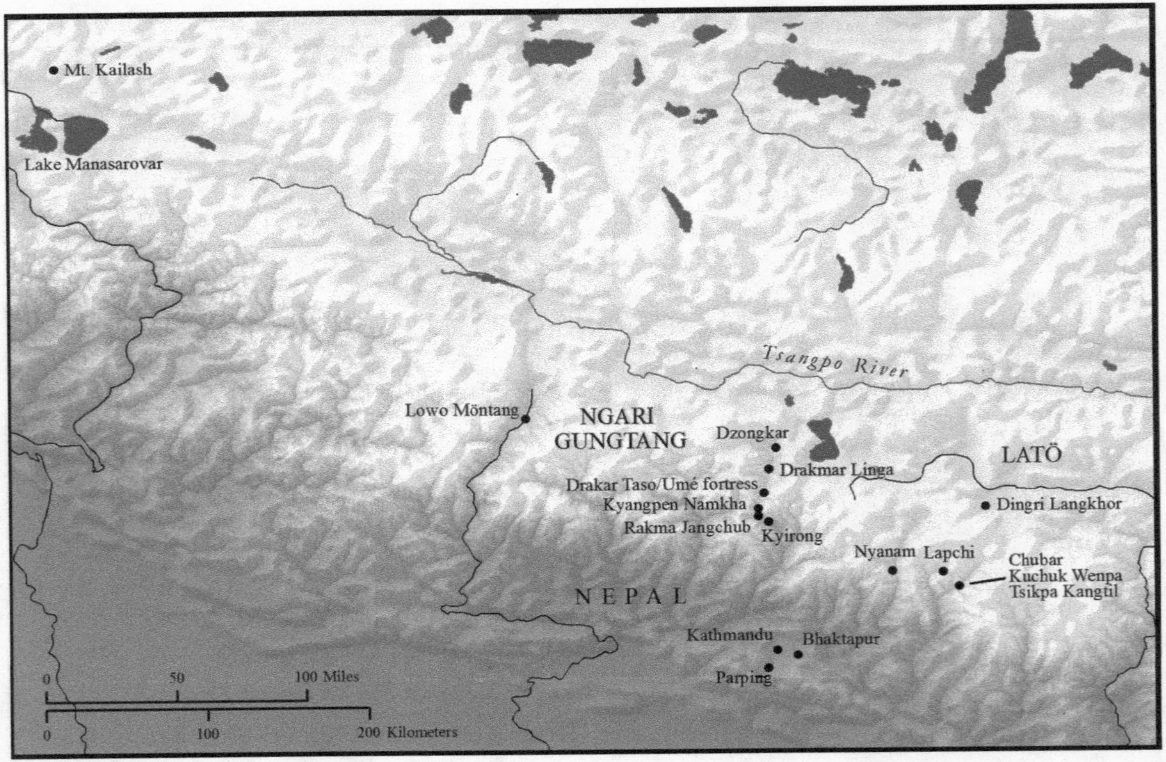

FIGURE 12 Tibet and the greater Himalayas

PART I

The Life Story of the Noble Küñga Zangpo, Glorious Holy Lama, the Preeminent *Siddha* Whose Practice Is Totally Victorious in All Respects, Called "That Which without Restriction Gives Goosebumps of Faith"

by Nyukla Peṇchen Ngawang Drakpa, 1494

1

Life before Monkhood

HOMAGE TO SARASVATĪ[8]

The Life Story of the Noble Künga Zangpo, Glorious Holy Lama, the Preeminent Siddha *Whose Practice Is Totally Victorious in All Respects, Called "That Which without Restriction Gives Goosebumps of Faith"*

I prostrate to the protector, lord of the world, Avalokiteśvara.

The singular embodiment of the collective body, speech, and mind
of all the Victors of the past, present, and future;
the father of every last one of the Sugatas;
whose body, appearing amid phenomena, is wisdom's magical
display—
at the feet of the lama, the preeminent *siddha*, I bow. {385}

The glorious Mount Meru[9] of your unmoving body, the substance
of all things;
intent upon illusionary, unifying play; as infinite as space,
completely tranquil from the start;
completely binding together saṃsāra and nirvāṇa, both the world
and its inhabitants, through the process of co-emergence, which
renders differentiated things equal—
at the feet of the lord of *siddhas*, the hero, the fearless protector
Künga Zangpo, I bow.

The one whose body is an apotheosis of amounts of merit
and wisdom
equal to those accumulated by an entire ocean of Victors, as
numerous as the sands of the Ganga;

the sole refuge and protector of the gods and all lesser beings
within existence and the tranquil beyond—
the life story of this glorious lama will here be told. {386}

Herein will be expressed the life story, the great roar of the lion in the wild,
which, when its wonder is beheld, gives goosebumps of faith—
but which is also the *vajra* thunder that smashes to bits the hearts and life-channels
of all the jealous ones bloated with arrogance and all manner of demons.

To express here just a little of *The Life Story of the Noble Künga Zangpo, Glorious Holy Lama, the Preeminent* Siddha *Whose Practice Is Totally Victorious in All Respects, Called "That Which without Restriction Gives Goosebumps of Faith,"* which is as vast as an ocean:

As for the area and setting in which the Great One was born, it was a place more than a hundred leagues northeast of India's Bodhgaya; east of the great Dharma *cakra*, the magical manifestation that is the glorious Jokhang temple in Lhasa. It was in the vicinity of the lord of snow mountains, Odé Gungyel, a short way up from the place called Drangyül Ölkha, in the settlement known as Ölsang Ngowo or Özang. The glorious garland of snow mountains appeared as if a white veil had been draped over them. The pastures and the different undulating hills and depressions, possessing the luster of sparkling emeralds, looked as if they had been laid out deliberately. {387} The melodious sound of bubbling waterfalls could be heard all around. There was a mist that interwove everything, like a sparkling necklace arranged into the auspicious symbol of an endless knot.[10] The area was adorned with potent and magnificent medicinal herbs, many-branched trees, flowers, and other types of plants. The area was a gathering place for birds and hummed with the sound of bees. It was indeed a locale endowed with the ten good qualities.[11]

As for the Great One's status, he was of the nobility, or was a commoner of more fortunate circumstances. His clan was Nyang. His father was called Özang Sega or Ḍangka. His mother was called Bapmo. Both were naturally of restrained passions, wealthy in both faith and dispensable things. They lived in a respectable manner. {388}

The youngest of their five sons, the Master, entered his mother's womb
1457 in the fire-female-ox year. At that time there were a variety of wondrous

good omens, such as his mother's and father's dreaming that the sun, moon and stars were all shining together; that they built and paid reverence to representations of enlightened body, speech and mind; that conch shells, drums and other instruments were blown and played and flew into the air; about a canopy of rainbow light, and other things—so it is renowned.

Then when he was born in the year called "abundant grain" in the Indian system, or the earth-male-tiger year in the Chinese, the infant was 1458
beautiful and pleasing to behold. His head was broad like a parasol, his brow was wide, and all of his limbs were fully articulated and lovely: one endowed with all the marks of a great being[12] had been born.

> As if merely moving from one divine palace into another,
> as if taking rebirth in this realm of existence at will,
> he was completely unblemished by the faults of existence,
> like a thousand-petaled lotus in the middle of a swamp.
>
> Until the allotted months had passed, his alluring, indestructible *vajra* body
> remained inside his mother's belly,
> shining as clearly as a butter lamp enclosed in a vase,
> his great bliss wisdom blazing like a forest fire stoked by the wind. {389}
>
> Then he was born fully developed,
> like the moon emerging from behind clouds all at once:
> thanks to his ability to bring welfare to others, the beams of this one with all the major and minor marks
> will certainly coax open the lily of the Sage's Teachings.

He was given the name Kyepo Dar. Nurtured on foods like milk and clarified butter, it was renowned that he grew like a lotus in a pleasure grove—so it is said. From the time he was a baby, he either assumed dancing poses or remained in the posture of meditation. With his melodious voice he sang different kinds of *vajra* songs. He would construct a ceremonial throne for himself, then sit upon it and pretend that he was teaching the Dharma. With the fierce look he had in his eyes, he overwhelmed all transmigrating beings with his glory.

Because his heart blazed with a great bliss wisdom that never diminished, even from the outside it looked as if he were having significant experiences within. {390} Without interruption, he experienced the luminosity of knowing all aspects of everything, which is indicated by such signs as seeing smoke, mirages, and apparitions in the sky. He comprehended the many different situations that the six types of sentient being can be born into. He imagined himself clearing out the hell realms, which caused immeasurable compassion to arise within him. Among other things, he could also see disembodied sentient beings traveling through the intermediate state between lives—so it is said.

He realized appearances to be false. Because his body consisted of rainbow light, time and again he was able to pass unobstructed through the walls of his family's home. On account of this, some feeble-minded people having no experience with this sort of thing declared, "He's possessed by a spirit!" and wrapped his head in a fishmonger's rags. Because of his smelling such a thing, and for other reasons, it appeared from the outside that the clarity of his vision became slightly obscured—so he has said.

From the time he was small, thanks to the strength of his internal *samādhi*, he was naturally free of the eight worldly concerns external to himself, and he thus completely abandoned all conforming to worldly ways. {391} Because he was never in agreement with any worldly person, and because of his zeal to integrate to the religious path anything that might arise before him, the other children would say, "This one doesn't get along with anybody—let's call him, 'Nobody likes him'!" Thus from a young age he had attainments that are difficult to fathom—attainments the likes of which others could not match in many lifetimes of training through study, contemplation, and meditation.

When he had reached the age of five or six, his mother would carry him on her back to Leu monastery, where he listened to many different teachings before the Dharma lord Yöngompa, who was a direct disciple of Dharma lord Götruk.[13] These included a collection of life stories of past lamas of the precious Kagyü, called *Brilliant Rays That Open the Eyes*; the *Mountain Dharma That Is the Origin of All Attainments*; as well as instructions on Cutting, and on Equalization of Taste. {392}

When he was eight or nine, at that same monastery he learned to read under *geshé* Darpo of Takshel and *geshé* Tashi Rinchen of Medro.

Then in the same way that not long after the birth of the Lord of Sages, his mother Māya departed for heaven, the Master's own mother went peacefully to a deep and vast celestial realm. Thus his mother departed from her lesser body.

Because they were "tax people" subject to Ölkha, the father and his sons had to experience the hardship of meeting their corvée labor obligations. What's more, in time the brothers took two wives, and the two women did not get along with one another at all. As the ten wearinesses,[14] corvée labor, and many other difficulties befell the family, the Master saw that the whole of saṃsāra has the nature of a pit of fire or an ocean of poison. He realized that all of life's worldly undertakings are like bubbles, like drops of dew on blades of grass. {393} Day and night he set his mind exclusively on the holy Dharma. With the intention of becoming a monk in the teachings of the Victor, he hoped to flee into the Dharma. His father and brothers became aware of this and prevented him from leaving, dissuading him by means of various threats. A year or two passed in this way.

Then one time, drunk on *chang*, a man named Sangyé Kyap—a servant of Gampo Pel, stablemaster of Taktsé[15]—punched, kicked, and bullied the young Master. "Kyema!" he thought. "The way of the world is such that the powerful beat on those weaker than them. They violate and abuse the feeble with harsh words. Being tormented in these various ways is what the three lower states of rebirth are like. If one does not renounce worldly activity, this cycle can never be broken. I really must go into the Dharma before too long." {394}

At all times, in all situations, the Great One thought, "All of the transitory appearances of the present world are like the dream you had last night, so why cling to a self as fleeting as this? This faltering, illusory human body is like a reflection on the surface of water, so why take joy in such a deception? Your happy, pleasant homeland is like a mirage, like a town inhabited by *gandharva* spirits, so why be attached to something so insubstantial? The relations and friends you hold so dear are like nothing more than travelers all happening to stop at the same inn, so why cling to anything so uncertain? The food and possessions you strive to accumulate can be snatched away, like the honey of powerless bees—so why amass what you do not need? {395} These temporary joys and pleasures are like the show you see in a dream—recognizing this uncertainty, where should one stay? The superior *siddha*s of the past subjected themselves to extreme difficulties and turned them into Dharma practice—they didn't just have the thought of doing so. The Dharma is not to be practiced in pleasant and peaceful settings. From now, even if heaven and earth were turned upside-down, I will fearlessly and authentically practice the holy Dharma!"

Like a lotus opening in the morning sun,
his holy body was ripened by fortunate conditions, both external
and internal.
Like a cloud laden with rain, he could fulfill the wishes of sentient
beings.

A fool would treat pure white sandalwood
as he would a clod of dirt—
would willfully scatter the beryl of the Victor's sons
as he would a pile of leaves.

But even while living within the household,
this one amazed and delighted those around him
by manifesting visions, clairvoyance, and miracles—
like precious metal buried under many layers of dirt:
although it is hidden, the gold still gleams.

Having achieved good fortune through lifetimes of training,
empowered by an awareness of the nature of saṃsāra,
he understood the happenings of existence to be like lightning
flashing in the sky,
and so developed the mind of renunciation. {396}

With his strength brimming like a lake in summer,
he threw away the pleasures of this life as if they were blades
of grass.
He took after the teachings of the Lord of the Śākya,
finding joy in the practice of holiness.

Such was the first chapter of *The Life Story of the Noble Künga Zangpo, the Preeminent* Siddha *Whose Practice Is Totally Victorious in All Respects, Called "That Which without Restriction Gives Goosebumps of Faith,"* relating the story of his life prior to becoming a monk.

2

Early Training

IN THE WATER-FEMALE-SNAKE year, when the Great One was sixteen, he ran away, joining up with some people who were traveling back to Tsari 1473 after gathering offerings on behalf of Yöndrel Bechungpa. Upon arriving at Tsari, the palace of glorious Cakrasaṃvara, the great meeting place of the heroes and *ḍākiṇīs* of the body, speech, and mind—the equivalent of India's Cāritra—his heart became filled with an unmitigated and inconceivable happiness. {397} He visited the various holy sites in succession.

Then he met the one who had been a teacher at Tsari over an uninterrupted succession of lifetimes, the *mahāsiddha*, the lord of yogins, Künga Namgyel from Chuwori. The Master was delighted, like when Nāropa finally met with Tilopa. Right then he took all of the layman's vows, and assumed the way of a pre-novitiate monk. Chuworipa gave him the name Künga Zangpo.

For the next three full years, Künga Zangpo served as an attendant to his master, following him like his own shadow. He continuously attended to Chuworipa while staying at the holy sites around the divine Khecara realm that is Tsari, at Dakla Gampo monastery in the east, at the Forest of Glorious Samantabhadra, Densa Til monastery, and other places.

Chuworipa conferred upon him the vow for generating *bodhicitta*, the mind of enlightenment, in both its aspirational and engaged aspects. The Master's mental continuum was ripened initially by means of the Vajravārāhī empowerment relying on the four symbols. Among the experiential instructions he practiced in their entirety were the Mahāmudrā of Co-emergent Union and the Six Dharmas, as they were transmitted by the superior being Barawa.[16] {398} For the preliminaries and all the subsequent practices, he would not just take in the words and receive the transmissions, but he would persist in his practice until incontrovertible experiences and realizations arose in his mind. After he had received the experiential instructions on the Mahāmudrā, while the Master stayed at various Dharma centers the ultimate experiences of the different Paths arose in him, without his having to proceed through all the steps of the visualizations. After he achieved certainty regarding the true nature of the mind, he saw all phenomena as being the unborn Dharma Body. By thus regaining his innate sovereignty, from that time onward he would experience everything as being of the same flavor, with no difference between meditation and non-meditation, remaining in a state of great non-conceptual bliss.

In like manner, during his training in the profound path of the Six Dharmas of the great Nāropa, he did not take merely progressing through the steps of the visualizations as sufficient. He would persist in the preliminary practices until the external, internal, and secret signs of accomplishment were produced. As for the actual practices, from the time he started doing *caṇḍālī* or *tummo* visualization, day or night he was never separated from his meditation belt. {399} He invigorated his body through the yogic exercises. He developed his power of speech by untiringly exerting himself in yogas concerning the subtle and coarse winds, especially the fourfold yoga. Even while performing the most detailed parts of the wind and body yogas, he never wavered from the external, internal, and secret *caṇḍālī* visualizations. Because he unfailingly maintained the yoga of stoking its flame with his winds, the *a*-stroke *caṇḍālī* naturally blazed within him. The syllable *haṃ* inside his head—which is a form of the supreme being Cakrasaṃvara, who is the nature of reality—would begin to melt, yielding a succession of drops. This stream of "camphor," conjoined with the warmth of wisdom Vajravārāhī, made the joys caused by the drops' descent to pervade his entire body, all the way down to his toes. Because of his skill in the yogic exercises, the joys of ascent reached to the top of his head. He felt the joy of ultimate thusness.

Once all the knots in his subtle body had become naturally undone—in the three main channels, the four *cakra*s, the channels corresponding to the twenty-four holy places, the seventy-two thousand channels descending from the thirty-two bodily elements, the thirty-five million minor channels, and so on—then the central channel, the channel of wisdom, assumed its natural supremacy. {400} The "nectar" elements of his physical body were completely purified into drops of wisdom. The twenty-one thousand karmic winds and the ten main and ancillary winds were also purified, and the wisdom wind became manifest as the indestructible sound. Thus like a snake shedding its skin, he completely cast off all the contaminated aggregates of the self, and his became an immaculate rainbow body, a *vajra* body. He became a *cakravartin*, a wheel-wielding king—a *vidyādhara* or "awareness-holder" with mastery over the external and the internal, the Stages and Paths, the holy sites and their neighboring areas, and so on.

By developing the luminosity of his experiences, his perceptions, and his realizations, he became able to see all objects, near or far, as clearly as a gooseberry laid on the palm of his hand. He had a variety of utterly supreme visions. Within spots of light he could see the bodies of deities, in their Enjoyment Body and their Emanation Body forms. {401} He saw inconceivable buddha realms and listened to Dharma teachings within them. He could see, exactly as it was, the layout of the channels within his *vajra* body; he could see the ways spiritual obstacles and attainments are generated; the circulation of the bodily elements, the winds, and the mind; as well as the colors of the different winds and the ways in which they circulate. Most important, he achieved the great non-conceptual wisdom that all of phenomenal existence, saṃsāra and nirvāṇa, is co-emergent with one's own innate mind. This is referred to as the true luminosity or the luminosity of realization.

As a result of his practicing the illusory body and dream yoga day and night without distraction, all things appeared to him in accordance with the eight analogies of illusoriness—appearing like rainbows in the sky, and so on. He became devoid of the ideations that lead one to indulge in the eight worldly concerns. He was like a heroic lion, whom internal and external disturbances such as illness, evil spirits, and ghosts could not bother. {402}

Thanks to the instructions on dream yoga, he became possessed of the ability to seize control of his dreams, to clarify and expand their contents, and so on. Able to do whatever he pleased, he reveled in his dreams. That which we call the dream reality was, for him, completely pure, having the nature of luminosity. Although some take achieving just limited abilities to control the content of their dreams as being really excellent, the Master was not satisfied with controlling only the nighttime dream, the analogical dream. Instead, he persisted until he was able to expand, manipulate, seize, and clarify the contents of the real dream, this great dream of waking life. Because of this, for him there was no difference between waking and sleeping, and the yogas of illusory body and dreaming were combined into a single practice.

When doing the illusory body and dream yoga meditations, he would sometimes leave through the window of his sealed retreat and travel to places like Tsari's Yülmé and Dakpa Shelri, the "Pure Crystal Mountain," arriving at his destination in a single instant. He would walk back and forth across great rivers as if they were solid land. He reveled with packs of predatory animals, leapt from one treetop to another, and so on. {403} Thus able to do anything he pleased, he displayed a variety of miraculous feats. He did all of these things without wavering from luminosity or from the state of the Mahāmudrā.

At the time of his performing these feats, Dharma lord Chuworipa told him, "Not doing religious practice, you go all over the place, just like a madman!" Although he outwardly pretended to scold the Master in this way, in private Chuworipa again and again declared, "This one has transcended what is conceivable to the rest of us!"

In that way, regarding the oral instructions for the main four of the Six Dharmas, as well as the ancillary oral precepts—on the transference of consciousness, and the intermediate state, on entering the dead, the "action seal," and the like—he became the equal of master Nāropa himself.

Even though the Master had already attained ultimate experiences and realizations in that way, because of his intention to help others he nevertheless received the reading transmissions for the Mahāmudrā and the Six Dharmas as transmitted by the superior being Barawa, paying close attention to even the most minor details of the practices. He also went through the motions of learning how to control his winds, do the yogic exercises, and other practices. {404}

The Master received an inconceivable body of teachings from the holy being Chuworipa. These included the experiential instructions for the Seven Day *Tummo*, instructions for Urgyenpa's approach-accomplishment practice as transmitted by the superior being Barawa, the life instruction called the Niguma Life Empowerment, as transmitted by Rechungpa, and the Eight Great Instructions, including the cycles on the Equalization of Taste and the Secret Practice. He received authorizations to do practices concerning the glorious four-armed wisdom protector, Mahākāla; the protector of the realm, Singhamukha, the "Lion-Faced" goddess; and the auspicious Five Long-Life Sisters. He received the reading transmissions for the *Golden Rosary of the Kagyü*, for the collected works of some past lamas of the precious Kagyü, and for various collections of songs, including the *Collected Songs* of master Milarepa. He also received the *Ship of Liberation*, the Jewel trilogy, and the *Application of Accomplishment*.

In the wood-female-sheep year, when the Great One was eighteen, he went to the Forest of Glorious Samantabhadra, which is indistinguishable 1475
from the Densely Arrayed Akaniṣṭha heaven. Amid that great Dharma community, the Master properly assumed the discipline of a novice,[17] becoming a monk in the *Vinaya* Dharma so excellently taught by the Buddha, the Bhagavan, the Supreme Being. Acting as preceptor[18] was the holy leader for this degenerate age, the lord of *siddhas*, the great abbot Sönam Tashi Gyeltsen Pelzang. {405} Acting as *ācārya* was the one completely free from the fault of arrogance, who had achieved perfection in living in accordance with the *Vinaya*, the great learned and meditatively accomplished ally of the Teachings, Sönam Tashi, who was from Sharmé. Also present were the requisite number of monks, including noble Chuworipa.

After this, the Master received some remaining Dharma teachings from the *mahāsiddha* Chuworipa. In the course of traveling as Chuworipa's attendant, the Master visited a number of monasteries, including Jang Taklung, where he received Dharma teachings before the great learned and accomplished Ngaki Wangpo, who hails from Taklung plain.

Then at Densa Til, from the one who had attained mastery in the infinite *sūtra* and mantra systems, the Dharma lord from Lhündé, Penjor Gyatso, the Master received the reading transmission for the great *paṇḍita* Abhayakara's three Garland cycles. He received the complete empowerment for the *Garland of Vajras*. {406} He also received empowerments pertaining to each of the four classes of tantras, and many minor authorizations. He received the expository transmission for the *Two-Parted*, the *Hevajra Tantra*. He received in its entirety the *Mountain Dharma* trilogy, written by the peerless victor, Yanggönpa the great. He received many instructions and reading transmissions, both specific and general, including the entire Aural Transmission of Rechungpa, the Aural Transmission of Ngendzongpa, the laying-bare instructions, the Mind Training, and the Three Core Meanings. He received the entirety of the experiential instructions for the Six-Branched Yoga, Vimalamitra's *Quintessence of the Great Perfection*, the Seventeen Tantras, and other teachings.

Then at Sapmo Drak, a hermitage associated with Densa Til, the Master went before the precious and realized Sönam Zangpo, who was also a direct disciple of Dharma lord Götruk. The Master received experiential instructions for Urgyenpa's approach-accomplishment—the profound Dharma of the *ḍākiṇīs*—and every last ancillary that accompanied it, including the notes on the yogic exercises. He also received many other teachings, including the Eight Great Instructions of the Drukpa, and the Six Cycles, including the *Summation of the Equalization of Taste.* {407} Notably, he received in their entirety the *Heart Essence of Profound Meaning*—the great instruction created by the Lady of Cutting, Machik Lapdrön[19]—some scattered supplemental teachings, the Son Transmission, the Meaning Transmission, and so on, all in the manner of experiential instructions. He practiced and became masterly in these Dharma teachings.

Over the course of a few different meetings, before the lord of yogins, the *mahāsiddha* Chupurwa, the Master received every possible cycle of Dharma teachings, including the Mahāmudrā cycle and the *Six Dharmas in Pure Gold,* as they were transmitted by the omniscient Karmapa. This delighted him.

Before the lord of the Dharma, the great bodhisattva Sharmepa, the Master received reading transmissions for the complete collected works of various past lamas of the glorious, peerless Dakpo Kagyü, including the succession of Chenngas. He also received many instructions, such as the Mahāmudrā of Co-emergent Union, the Five-Parted Mahāmudrā, the Mind Instructions, and the Six Dharmas.

Then he arrived before the one who had been his teacher over many lifetimes, since beginningless time: the lord of the families, sovereign over the world and its inhabitants, the holy primordial buddha, the *mahāvajradhara,* lord of the dance—Rinchen Zangpo, the precious one from Drakchok. {408} The first time he saw Drakchokpa's face, his perceptions were transformed. By merely hearing Drakchokpa speak, the fettering fog of dualizing fixation was dispelled, and wisdom derived from experiential realization blazed within him. Benefit to himself and others were achieved simultaneously.

After pleasing his teacher in the three ways—through giving, service, and practice—the Master received Dharma teachings in their due order. As for ripening initiations, he was given the complete empowerment for the sixty-two-deity maṇḍala of the supreme being Cakrasaṃvara; the empowerment for Akṣobhyavajra, of the glorious *Guhyasamāja Tantra;* the empowerment for the nine-deity Hṛdaya Hevajra maṇḍala; and the complete empowerments for the five tantra classes of the glorious Shangpa Kagyü; as well as for the father teachings and the mother teachings of the Aural Transmission.

He received the liberating Generation Stage teachings, with their ancillaries.

For the Perfection Stage, he received the respective Perfection Stage teachings for all four classes of tantras. He learned the profound path of the Six Dharmas of Nāropa based on the instructional text by *chennga* Nyernyipa, Sönam Gyeltsen, called the *Thousand Rays Clarifying the Great*

Bliss.[20] {409} He received in their entirety, by the same author, the instructional text on the Mahāmudrā of Co-emergent Union, *Dispelling the Darkness of Ignorance*; the instructional text the *Wish-Fulfilling Jewel of Mind Instructions: The Rain Cloud That Fulfills Every Need and Want*; the instructional text on the Five-Parted, *Drop of Ambrosia*; and other texts.

He received every possible teaching, including the Six Dharmas of Niguma; the laying-bare instructions of the Tsembupa tradition, of the Dawa Gyeltsen tradition, and of the Pelmo tradition; as well as the five stages of the *Guhyasamāja, Finding Ease in the Nature of Mind,* the Aural Transmission, and the approach-accomplishment. He also received in their entirety every possible authorization, initiation, reading transmission, esoteric oral instruction, and so on, for deities of discernment, like Mañjuśrī; for deities of longevity, like the protector Amitāyus; for Kurukullā; for deities of wealth, like Vaiśravaṇa Jambhala; for Dharma protectors like the glorious wisdom protector Mahākāla in his four-armed and four-faced forms, and for Tseringma, the Long Life goddess; and for others. {410}

He received the root text of the *Hevajra Tantra*, the *Synopsis of the Empowerments*, the great commentary on the *Hevajra Tantra* by Nāropa, the earlier and later *Primers*, the *Vajra Songs of the Six Dharmas*, the *Vajra Verses on the Aural Tantra*, and the *Essence of Accomplishments.* He also received the *King's*, the *Queen's*, and the *Commoners' Dohās* by Saraha; the *Alphabet Dohā*, with its root text and commentary; the *Dohā That Is like the Flame of a Butter Lamp*; the *dohā* of the body treasury, called *Immortal Vajra*; of the speech treasury, *Mañjughoṣa Vajra*; of the mind treasury, *Unborn Vajra*; the *Dohā on Paying No Attention to Body, Speech, or Mind*; the *dohā* called *Song of the Esoteric Oral Instruction of the Inexhaustible Treasury, Completely Full*; the *Dohā on Dying*; cycles of *dohās* by Tilopa, Nāropa, Virūpa, Lohipa, and Śawaripa; the *dohā* of noble Avalokiteśvara; the Nāropa–Maitripa *dohā*; and the *vajra* songs of the eighty *mahāsiddhas*, along with their accompanying commentaries. He also received the greater and the lesser Secret Practice of India by Maitripa, the Secret Practice of Nāropa, and the Pebble Cycle of the Mahāmudrā. {411}

In short, like a vase being filled to its brim, the Master received and mastered all of the empowerments, tantras, reading transmissions, and oral instructions, including, in particular, all of the esoteric oral instructions of the precious Kagyü.

At Sapmo Drak, before the lord of yogins Bangrimpa, he received every possible profound and vast teaching, including the Five-Parted Mahāmudrā and the wish-fulfilling jewel of Mind Instructions. From the lord of the

Dharma, the precious learned and meditatively accomplished one, Namkha Lodrö, the Master received every possible empowerment, instruction, reading transmission, and esoteric oral instruction. Before the omniscient Lochen he received some Dharma teachings of lesser importance.

Finally, at snowy Mount Shampo, before the feet of the *mahāsattva* bodhisattva, the noble Miyowa, he received many limitless and profound Dharma instructions, including the *Seven Points of Mind Training*, the *Peacock in the Poison Grove*, the *Wheel of Sharp Weapons*, the *Stages of Bodhisattvahood, Defeating Conceptuality*, the Eight Session practice, and the One Session. {412}

The empowerments, instructions, reading transmissions, and esoteric oral instructions that he received were limitless in scope; for fear of getting too long, I will not write about all of them here. These things can be known more fully from the great volume listing all the teachings the Master received.[21]

In that way he obtained from his teachers empowerments, tantras,
and esoteric oral instructions of profound meaning—
like taking a garland of jewels from the king of the *nāgas*—
and satisfied the entire community of worthy beings with the
pleasure he took in the Dharma.

Although he commanded a throne on the solid ground
of first benefiting himself,
for the sake of others he crossed the ocean of learning
in the ship of analysis and zeal.

The crystal vase of his mental continuum became filled with the
jewels he retrieved—
jewels with the power to extract the essential nectar from
ambrosia.
He became like a marvelous cloud of Dharma, unsurpassingly
amazing,
capable of fulfilling the hopes of all worthy beings.

Such was the second chapter of *The Life Story of the Noble Künga Zangpo, the Preeminent* Siddha *Whose Practice Is Totally Victorious in All Respects, Called "That Which without Restriction Gives Goosebumps of Faith,"* relating the story of how he became a monk in the teachings of the Victor, and crossed the ocean of great learning. {413}

3

Meditation

THE MASTER HAD obtained all of the oral instructions. He knew how to sustain his religious practice. He had no fear or apprehension concerning anything. The effects of any danger that might appear in this world had been forestalled. He had been accepted by a qualified lama. *Ḍākiṇīs* of the body, speech, and mind swarmed around him.

At this point he thought, "Now, in order to further cultivate these realizations, I should go to great holy places like Lapchi and Chubar."

He traveled there by stages, accompanying a hermit from Densa Til. Then for three whole years the Master did nothing but practice meditation in sealed retreats, alternating between the place called "the snowy enclave of Lapchi"—the snow mountain of glorious accomplishments, itself like a crystal stūpa—and the place called "the divinely emanated palace of Chubar." {414}

Once he had firmly planted the victory banner of practice, the Master was able to finish his training in the Generation Stage. As a result, he cast out from its very root all attachment to ordinary perceptions, so that subsequently everything appeared to him as being the play of the gods. He had a vision in which the sky was filled with the divine assembly of glorious Cakrasaṃvara. On many occasions he had visions of and received prophetic assurances from his tutelary deity.

On the ordinary level of the Perfection Stage, involving elaborative elements, the Master gained complete control over his bodily processes: he achieved the ability to hold each vase breath for a whole day, to force the elements from the left and right channels into the central one, and so on. The qualities and the movements of the different winds became clear to him. Sometimes the winds would pass out through his fingertips. Because the blissful warmth of *tummo* blazed within him, for clothing he did not have to wear anything more than a single piece of cloth, and even spent most of the time naked. {415} Nothing ever felt cold, so he could stay in caves or thatched huts, with warmth continuing to blaze from within. As a result of experiencing the bliss caused by the melting of the yogic drop, his body became as clear as crystal. His mind became free of any obscuration, like the surface of a mirror. He would smell phantom odors of Indian *valerian* and of lotus flowers. His body gave off an abundance of brilliant light. And so on. Because of all this, the heroes and *ḍākiṇīs* of the body, speech, and mind swarmed around him, passing unhindered through the window to his retreat as easily as a sword cutting through a rainbow.

On the extraordinary level of the Perfection Stage, free of elaborative elements, day and night the Master never wavered from a continuous state of luminosity. In his clarified perception he knew the thoughts of others. The Master recalled many of his previous lives. He could accurately foretell that this or that tumultuous worldly event would take place. Most of the time he experienced the true luminosity, in which he perceived all phenomena in a way that was as free from dualizing fixation as the center of a cloudless autumn sky is clear—so he has said. {416}

Again and again he saw good omens regarding the prospect of his going before the peerless Dharma lord Drakchokpa at the Forest of Glorious Samantabhadra. These were in accordance with the prophecies given by his tutelary deity and the *ḍākiṇīs*, and with the visions he saw within his luminosity. So the Master traveled back to Tartsa Cave, which was once inhabited by glorious Pakmodrupa, again accompanying a hermit from Densa Til.

When he went before his master, it was like when Maitripa visited glorious Śawaripa. The Master and Drakchokpa had a number of conversations about the Dharma, in the course of which the son greatly pleased his father. He made offerings of the practice he had done, the realizations he had had, and so on. Drakchokpa was delighted. He taught the Master all of the remaining Dharma teachings, his most intimate esoteric oral instructions, the critical points of the oral instructions, and all the implications of the essential and the definitive meanings. It was just like the Lord of Sages teaching the *Extensive Perfection of Wisdom Sūtra* to the assembly of his spiritual sons at Vulture Peak.

Then the Master pledged to do a strict retreat for some time. {417} He was abiding, focused single-pointedly on practice, in a mountain cave behind Densa Til called Chöjung Puk—"Matrix of Reality Cave"—which had been blessed by Vajrayoginī. At one point, a Dharma brother named

Gepel arrived. He asked, "Are you still staying here? The precious Dharma lord has come back to Densa Til and is giving many profound and vast Dharma teachings."

As soon as the Master heard this, he began to long palpably for his lama. With tears streaming down his face, he abruptly left his retreat. When the Master arrived before Drakchokpa, he was asked, "Why did you come here from Chöjung Puk? Are you not staying in retreat?"

"I was," he answered. "But I missed my master, so I came."

"After you decide to stay you want to go, and after you decide to go you want to stay: that is truly a distracted mind!" Drakchokpa said in a scolding manner. {418} "If you had listened to what I have taught, this kind of uncontrolled thought should have been cleared up by now. Looking off into the distance, not distracted by different things, set your mind at rest in its natural state."

As soon as the Master heard those *vajra* words, like the roar of a lion in the wild, all the waves of mental disturbances and all ideational constructs dissolved back into a state of thusness. All of the conceptual attributions related to dualizing fixation and dualistic perception floated away like feathers, were dispelled like clouds. The Dharma Body—completely non-conceptual wisdom—became manifest in his mind. As naturally as if he were meeting people he already knew, he achieved reflexive awareness and saw the nature of the mind as it truly was. All phenomena became as vibrantly clear to him as a silk brocade laid out at noon. He achieved absolute control over all the workings of dependent origination. Everything that is perceived within phenomenal existence, saṃsāra and nirvāṇa, whether brought together under the notions of "self" or "other"—from the moment they appear, they are

> sparkling, sparkling, self-liberated from the four extremes;[22]
> shifting, shifting, in the form of the four Bodies of buddhahood;[23]
> exceeding, exceeding, in the form of the five types of wisdom;[24]
> upright, upright, inseparable from the Three Refuges.[25] {419}

In that way the Master achieved the yoga of perceiving the sameness of existence and the tranquil beyond. He understood the inseparability of saṃsāra and nirvāṇa. He had non-dualistic self-liberating realization. He saw that, by nature, the infinitely vast disk that comprises the three realms of existence—the Desire Realm, the Form Realm, and the Formless Realm[26]—has been completely pure since the very beginning.

Drakchokpa instructed the Master to spend the next year with him. Staying as near to his master's body as its own shadow, day and night he continuously received every last instruction, with all of their respective follow-up teachings. Drakchokpa eradicated, then and forever, all of the easy- and difficult-to-resolve questions and concerns that the Master needed to ask him about. In that way the Master attained the state of non-reversion.

Then Drakchokpa Ratnabhadra, the lord of *siddhas*, the peerless king of the destroyers of illusion, gave him the following prophetic command: "Son, you have trained in the important things that must be learned. Every last instruction and follow-up teaching has been given to you. You have experience in all the profound Dharma teachings of the *ḍākiṇīs*, which are the quintessence of the secret oral teachings. You have reached a state of completion in most aspects of the experiences and realizations that lead to mastery in skillful means and discernment. {420} You have become like a keeper of the teachings of the Meditation Tradition.

"It is now time for you to travel to the Three Great Abodes—Tsari, Lapchi, and Mount Kailash—the Six Fortresses of Milarepa, and so on, and as far as Nepal and 'Indian' Parping. All the while, stay in monasteries high above the villages, apart from those who are mired in human lives defined by the eight worldly concerns. Further increase what you have achieved in terms of renunciation and realization. Finally, through the four types of enlightened activity,[27] you must take care of transmigrating beings."

After reciting some prayers and good wishes, the Master departed. He passed through the heart of Kyishö and headed toward Tsurpu monastery, in Tölung valley. At that time, the omniscient Karmapa—the divine emanation, the self-arisen, invincible, all-knowing king of the Dharma—was giving a public Dharma teaching at Tsurpu. The Master listened for one teaching session, made some prayers, and so on. Meanwhile, the invincible Karmapa watched everywhere the Master went, regarding him as an object of amazement.

Then, focusing single-pointedly on his meditation practice, summer and winter, fall and spring the Master would alternate between such locations as Lapchi, the great holy place that gives rise to spiritual accomplishments; Chubar, the palace of the *ḍākiṇīs*; the Six Fortresses of Milarepa; Mount Kailash, the king of the snow mountains and the hub of the physical world; the Kathmandu valley; Kyirong; and "Indian" Parping. {421} During this period he took on additional austerities. He assumed the burdens of the spiritual path. He discarded all concern for his body and life. He dispossessed himself of all food and clothing. For the sake of the Dharma, he endured extreme hardships that could well have killed a person. These trials enabled him to toss into the wind all designs for the future of his current life. From that point onward, hot and cold, hunger and thirst, weariness and fatigue, pleasure and pain, praise and criticism, good and bad, the turning of the seasons, injuries from without or within, harm caused by human or nonhuman beings, by the four elements, and so on—all became like mere illusions to him. By entering mental states such as the Going Heroically and *Vajra*-Like *samādhis*, he was able to overwhelm everyone with his glory. He danced on water like the reflection of the moon. He spoke the language of echoes. He performed magical tricks with his wisdom. In these feats he was unsurpassed.

Throughout this time the Master did further practice in the winds, the yogic exercises, and other yogas pertaining to the Generation and Perfection Stages of the astonishing, short path of the Vajrayāna. {422} The lama and the *ḍākiṇīs* dispelled some minor obstacles and potential pitfalls for him.

While staying at Drakar Taso, meditating with single-pointed diligence, the Master had inconceivable experiential realizations involving bliss, luminosity, and non-conceptuality. As for bliss, at first he experienced a corporeal bliss that was still tinged with the basic afflictions. Then his entire body became pervaded by a bliss that was free of the afflictive emotions: whatever he touched—hot, cold, or whatever—he experienced as blissful. Even if he sat on a pile of nettles or thorns, he still felt entirely blissful. He also experienced a mental bliss of happiness and contentment. Meanwhile, the unmitigated great bliss, by which one transcends all discomfort, increased ever more within him.

As for luminosity, he experienced the luminous aspect of each of the five senses. He had perceptions of smoke, mirages, butter lamps, suns, moons, rainbows, lightning, eclipses, spheres of light, and so on. {423} He had some fully detailed visions, including visions of the different types of transmigrating beings. He could hear everything, whether the origin of the sound was near or far away. By the end, he exclusively experienced imperishable reflections—endowed with all the qualities of luminosity—of sounds, smells, tastes, objects of touch, and so on. As for the luminous aspect of the mind, there arose the respective antidote to each thought that needed to be abandoned. He knew that understanding, mental projections, tranquility, and the like are each concordant with the factors on which they depend. Pure and clear, without torpor or fogginess, he accurately perceived all phenomena, both internal and external, as clearly as a gooseberry laid on the palm of his hand.

As for non-conceptuality, his mind took hold of whatever it was directed toward. Because ideations had subsided, his mind would remain wherever it was set. By the end, all of the mental factors that typically lead to ideation were pacified. He thus achieved a state of non-conceptuality that was as still as a mountain—neither increasing nor decreasing, like the ocean; unobscured, like a cloudless sky. {424}

Because he beheld his bliss, luminosity, and non-conceptuality with a completely pure discernment that had the nature of wisdom marked by reflexive awareness, he knew that the bliss he felt lacked a true nature, and he did not savor it. He realized the causes and the effects of luminosity, and therefore never became scattered or agitated. Although he had achieved an unwavering mind that was free of conceptuality, he nevertheress remained aware of the various mental factors, immediately recognizing the ways they arose or ceased. As such, the Master avoided the pitfalls of desiring and becoming attached to the experience of bliss; of the complacency that can result from taking pride in one's achievement in luminosity; and of the disregard for causes and effects that can result from non-conceptuality integrated with the experience of emptiness. Thus he did not stray into any of the three realms of existence or the four levels of concentration.[28] All of the other dangers were also forestalled, such as mistakenly taking emptiness, compassion, or thoughts about cause and effect to be the enemy. Stamped with the seal of emptiness, he did not cling to the experience of bliss. When mental projections appeared within his clarified perceptions, he reconciled them into non-conceptual clarity. {425} The luminous aspects of the five senses, the ten signs that indicate them, his clairvoyant perceptions, and so on, were all definitively resolved to be of his own mind. All clinging to conceptual attributions as being truthful was thus cast off. He thereby passed into his own nature, free from all mental constructs.

The Master avoided the pitfalls of viewing phenomena as permanent, of taking the view of nihilism, of ideating a self, and of the confusion that is ideating the existence of an external object that must be negated. He also avoided the pitfalls of waning in his critical analysis or happiness, of wavering from presence of mind, and of mistakenly taking a state of concentration that involves the cessation of the breath to be the ultimate concentration. In his clear and non-conceptual thought, he no longer made conceptual attributions with respect to objects. He avoided the pitfalls that send one to the Form Realm or the Formless Realm, such as accepting the Sky-like, Limitless Consciousness, Nothing-at-all, or Notionless-yet-not-notionless states of mind as being the ultimate. In short, he completely abandoned all incorrect views regarding the transitory assemblage of things that is the three realms. Because he had trained in the four levels of concentration, the four formless states of mind, and how to terminate them, all obscuring notions resulting from ideation in terms of the three spheres of actor, action, and object were fully quelled. {426} Upon directly realizing all phenomena to be empty and lacking an inherent nature, he became a preeminent *siddha*, with mastery over all phenomena—both external and internal—and thoughts.

Because the Master remained unwaveringly in that state day and night, while awake his mind enabled him to perform many different sorts of miraculous feats, such as assuming whatever bodily form he pleased, making his body disappear, and soaring through the sky. While asleep, he was able to see and rove unhindered from the highest peak of existence down to its very bottom. After he emanated hundreds of manifestations of his body, speech, and mind, they would travel individually to innumerable buddha realms, where they would teach the Dharma and generate numerous clouds of offerings. They taught the Dharma to an inestimable number of transmigrating beings. The Master manifested every other ability, including the ability to make water pour down from the upper half of his body while fire blazed up from the lower half. {427}

Thanks to the heroism and the power that arise when awareness and wisdom blaze co-emergently within, his actual body would fly through the air! The Master flew from Drakar Taso to Minkyuk Drip fortress. He stayed for a few days at Minkyuk, then winged it to Lagö. Then, riding on a rainbow, he flew back to Drakar Taso. This sort of thing occurred many times. Hunters and other people were witness to them. In like manner, at Minkyuk, Taso, and other places, on the sides of great precipices with rock faces as smooth as mirrors, he danced, ran, leapt, and flew about. In doing so he was like noble Milarepa when he sang,

> Over Drakar Taso and Umé fortress,
> the vulture flies, wingtips fluttering.
> When I, the yogin fly, I fly like that. {428}

When the Master was staying at Kyidé Nyima fortress, a hunter arrived. Upon seeing him, the hunter asked, "Who are you? How long have you been here?"

"I am an ascetic yogin from Ü, that distant place down there," he replied. "I arrived here a while ago."

"Your brilliant complexion is evidence of great abilities," the hunter declared. "You would be happier living as a worldly person than you will staying here like this. Even if you continued to practice the Dharma, if you stayed in populated places where there are patrons, it would be more pleasant for you."

"I have met the likes of the noble, precious Drakchokpa," the Master began. "I have obtained many profound Vajrayāna instructions. Since renouncing my life, I have stayed continually in isolated abodes. I have no wish to roam about in the world, especially not in populated places. I know the world of you people—I have seen it. In this lifetime, having for once attained a human body, I must strive to disassociate myself from saṃsāra forever. There is no time to pursue other concerns." {429} Hearing this made the hunter faithful and happy.

When the Master was staying at Drakmar Linga fortress, some non-human spirits caused a great disturbance that put him to the test. But thanks to his Illusion-like *samādhi*, to his ability to endure hardships that could have hurt or killed an ordinary person, and to his realization of the Mahāmudrā, he was able to overwhelm those spirits with his glory. As the Master himself has described it, "Those disturbances passed into their natural tranquility, their natural purity."

At that time he saw inconceivably amazing signs, such as having visions of his tutelary deity and hearing the sound of mantras recited by the heroes and by the *ḍākiṇīs* protecting the realm. Nevertheless, as the Master has said, "Viewing things from the perspective of the Mahāmudrā, I experienced everything as being of the same flavor, and therefore did not have any attachment or fascination toward these things."

After staying there for a while, the Master went to Drakya Dorjé fortress. There he recalled some of his previous lives, such as the lifetime in which he was born as the realized one Tsachungpa.[29] He had various visions, including one in which he was sitting in noble Milarepa's own Dharma assembly.

He spent the winter at Dröpa Cave in Nyanam. {430} Day and night he continuously remained in a state of sky-like realization. He has said that he was able to remain in this state without even having to be conscious of it.

That spring he meditated at Rakma Jangchup fortress. The entire day would pass while he sat in a single session of practice. At night, the nonhuman spirits would cause a racket, which slightly distracted him from his religious practice temporarily. But this was actually of great benefit to his meditation.

One time while staying at Kyangpen Namkha fortress, he supplicated with a single-pointed focus the noble lord of yogins, Milarepa. As a result, their minds became melded together as one. In the clarified perception that was enabled by his being in that state, the Master recollected and foreknew the stories of many of his past and future lives.

His meditation also improved greatly while staying at Kuchuk Wenpa fortress and Tsikpa Kangtil fortress.

In that way the Master practiced with single-pointed focus at the six external fortresses, the six internal fortresses, and other places that had been blessed by the "*ācārya* from Oḍḍiyāṇa," Padmasambhava, and by noble "Laughing Vajra," Milarepa. {431} Once he had prevailed over the great army of things that one must abandon, and once he could simultaneously benefit himself and others, he traveled as far as the Kathmandu valley and "Indian" Parping. Living in the manner of a covert yogin, he took care of many transmigrating beings.

After staying at Lapchi for a while, he went that spring to Mount Kailash—the great abode of Cakrasaṃvara, hub of the physical world, the king of the white snow mountains. He stayed there for about a year. On account of the great force of his yogic winds, he could carry a boulder the size of a full-grown yak on his shoulders. Although for food he had nothing except essences that he extracted from flowers, his body's radiance and vigor were maintained. During his stay at Mount Kailash, he had visions of glorious Cakrasaṃvara and many other tutelary deities. He bound under oaths many nonhuman spirits and ghosts. Dharma protectors, including the protector of the realm, Singhamukha, helped to carry out his enlightened activity without hindrance. {432}

In that way the Master practiced for a period of five whole years at Mount Kailash, Lapchi, Chubar, the Six Fortresses, the Kathmandu valley, and even distant "Indian" Parping. His meditation improved greatly throughout this time. In waking life, his visionary experiences, and his dreams, the Master saw inestimable buddha realms, from whose Victors and their sons he received the Dharma. He saw his tutelary deity surrounded by his retinue, filling the whole sky above. He achieved good qualities that cannot be fully described, including the Attainment of

Appearance, the Five Eyes—including the eye of the flesh—and the six types of higher perception.[30]

Concerning the understandings of the nature of the mind and the nature of the Dharma Body that had been established under lord Drakchokpa, there was no need to correct or improve upon them. However, the Master did have a subtle notion of there being a difference between the object of meditation and the act of meditation. Because of this, at times his religious practice ceased to improve, and his experience became somewhat uneven. This mistaken understanding clung to him like a bad smell, or like a layer of dead skin that needed to be shed again each day. {433}

Following a prophetic command from the *ḍākiṇīs*, the Master went to Dechen Ding. When sitting in meditation one morning, he completely did away with the notion of there being a difference between the object of meditation, the act of meditation, and the meditator. All the phenomena of saṃsāra and nirvāṇa were resolved into thusness. Because the essence, the nature, and every last characteristic of the mind became fully apparent to him, all the disquietude of his own mind was brought to an end. With an understanding not subject to any limitation or bias, he experienced all the insubstantial phenomena of existence as neither existing nor not existing, as being neither as they appear nor utterly void, neither permanent nor nihilate, neither delusory nor liberated by nature. He knew phenomena to be neither created by a buddha nor contrived by sentient beings—not actually purified by means of the path, never changed in their color or form. He realized that the path is self-traversed, that meditation is self-settled, that faults are self-resolved. Limitless good qualities have already been possessed since the very beginning. The three Bodies of buddhahood exist of their own accord. In terms of renunciation and realization, the Master had nothing more to achieve. He was radiant with knowledge that encompassed both the full extent of all things and their true nature. {434} The door to innate, sparkling, fundamental awakening, which has existed of its own accord since the very beginning, became opened. He transparently saw his own nature in its nakedness. He did not partition things as being of saṃsāra or nirvāṇa by their nature. He fully achieved the Mahāmudrā—an understanding of reality in which phenomena are neither superimposed upon nor negated by conceptions of existence or emptiness.

All phenomena fell away before him. He swallowed saṃsāra and nirvāṇa whole. He arrived at buddhahood in a single day. He bore the burdens of phenomenal existence. He shook all the sentient beings out of saṃsāra. Among all the phenomena of saṃsāra and nirvāṇa, he found not even the tip of a hair's worth that was to be rejected, seeing everything as the shifting display of the three Bodies of buddhahood. By thus pursuing his individual aims, he captured the great stronghold that is the Dharma Body.

Around this time, the Master also had specific luminosity and Mahāmudrā experiences in which appearances were unified with their inherent emptiness. These included the experiences referred to as "fabrications being carried off by the wind," "the words of the teachings floating off into the sky," and "yogic bliss during the state of non-meditation." {435}

With the great sail of your dauntless fortitude raised and full,
impelled by the wind of enthusiastic perseverance,
the swift ship of the Master's perfected body, speech, and mind,
ventured out into the ocean in order to learn and practice the sūtra
 and mantra systems.

You approached the unsurpassed lama, the king of the *nāgas*,
and grabbed the supreme wish-fulfilling jewel:
realizing your own true nature.
After returning to your home territory,
you satisfied every need and want, the ultimate fulfiller of wishes.

Just as the reflection of the moon, dependently arisen, dances
 upon the water,
you—a moon full in all its sixteen increments of courageous
 asceticism,
a glowing treasury of camphor refined from blissful winds and
 mentation—
you flitted magically about on the peak of Mount Kailash,
the navel of the physical world.

By filling the Twelve Fortresses—six internal, six external—
with the white light of the experiential realization contained
 within you,
you coaxed open the lily that is the *ḍākiṇīs'* definitive secret,
as well as the storehouse of non-dual mental clarity. {436}

While maintaining the lay, monastic, and tantric vows, you were
 like a grove of lotuses
resplendent with the anthers of your experiential realization:

the sweet honey of your realization
attracted bees, your fortunate disciples, for a veritable feast.
Your fame, the sound made by the jangling anklets of those bees,
adorns the garden of the Kagyü teachings.

Within the state of great bliss, the wind of wisdom blows away
deluded understandings and deceptive appearances.
Achieving the mind of the Victors of the past, present, and future,
experiencing everything as being of the same flavor—
who but you can understand such things?

Such was the third chapter of *The Life Story of the Noble Künga Zangpo, the Glorious Preeminent* Siddha *Whose Practice Is Totally Victorious in All Respects, Called "That Which without Restriction Gives Goosebumps of Faith,"* relating the story of how, after receiving many Dharma teachings—crossing the great ocean of learning—he took meditation as the essence of practice, and lived dressed in the attire of a monk.

4

Taking on the Observance

IN THAT WAY the Master dispossessed himself of food and clothing. By submitting himself to an inconceivable regimen of asceticism, he expelled from his mind all calculations for what may occur in his future within this world, casting such thoughts to the wind. {437} Like the king of the noble ones, Mila Laughing Vajra, he applied himself with single-pointed focus to the various concentrative *samādhis*, and to the yogas of the Generation and Perfection Stages. He thereby attained all of the positive attributes that can result from realization.

At that time, when the Great One had become a great preeminent *siddha*, never to revert from that state, in succession he received prophetic assurances from his lama and the *ḍākiṇīs*, leading him to think, "My continuum is ripened and liberated, so whatever I do is just as well. However, in accordance with the prophetic commands given by my lama and the *ḍākiṇīs*, I should give up the indicators and attire of monkhood and take on the accoutrements of the Heruka. Having combined practice with an 'intimate one'—a consort—with the yogas of the Generation and Perfection Stages, which are derived from the short path of the Vajrayāna, the swift path of the definitive secret of the *ḍākiṇīs*, I will enhance the aspects of my method visible to others, and show the manner of traversing the stages of the Stages and Paths as easily as if they were mere illusions. In one life and one body I will make manifest the body of a sovereign *vajradhara*." {438}

In order to overwhelm all of phenomenal existence with his greatness through the Practice; in order to subdue all the nonhuman spirits that are enemies of and obstacles to the Teachings; in order to take care of every last worthy being and set them on the Stage of Accomplishment; in order to proclaim the greatness of the Vajrayāna and highlight the profundity of its essential meaning; in order to fulfill the intentions of the heroes and *ḍākiṇīs* of the body, speech, and mind;[31] in order to project heaps of offerings like Samantabhadra for the Victor and his sons; in order to spread and increase the teachings of the Victor in general; and especially to initiate a tradition dedicated to the definitive meaning of the precious Kagyü, the master laid down the indicators and attire of monkhood before an image of the Lord of Sages and took on the accoutrements of glorious blood-drinking Heruka.

Upon his naked body he was adorned with a crown of long hair, as well as a circlet, earrings, a necklace and bangles made of bone, a sash, and a Sacred Thread—the Six Bone Ornaments—as well as clumps of ash, drops of blood, and smears of grease from human tissue. {439} For a shawl he wore a human skin, with hair and nails still attached. He wore a tiger's hide as a skirt. He wore a *brahmin*'s cord made from human hair. He took up a *ḍamaru* made of *catechu* wood, a smaller hand drum made from the tops of skulls, a trumpet made from human bone, and an authentic *kapāla* or skull cup that was fissured and yellowed. He had a *vajra*, a bell, and a "sky-staff" or *khaṭvāṅga*, which was decorated with bells, strips of silk, and so on. All of these were associated with *samaya* vows.

Thus he was adorned with the Six Accoutrements of the Heruka, or the Eight Accoutrements of the Great Glorious One. For his *samaya*s he drew from such volumes as the root text of the *Hevajra Tantra*, the *Cakrasaṃvara Tantra*, and the *Dohā Trilogy*. For his appearance he drew from the forms of Hevajra, Cakrasaṃvara, the glorious four-faced vitality-sapping Mahākāla, and so on. He would consume *samaya* substances. . . .[32] {440} He also took up a sword symbolizing Wisdom, an arrow and a bow symbolizing Means and Discernment, and so on.

After taking on all the accoutrements of the charnel ground in that way, the Master cultivated his meditation for some time at Lapchi, Chubar, and the Six Fortresses. He would preside over whole assemblies of heroes and *ḍākiṇīs*.

Then the Master saw various signs, both external and internal, which made him think as follows: "Here lives the king of Ngari Gungtang and his sons. They have a stainless ancestry that includes, from long ago, the king of snowy Tibet, Lhatotori Nyensheltsen; and the Three Dharma Kings: Songtsen Gampo, Trisong Detsen, and the ruler Tri Relpachen. If I overwhelm the present king with my glory, all of the gods, demons, and people of Tibet will also be overwhelmed. If I subdue him, all the others will naturally become subdued. {441} This would bring extensive benefit to the teachings of the Buddha and to sentient beings." He saw external and internal signs indicating that this was so, and also foreknew it with his clairvoyance.

So, wearing the accoutrements of the Heruka, he stole his way into the king's palace in Ngari Dzongkar, unhindered and unnoticed. Having put himself in the *samādhi* called "Overwhelming All of Phenomenal Existence, Saṃsāra and Nirvāṇa, with Glory," he passed straight through, without paying any heed to the guards, eunuchs, dogs, or anyone else who was there. Everyone was so panicked with fright that it was as if they had blacked out. In that kind of state, with no one capable of touching him, while letting loose a loud howl the Master passed through an intermediary gatehouse to the palace. The king and his retinue of ministers and commoners were all scared. They were dumbfounded by fear. {442} A number of people emerged from the gatehouse, grabbed the Master, and threw him out onto a large courtyard of flat stones. A great many ministers and commoners cast a rain of weapons at him, including daggers, knives, swords, rocks, and staffs. But no matter how fiercely they beat him, the Master's rainbow, *vajra* body experienced no pain or harm whatsoever. Then his meditation deepened and his entire body became pervaded by an unmitigated bliss. In a state of realizing that all of phenomenal existence is as foundationless as the center of the sky is clear, he abruptly got up and performed a dance while intoning *hūṃ* and *pheṭ*.

The king, ministers, and commoners were moved to faith by this indication of the Master's *siddha*hood. In a state of amazement, the king invited the Master into the palace, where he paid him reverence and made inestimable offerings. The king confessed to the Master, entreating him to forgive all his sins, obscurations, faults, and failings—especially that of so disrespectfully abusing the Master. {443} The king's joy and his dedication and faith for all time were inestimable. In the same fashion, all of the ministers and commoners invited the Master to their respective homes, in the order of their rank. They paid him reverence, made offerings, did prostrations, circumambulated him, and so on. The Master gave profound and vast Dharma teachings in accordance with their individual wishes.

In that way, through his practice that is totally victorious in all respects, he overwhelmed those people with his glory. From this time onward, the name "the lord of yogins, the Madman from Ü" became fully renowned everywhere.

After that, the Master spent time at such places as Drakar Taso, Shelpuk Chushing fortress, Chonglung Kyung fortress, and Drakmar Linga fortress. That winter he went to the Kathmandu valley, the Swayambhūnāth stūpa, and even "Indian" Parping. He went even beyond that, traveling far enough to set his eyes upon Bodhgaya in India. {444} Inconceivable numbers of heroes and *ḍākinīs* flocked to those holy sites. The Master held *gaṇacakras* or tantric feasts with them on many occasions. Thanks to the marvelous short path of the Vajrayāna, he could progress through the Stages and Paths in whatever fashion he liked.

When the Master stayed in fearsome charnel grounds, he bound every last gang of demons that might otherwise have led one astray, whether external or internal, with oaths to obey his commands. He took an accounting of the promises they made.

One night, while the Master was staying at the very intimidating and frightening charnel ground called Dhana, the remover of obstacles, Lord of the Divine Assembly, Gaṇeśa, appeared before him. With the wisdom of coemergence, he experienced everything as being of the same flavor, seeing himself and the Lord of the Assembly as undifferentiated. Upon being overwhelmed by the glory of the Master's non-conceptual Mahāmudrā wisdom, the Lord of the Assembly bowed in respect and promised to protect the Teachings. After prostrating and making offerings to the Master, the Lord of the Assembly transformed into moonlight and disappeared. {445}

In the same way that the lord of yogins Virūpa used his powers and the performance of miracles to smash the non-Buddhists' idols and teachings to dust, by striking them with stones, hammers, and other implements the Master reduced to powder most of the idols of the *tīrthikas* or Hindus, including an image of Śiva and a statue of Viṣṇu. He stood atop the heads of other statues, urinated on them, and smeared them with unclean things. Other statues he toppled over and buried upside-down in the dirt, detaining them underground. Upon the heads of the larger statues of the great gods, he sat cross-legged, danced, performed the yogic exercises, and so on.

On account of his doing these things, the people living near those temples and in fact the entire populace of the city gathered together, numbering many hundreds of thousands. {446} For an entire day they tormented the Master's body using all sorts of weapons, including swords, long arrows, short arrows smeared with poison, knives, battle-axes, hammers, and a great rain of stones that nearly blocked out the sun. After this they put a sturdy noose around his neck and hanged him from a tree branch. Using dry wood, they lit a large fire beneath where he hung, roasting him. At that time the Master performed the manner of departing into tranquility. Satisfied, the people all went back to their homes.

Before even a day had passed, the Great One returned, like the rising sun, dancing, blazing with a radiant complexion. The fear that was caused by his chasing and beating people made the entire populace fall senseless from shock. Then the Master let out a roaring bellow, like that made by an earthquake pervading both heaven and earth, and the people scattered in every direction.

After some time had passed, the locals came back to their senses and reassembled. {447} Again they tormented the Master's body by casting a whirling snowstorm of weapons at him. With twisted-up cloths, ropes made from hemp and roots, and other things, they tied up every inch of his body, so that he could not even move. Then they tossed him into a large river that eventually empties into the ocean. Having done all of this, the Mön and Nepalese people felt satisfied. They were pleased by the thought that the Master certainly would not return this time.

Because of their attachment to the land of Tibet, the Tibetan merchants, monastics, and beggars who happened to be in the Kathmandu area at the time all felt somewhat dejected. They began to act based on their certain belief that the Master had passed away. With the intention of performing funerary activities on the Master's behalf, the Tibetans all got together and began to eat and drink. They were seated in a line with a mendicant placed at the head, in the position of the lama.

Right when they were in the middle of declaring that any merit they might generate should be put toward benefiting the deceased, the Great One quickly arrived there, unhindered and unnoticed. {448} He stepped on the head of the person making the dedication of merit and slapped him in the face, then performed the dance of the six syllables.[33] This made all the Tibetans and Nepalese flee in every which direction. They all fell down, stupefied, their arms and legs paralyzed. They let out great cries of anguish. Their combined wailing was so loud that it caused the ground to reverberate.

The local lord, who was referred to as "the king of Khokhom"—Bhaktapur—assembled an army complete with the four divisions—infantry, as well as soldiers mounted on horses, elephants, and chariots. They battered the Master with an inconceivable variety of weapons, such that one could not possibly get another hand in. The attack raised a cloud of dust so thick that it blocked out the sun. The air was so full with the rain of weapons and stones they cast that there was not space for even a small bird to fly. {449} The combined sound of the diverse instruments played by that army made the entire world and all its inhabitants tremble. Its volume left all living beings completely deranged. While that was happening, the soldiers tightly bound up the Master's body with hempen rope. They pierced his mouth, eyes, ears, and other parts of his body with thorns and bamboo shards. They smeared his mouth, eyes, and so on with many different kinds of poison. After laying him on top of some kindling and many loads of wood, they chopped him up using axes and hatchets. Then they hit those chunks with hammers and finally roasted them over a fire. Then, chattering with laughter, the soldiers all left their separate ways, satisfied with what they had done.

At the end of the night, just before dawn, the Master arrived in the middle of town with the charnel ground accoutrements he wore jingling and rattling, blowing his thighbone trumpet, intoning *hūṃ* and *pheṭ*. He performed a dance. He reveled in an unsurpassed array of magical displays of his wisdom. {450} At this everyone was amazed and got goosebumps of faith. While crying and prostrating, they admitted their faults. They filled the space around the Master's person with a succession of offerings, indications of their reverence, and things to eat and drink. Because the Master had performed his feats in plain sight, everyone, even the king of Khokhom, revered and pleased him with many clouds of offerings. The wicked king and his retinue were even set upon the way to virtue.

This course of events frightened all of the *tīrthikas*. Worried that their idols might be destroyed, they tightly closed and locked all the doors to their various temples. That night the Master passed unhindered into those very temples and sat with his feet on the heads of the statues. No one could defy, intimidate, or harbor any doubts about him. {451} From that moment, the Master put an end to the locals' performance of animal sacrifices. Inestimable numbers of goats, water buffalos, and other animals were thus given the gift of protection from the fear of having their heads cut off. Atop the heads of all the *tīrthikas*' idols, the Master placed statues of the Lord of Sages, of Avalokiteśvara, and other figures. What's more, after conducting their trade in Nepal, many Tibetans used to stay on to work as servants and maids. The Master put an end to this practice. He impelled these people to enter the door to the Dharma, setting them upon the way to virtue.

The Master visited all of the important holy sites in Nepal, including the places blessed by the eighty-four *mahāsiddhas*. With *gaṇacakras* and heroes' feasts, he delighted all of the heroes and *ḍākiṇīs*. His meditation continued to improve as a result. His very name made the teachings of the Victor shine like the sun.

One time the Master encountered the daughter of a Nepalese nobleman traveling down the road. She was being carried on a palanquin, surrounded by her retinue and many commoners. {452} By making a fierce look, the Master overwhelmed them with his glory. He threw the girl right out of the palanquin. She and her retinue fled, unable to even look at him.

In that manner, the Master discredited all of Nepal's *tīrthikas*, protected the lives of all her animals, and set all of her people upon the way to virtue. He ferociously defeated those who did not heed his commands, forcing them into the way of the teachings of the Victor.

Because the Asura and Yangleshö caves in "Indian" Parping had been taken over by *tīrthikas*, no Buddhist was fortunate enough to visit or to reside within them. The Great One traveled there and, using the Practice of the Fierce Observance, passed unhindered into the caves. He punched the non-Buddhist shrine keeper and threw him out. He chased away and subdued all the *tīrthikas* residing there, forcing them into the way of the Buddhist teachings. {453}

Thus by means of his practice that is totally victorious in all respects, the Master overwhelmed with his glory all of the beings residing in those places—god, human, or otherwise. After completing all of his enlightened activities there, the Master went back to the snowy enclave of Lapchi, where he stayed for some time.

Then the Master thought that if he went to the glorious Khecara realm that is Tsari, it would be of benefit both to the Teachings and to sentient beings, and his own meditation would also improve. This thought was in accordance with the prophetic commands of the *ḍākiṇīs* and with the clarified perceptions he saw during his meditation.

When the Master was traveling across the Pelmopel plain, different kinds of predatory animals set about to cause him harm. However, they were all paralyzed by the mere sight of the Great One's finger pointed threateningly at them.

Somewhere near there, the Master came across a formidible bandit as he was roving about. The Master overwhelmed him with the splendor of his Heruka accoutrements and the brilliance of the fierce look in his eyes. {454} Unable to even lay a hand on him, the bandit was left there, staring off into the distance, chattering in shock.

In the middle of the plain, the Master met a monk who was afflicted by an illness that was caused by an earth spirit. He immediately grabbed and beat the monk. Like wiping dust from a conch shell, the illness was dispelled and the monk got better. He subsequently held the Master in great respect.

The Master went to Dingri Langkhor monastery, where he stayed for a few days. He made prayers before the White Mausoleum, meditated in the House of Dependent Connections, and so on.

Then he went by stages to Tanak, "Black Horse," where he met peerless Tsachungpa the Great, Khyenrap Yönten Penjung. The Master received every last empowerment, instruction, esoteric oral instruction, and reading transmission for the cycle of teachings passed on by the Later lineage of the Pacification practice. He also received all of the esoteric oral instructions relating to the cycles of the Early and Middle lineages. The Master became especially certain and faithful with respect to these cycles of Pacification teachings. {455}

While practicing at the House of Dependent Connections, the Master encountered the precious Padampa Sangyé. Padampa gave him his authorization and many prophetic assurances. The Master received prophecies stating that the victor Tsachungpa was in fact an emanation of precious Padampa, and that the Master himself was an emanation of Padampa's mind. During the time when the Master was receiving empowerments for the five paths and the three paths,[34] he had many visions, including one featuring the glorious wisdom protector, Agora Mahākāla.

At that time he received, for experiential instructions, the entirety of the Six Dharmas of Niguma—the very heart essence of the wisdom *ḍākiṇīs*. He also received Niguma's ancillary instructions; empowerments for the five classes of tantras; a general teaching on the illusory body; teachings on each of the Six Dharmas; the empowerment for the five deities, featuring Cakrasaṃvara; teachings on Khecarī, in both her white and red forms; four exoteric teachings, including the empowerment to perform the *torma* of the glorious wisdom protector Mahākāla in his six-armed form, which has the capacity to remove any obstacle; the entire cycle for the six-armed one, including instructions on the white protector, the wish-fulfilling jewel; and also the yogic exercises and teachings for achieving a deathless body; the instructions and teachings for a deathless mind; the instructions and teachings on the three types of non-erring; as well as the experiential instructions, the empowerment, the teachings, and the reading transmission for the Amulet-box Mahāmudrā. {456} In short, like a vase being filled to the brim, he received all of the available instructions and reading transmissions for the special Dharma teachings of the Shangpa Kagyü.

The realizations that the Master had internally throughout this time were limitless like the sky, and therefore cannot be fully encompassed in writing. However, in order to foster different individiuals' personal stakes in the Dharma, I will mention some of them here.

While receiving those various empowerments and teachings, the Master had visions of the principal deities featured in their respective maṇḍalas. He saw those deities as indistinguishable from his own lama. He fully understood the wisdom that was expressed by each initiatory empowerment ritual, and by the different symbols used within each empowerment. He also understood the wisdom expressed by the relationships between the individual symbols and their respective meanings.

Wherever the Master was staying, the six-armed wisdom protector and his attendant deities would come before him. They obeyed him as if they were serfs.

As for the state of dreaming, the Master could seize control of his dreams through meditation. This enabled him to revel in tantric feasts along with the heroes and *ḍākiṇīs* of the western land of Oḍḍiyāṇa, during which he would sing *vajra* songs expressing his experiences and realizations. {457} Upon traveling to the eastern pureland of Abhirati, he received the Dharma from the buddha Akṣobhya. In the western pureland of Sukhāvati, he offered the seven aspects of worship,[35] plus some prayers. In the pureland of Akaniṣṭha, he made an offering to the primordial buddha Vajradhara, which consisted of his own realizations concerning bliss and emptiness. Then the Master dissolved into Vajradhara's heart and the entire dream experience was transformed into luminosity. He rested in equanimity within the obscurationless Dharma Body. Then he rose up from that state, like a fish jumping out of water, and projected heaps of offerings like Samantabhadra for all the buddhas of the ten directions, in the hundreds of buddha realms. This caused the ripening of all transmigrating beings. Riding on the sun and moon, he circled the four continents, received Dharma teachings from the eighty *mahāsiddhas*, and so on.

At one point he assumed the form of a tiny Vajrayoginī and entered into master Tsachungpa [Yönten Penjung] by way of his nose. {458} Inside, he saw the complete maṇḍala of the lama's yogic body. While stopping at the individual *cakras*, the Master received different empowerments from the lama, who had assumed various forms, including those of the four Bodies of buddhahood and the respective appearances of the different members of the five buddha families.

As the strength of his luminosity increased, on a few occasions the Master was able to see all of the billion worlds of the universe. From afar, he continuously saw whatever his lama and his Dharma brothers were up to, as clearly as if he were looking at a gooseberry laid on the palm of his hand. The different miraculous feats he performed, without ever wavering from a state of sky-like realization, are beyond enumeration.

The Master received many other empowerments and authorizations from the victor Tsachungpa, including many cycles of *dohās*, which are so essential for spiritual accomplishment; reading transmissions for the *Completely Non-abiding Mahāmudrā* and the *Mahāmudrā Drop*; the Secret Practice of India; and the Great Perfection cycle.

After this he went to Yarlung, traveling in stages by way of the southern route. He stayed at Densa Til for a few days, during which time the son was reunited with his spiritual father, Drakchokpa. {459} In the course of their conversations, the Master made offerings of his experiential realizations, which were to the amazement of all.

Then, traveling by way of the Dakpo area, the Master entered the divine abode of Tsari. He was welcomed to the area by the glorious king ruling over all the divine protectors of the realm. An inconceivable number of heroes and *ḍākiṇīs* gathered around him. Beginning that night, inside that abode, they held an inconceivable tantric feast lasting for days. The moment when the Master drank some alcohol from the implement known as the Authentic Small Maroon Skull Cup, the "nectar" began to boil, making a crackling sound. Meanwhile wisdom blazed within all of the congregants. With his body, the Master performed an inconceivable array of dances. With the *vajra* laughter of his melodious voice, he sang many songs of experience. In his mind, utterly non-conceptual wisdom co-emerged with great bliss, which allowed him to remain in a state of experiencing saṃsāra and nirvāṇa as being of the same flavor, of experiencing the sameness of existence and the tranquil beyond—a state that cannot be fully described in writing.

The Master departed from Pangchung, traveling stage by stage. {460} Alongside various lakes and abodes, he would perform meditations on and make offerings to the particular deities associated with those individual sites, connecting what is external, what is internal, and what is secret. He also held amazing tantric feasts in those places. As a result of his performing those and other fitting meditations, spiritual gains and clarified perceptions arose in the following manner:

At what is called the "Mansion of the Dharma Body of Appearances" or the "Cāritra of the Baseless Nature of the Mind," he was blessed by the lamas of the Kagyü, discovering the lama and the Dharma Body within his own mind. As a result, the true form of Tsari, as the divine Khecara realm, became visible to him.

At what is called the "Mansion of the Pure Enjoyment Body" or the "Cāritra of the Unified *Vajra* Body," he was blessed by the divine assembly of his tutelary deity's maṇḍala, discovering the entire divine assembly mentioned in all the secret tantras to be inside his very own *vajra* body. As a result, the "Cāritra of the *Vajra* Body Within" became visible to him.

At what is called the "Mansion of the Body, Speech, and Mind" or the "Cāritra of the Object Emanated Externally," he was blessed by the glorious protectors of the three buddha families—Avalokiteśvara, Mañjuśrī, and Vajrapāṇi—and all appearances within the infinite expanse of purity became the stuff of unceasing potentiality. {461} As a result, the "Cāritra of the Object Emanated Externally" became visible to him.

At what is called the "Mansion of the Five Poisons, Completely Purified" or the "Cāritra of the Five Families," he was blessed by the fathers, the Victors of the five buddha families, discovering amid the ordinary aggregates and elements—which are pure from the very start—all the members of the hundreds of external and internal divine families. As a result, the "Cāritra of the Five Secret Families" became visible to him.

At what is called the "Mansion of the Five Wisdoms" or the "Cāritra of the Channels and Elements, Completely Purified," he was blessed by the mothers, the five classes of *ḍākiṇīs*, discovering all of the field-born and mantra-born messengers[36] to be co-emergent with his own yogic channels and drops. As a result, the "Cāritra of the Unification of Bliss and Luminosity" became visible to him.

At what is called the "Mansion of the Tsari Maṇḍala" or the "Cāritra of the Khecara Palace," he was blessed by Secret Mantra's divine assembly within, discovering the entire array of the amazing realm of karmic appearances to be an unrestricted magical display. {462} As a result, the "Spontaneously Arisen Cāritra" became visible to him.

At what is called the "Mansion of the Turquoise Lake Palace" or the "Cāritra of the Twenty-Four Holy Sites," he was blessed by the divine assemblies emanated both externally and internally, discovering all the amazing aspects of the divinely emanated place known as Tungchö—"Quenching Thirst"—while in a profound and clear *samādhi*. As a result, the "Cāritra of Purpose in Whatever One Does" became visible to him.

At the supreme external abode of Dakpa Shelri, he was blessed by 2,800 deities, which purified his *avadhūti*, the central channel within, leading to his casting conceptual attributions out from their very root. As a result, his own mind became apparent to him as being the Dharma Body.

At the external "Mansion of the Hero of the Great Corpse," he was blessed by an entire ocean of gods and heroes, which internally purified the very top of his head—which corresponds to the holy site of Puliramalaya in India—and completely eradicated clinging to perceptual experiences. As a result, he had a realization concerning the great bliss of reflexive awareness. {463}

At the external "Mansion of the Heroine of the Lesser Corpse," he was blessed by an ocean of motherly *ḍākiṇīs*, which internally purified the crown of his head—which corresponds to Jālandhara—and completely eradicated conceptual attributions that he might have grasped on to. As a result, everything appeared to him as the play of luminosity.

At the external "Mansion of the Four Mountains of Khecara," he was blessed by the entire assemby of divine pairs enacting the unification of skillful means and discernment through their sexual embrace, which internally purified the *cakra* at his crown protuberance, and completely eradicated the aspects of saṃsāric existence that he had not already left behind. As a result, he achieved the state of the pure Khecara realm.

At the external "Skull, the Spirit Lake of the Kagyü," he was blessed by the fathers, the Kagyü lamas, which internally purified the *cakra* of great bliss at the top of his head, and completely eradicated the potential flaw of following mistaken paths. As a result, the blessings of his root and lineage lamas were established in his mind.

At the external "Mansion of the Great Palace," he was blessed by the divine assembly emanated within, which internally purified the emanation *cakra* at his navel and completely eradicated clinging to ordinary appearances. {464} As a result, everything appeared to him as the bodily play of the deities.

At the external "Mansion of the Crooked Palace," he was blessed by the queen mother, Vajravārāhī, which internally purified the vessel that houses the *a*-stroke—the abode of fire—and caused his physical body composed of the four elements to ripen into its pure form. As a result, *tummo*, the fire of wisdom, blazed within him.

At the external "Mansion of the Great Lake of Blazing Light," he was blessed by the emanated divine assemblies of Hevajra and Guhyasamāja, which internally purified his protector-of-bliss *cakra*—the abode of bliss—and made the three appearances[37] dissolve into a state of luminosity. As a result, his wisdom of the four dispositional joys increased.

At the external "Mansion of the Spirit Lake of Cakrasaṃvara, He of the Supreme Bliss," he was blessed by his tutelary deity, Cakrasaṃvara, which internally purified the Dharma *cakra* at his heart and eliminated the fetters that are the three poisons. As a result, the great bliss wisdom of co-emergence arose within him. {465}

At the external "Mansion of the Spirit Lake of Tārā," he was blessed by the mother, Amogha Tārā, which internally purified the *cakra* of great bliss at his "secret place" and eliminated the obscurations to the Four Appearances.[38] As a result, he became capable of the four types of enlightened activity.

At the external "Mansion of Kala Dungtso Lake," he was blessed by the mother, the *ḍākiṇī* of the body, which internally purified the maṇḍala at his forehead and eliminated the bodily obscuration that is physical habituation. As a result, the *ḍākiṇī* of magical bodily display became visible to him.

At the external "Mansion of the Copper Matrix of Reality Lake," he was blessed by the mother, the *ḍākiṇī* of speech, which internally purified the maṇḍala at his throat and eliminated the obscuration in his yogic winds that is caused by exhaling and inhaling. As a result, the *ḍākiṇī* of indestructible speech became visible to him.

At the external "Mansion of Lapis Lazuli Lake," he was blessed by the mother, the *ḍākiṇī* of the mind, which internally purified the maṇḍala at his heart and eliminated the mental obscuration that is dualizing fixation. As a result, the *ḍākiṇī* of non-conceptual mind became visible to him. {466}

At the external "Mansion of Yellow Origin-of-All Lake," he was blessed by the mother, the *ḍākiṇī* of good qualities, which internally purified the maṇḍala at his navel and eliminated the obscuration that is mental fabrication. As a result, the *ḍākiṇī* of effortless good qualities became visible to him.

At the external "Mansion of Dramozik Lake," he was blessed by the mother, the *ḍākiṇī* of enlightened activity, which internally purified the maṇḍala at his "secret place" and eliminated the obscuration of endeavoring under the notions of "actors" and "actions." As a result, the *ḍākiṇī* of spontaneously achieved enlightened activity became visible to him.

At the external "Mansion of the Spirit Lake of Māranatha," he was blessed by the divine assembly emanated by Māranatha, which internally purified his bliss—the conqueror of Māra—and eliminated the external, internal, and secret obstacles. As a result, he attained both the supreme *siddhi* and the mundane *siddhis*.

At the external "Mansion of Blazing Fire Lake," he was blessed by the garland-of-flames *ḍākiṇī*, which internally purified the hub of his fire *cakra* and eliminated the dross of the four elements. {467} As a result, he attained a pure illusory body.

At the external "Mansion of Marnak Rakta, Dark Red Blood," he was blessed by the mother, Ekajaṭī, which internally purified the letter *kṣa* and eliminated the fetter that is the karmic wind. As a result, his life force and the downward-voiding wind became melded together as one.

At the external entrance to the "*Vajra* Enclave of the Sexed Stones," he was blessed by the mother, the secret *ḍākiṇī*, which internally purified the opening of his *liṅgam* and eliminated the fetters that cause difficulties in traversing the Paths. As a result, he discovered the supreme path, the forceful method of quick bliss.

At the external entrance to Angé gorge in Yülmé, he was blessed by the mothers, the three Angé sisters, which internally purified the three channels and the places where they meet and enabled him to hold the bliss of ejaculation within the *avadhūti*, the central channel. As a result, he attained the *siddhi* of "not transferring the yogic drop."

At the external "Perilous Gorge of the Fearsome Goddess," he was blessed by the three guardians of the Teachings—the mother protector and her siblings—which internally purified his lesser channels and eliminated the obstacle that is the very thought of ejaculation. {468} As a result, he achieved the *siddhi* of conquering the demons that are the basic afflictions.

At the external "Wish-Fulfilling Mansion of Parpata," he was blessed by the mother, the field-born *ḍākiṇī*, which internally purified all of his skin and eliminated delusory perceptions. As a result, he attained the *siddhi* of seeing buddha realms in his purified visions.

At the external "Mansion of the Entrance to Taktsang Gorge," he was blessed by the mother, the karmic *ḍākiṇī*, which internally purified the spot that corresponds to the supreme abode of Suvarṇadvipa and eliminated the obscurations that lead to bad transmigrations. As a result, he attained the *siddhi* of the three spheres of the expanse.[39]

At the external "Mansion of the Four Entrances to the Perilous Path," he was blessed by the gatekeepers of skillful means and discernment, father and mother, which internally purified his four upper and lower orifices and enabled him to completely conquer the armies of the four demons. {469} As a result, he attained the *siddhi*s of the four liberations and the four immeasurables.[40]

Thus, upon seeing the different parts of the landscape around there, or upon being told, "This place is this . . . ," the Master encountered the many holy sites at Tsari. When he was not viewing the external abodes he visited on the level of their essential nature, he delighted the deities of the maṇḍalas of those places by doing meditations on and making offerings to them. Thanks to the blessings they bestowed upon him, his mental continuum was ripened and liberated. The knots in the outer and inner channels—which correspond to the holy sites, their surrounding areas, and so on—were all undone. The vital wind associated with the passing of time was arrested. He attained the different Stages in succession. These and other things were achieved in accordance with the ways they are explained in the different classes of tantras. Recognizing this abode called "the unrivaled Tsari" as being the actual pure Khecara buddha realm, and not separating it off as external to himself, he was able to see the essence of his own mind as being wisdom that is completely free from conceptuality. {470} While remaining in a state of non-duality, he achieved perfect understanding.

He spent about a year at Tsari in that manner. The Jozang people,[41] the community of monks, and the great meditator yogins and yoginīs of Tsari all became unanimously dedicated and faithful toward the Master—for once able to put aside their jealousy over their status relative to one another.

After giving the Mahāmudrā to many pilgrims circumambulating Tsari that spring, the Master went by stages to Turquoise Lake. Along the way, he stopped to offer extensive feasts and *tormas* at whatever notable holy sites and divine images he came across. To a subset of his retinue, he began to give instructions on the Six Dharmas and the Mahāmudrā, with a different corresponding topic for meditation each day.

When they were on the bank of the vast Dokhar Lake, a large rockslide was set off above them. A boulder the size of a yak was rolling down, headed straight for the Master and his students. The Great One blew a fierce puff of air from his nose, snapped his fingers, and pointed at the boulder. The boulder stopped rolling and came to rest right there on the side of that mountain. {471}

Then the teacher and his students spent a day in Taktsang gorge. When he was performing the leftover *torma* portion of the tantric feast, a naked creature with the body of a woman and the beak of a bird appeared. She picked up the leftover *torma* and walked off with it, making a whistling sound.

When the Master was offering a *torma* dedicated to his tutelary deity at Marnak Rakta, an invisible hand emerged from a circle of light and lifted up the *torma*. Among other things, the invisible hand also picked up the pebbles and *sindoor* being used in the ritual and delivered them into the Master's hands.

At the holier sites, the Master constructed Dharma thrones of varying sizes, as appropriate for each place. He taught the Mahāmudrā, the Six Dharmas, the *Dohā Trilogy*, and other things, depending on what was suitable and timely.

It is said that when he shot an arrow at a rock face in Gönpo gorge, the arrow sank halfway into it.

Amid those and other inconceivable and amazing things that appeared externally, internally, and in secret, the Master saw signs indicating that if he went to Gyel-la in Kongpo, it would be of benefit to transmigrating beings. {472} So he developed the intention of continuing his Secret Practice and taking care of both human and nonhuman transmigrating beings in that area. While traveling there, he left the monks and mendicants behind: while holding in a vase breath with his mouth closed, he entered the swift-foot *samādhi* and took off. In an instant he arrived at a place in Kongpo called Tongshong.

When the Master was traveling near the outskirts of a town in Kongpo, he came across a couple of youngsters who were playing an archery game, drunk on *chang*. One said, "Hey yogin, show me that bangle on your left wrist." The Master took off his ivory bangle and handed it to him. The two youngsters took it and would not give it back. {473}

"That is the body ornament of a yogin, so I really need it," the Master told them. "You should give it back." When they did not hand it over, it seemed as if the Master was about to hit them. The youngsters took up their bows and arrows and made ready to stick the Master right in the heart. Then the Great One targeted a fierce look and pointed threateningly at them. They both became completely paralyzed, falling senseless with their bows and arrows in their hands. After a little while, the Master spit and they were revived.

The Master stayed in the area for a while after this. One time he met a monk called Jozang Sthavira[42] as he was returning from doing pilgrimage and gathering offerings, accompanied by many people. That protector of beings asked the Master some questions about Dharma jargon, with the intention of discrediting him. Even though the Master gave only correct responses, the monk said, with a look of disrespect, "Yogin, all of this crude behavior of yours does harm to the Teachings. In particular, it is sickening that you should drink so much alcohol." {474}

The Great One responded, "You are not the only one who gets to say and recognize what is the Buddha's teaching. I wonder if any of us upholds the essence of the Victor's teachings? I do not harm the Teachings. You be careful!" He continued, "If you are so sickened by the drinking of alcohol, let's see if it is I, the yogin, who has been drinking, or if it is you, Jozang." Then the Master caused a wave of alcohol to issue forth from the syllable *maṃ* inside the monk, and a pool of milk from the *baṃ* at his own navel. The monk became nauseous from the alcohol and vomited it up in an uninterrupted stream. Meanwhile just a small bowl's worth of milk poured forth from the Master's own mouth. All were amazed, and became faithful toward him.

Some time after that, an inconceivable number of people had gathered near the turbulent rapids at Shinjé Dongkha, "the Mouth of Yama's Well." {475} Impelled by the force of the experience that blazed in his mind, the Master jumped from among the crowd right into the rapids. Everyone was both frightened for him and amazed. While chattering loudly, he danced gracefully over to the far bank of the river and back again, as if he were on solid ground. Everyone saw him as an actual buddha. The people did prostrations and paid him reverence with dedicated and faithful zeal. He accepted the offerings that were made with such insistence, then satisfied everyone by pronouncing a completely pure dedication of merit. Then, without making a single mistake, he returned the offerings that were made by each respective individual. "An ascetic yogin like me has no need for wealth," he declared. This gave goosebumps of faith to every last person there.

At a place in Kongpo called Dru Dorjé Den, there was a *geshé* who harbored doubts about the Master. {476} With the intention of putting the Master to a test, the scholar-monk expressed faith in him, then invited him inside and called for a tantric feast. Later, the *geshé* invited him to spend the night there. As if he knew the *geshé*'s true feelings, the Great One said, "I won't stay." He walked toward a part of the building where there was no door, then passed unhindered through the solid wall. The monk became very faithful toward the Master and his fame spread to one and all.

After that, the Master went to Kongpo's beautiful northern Draklé. When he was staying in an isolated mountain retreat in the upper part of the valley, one day a number of hunters native to Kongpo were getting ready to kill an old buck. Hunting dogs blocked off the rocky path while the men closed in with their arrows. With no place to flee, the deer was in a helpless situation. At that very moment, the Master leapt right into the midst of all the hunters and their dogs. The Master pointed threateningly at all of them, causing the dogs to tumble off the cliff and the men to become paralyzed, their mouths mute, not knowing what to do. {477} The buck laid down at the feet of the Master as if beseeching him for protection.

There was another occasion in Draklé, not long after that, when many people from Kongpo were repeatedly plying the Master with *chang* and strong liquor. Although he drank at three times the ordinary rate, he did not get intoxicated and was actually physically very well—so he has said.

At Tatok Khar in Kongpo there is a narrow passage between two rock faces—so narrow that a single very fit person can barely manage to squeeze through it. The Great One mounted a good Kongpo horse, holding a sharp sword with his right hand. Using the sword in the place of a whip, he hacked wildly at the horse. They galloped down the narrow passage, cutting straight through the rock. The Master found himself in the middle of a forest so thick with conifers that a person could not pass through it or even see where it ended. {478} The Master traveled a great distance through that forest, laughing an audible "Ah la!" the whole way. This made all the people of Kongpo very faithful. They beheld him with amazement and wonder.

After that, as presaged by the clarified perceptions he saw during his meditation and by the prophetic assurances given to him by the heroes and the *ḍākiṇīs*, the Master went to Dakla Gampo monastery by way of upper Dakpo. Doing the Fierce Practice, he was able to pass unhindered into the offering chapel. The shrine keeper, of a malicious and unruly mind, began to punch the Master and hit him with a staff. Then he beat the Master about the face and chest with the leg of a footstool, berating him with a roar of unpleasantries all the while. At first, the Master patiently endured this hardship. Then he thought, "Although it is easy for me to withstand this sort of trial, this shrine keeper will surely do real harm to other mendicants and great meditators who come here in the future. So I should put a stop to this now."

The Master stood up and offered him a challenge, saying, "If you would treat an ascetic temple visitor like me in so ruthless a manner, let's see how much you yourself can take." {479} The Master grabbed the shrine keeper by the neck and began punching him. Unable to do the slightest thing in return, the shrine keeper cried out in pain. He ended up pledging not to treat people that way anymore.

While at Dakla Gampo, the Master made prayers and supplications before representations of enlightened body, speech, and mind. When he did this at the foot of a certain statue made from precious materials, it miraculously spoke—so it is renowned.

Then the Master went by stages to the Ja area. On account of the inconceivable enlightened activities he had performed and the faith that everyone had in him, he received magnificent offerings and reverence, as well as many requests to teach the Dharma. The great patron of the Teachings, Tashi Dargyé Lekpé Gyelpo of Ja, offered him inconceivable reverence. In the course of their conversations, Tashi Dargyé asked the Master, among other things, to resolve the uncertainties he had concerning many difficult points on the level of definitive meanings, and to give him an introduction to the essential meaning. {480} Out of their immeasurable devotion, the other officers of Ja all requested the Master to give further Dharma teachings relating to what had been discussed in his conversations with Tashi Dargyé. They offered him a robe made of red *eren* fabric and adorned with sequins. They served and made offerings to him in every appropriate manner.

After staying there for a while, the Master went to Densa Til, traveling by way of the Yartö area. The son met with his father-lama, of the same nature as the victor Vajradhara. Before representations of enlightened body, speech, and mind—including the two statues made from precious materials—the Master made offerings of butter lamps, clothing, and the like. In a state of delight, he received before the *mahāsattva* Sharmepa many well-spoken teachings and oral instructions of the precious Kagyü that he had not received before. He also received all of the unwritten oral instructions of the Aural Transmission, which had remained as an aural transmission from the time of the protector of beings Pakmodrupa, "the Great One Who Resided at Tartsa Cave," down to the noble and precious Drakchokpa. These included the empowerment and authorization for the four-armed wisdom protector Mahākāla, and the instructions on the protectress Kurakma. {481}

After spending some time there, the Master went to the Kyishö area. Intending to visit the precious Jowo statue, he went directly to the magical manifestation that is the Jokhang temple in Lhasa. But the shrine keeper would not open the gate. The Master caught a glimpse of the Jowo through a chink in the locked gate, seeing the statue as the actual peerless Lord of the Śākya. A faith of unlimited zealousness arose within him, which made the appearances of this world subside into reality. Thus invigorated, the Master was able to slip through a tiny opening in the gate and go before the Jowo unhindered. Loudly praying and supplicating, "Oh precious Jowo!" he threw his arms around and bowed before the statue. {482} This was performed in plain sight of everyone.

At that time many people arrived to show the inconceivable reverence they had for the Master. They did this by offering him things like tea, hospitality, and "inner offerings of nectar." Among those people there was a woman, utterly different from the others, wearing a shawl of fine silk. She had arrived there without being noticed by anyone. She carried a cup of "inner offerings," which she presented to the Master. She then performed many prostrations, prayers, and circumambulations. Then she spoke of her need for a Dharmic link. So the Great One imparted to her the practice of arousing the *bodhicitta* mind of the Mahāyāna, along with a guru yoga meditation. Upon promising to reverently serve him for as long as he should live, she vanished instantly. The Master has said that the one who thus pledged to increase the number of his disciples and to reverently serve him was the glorious goddess Machik herself. {483}

The Master went by stages to the Tsang area. He stayed briefly at Jak, Bara Döndrup Ding, and other places, giving whatever profound and vast Dharma teachings suited the many superior and ordinary beings he met. Before the victor Tsachungpa, he received some remaining Dharma teachings. Father and son exerted themselves in activities exclusively Dharmic in nature.

At one point early on in this period, the Master intended to go to the upper Tanak area. Along the way, he saw a pack of brigands sitting along the bank of the Shang river, their horses grazing nearby. Doing the Practice of the Fierce Observance, the Master descended unhindered upon them. The horses ran off in different directions. The frightened brigands jumped up and began to shout. Right away they started hacking at the Master with their weapons. They chopped off his right arm, then each of his legs, then his left arm, then his head. {484} Then they scattered the pieces about, stabbing at his head with a number of swords. After they had smashed his body to dust, the brigands dispersed. Then the Great One restored his body to the way it had been before, bearing no sign of harm whatsoever. As a result, all of the brigands became faithful toward him, and the white banner of his fame became visible as far away as the ends of the earth.

The Master stayed in many of Tanak's more isolated holy sites, where he deepened his meditation and greatly benefited transmigrating beings.

While traveling to the Shang area, the Master walked unhurriedly across the surface of the Shang river. Many people saw this happen. As a result, indications of people's unrestricted faith in him reached to the very ends of the earth.

One time, Rinchen Pelzang—the Indra of this earth, the great king wielding the wheel of power, the protector of the realm—was at the hot spring in the pastureland of Gyatso. The Great One and his students went right to where the lord was sitting. With a single look, the Master overwhelmed everyone with his glory. {485} Then he sat down and entered a meditative state in which any distinction between a perceived object and its perceiving subject was negated, thus resolving the challenge he faced at that moment. Because of this, that lord of men achieved a perfectly purified vision of the Master. He offered the Master reverential service, displays of his respect for him, and so on.

In autumn, the Master went to a place in Khartsé where people were busy reaping the harvest. He did a dance on top of the lunch that had been prepared for the workers, then slapped the people who became hostile toward him for doing so. The lord of the estate and his servants stabbed the Master with daggers, knives, sickles, and other implements. They cast a great rain of stones, stopping only after the Master was completely buried under a pile of them. After a moment, he shouted *pheṭ*, arose from the pile of stones, and performed a dance. Every last person gathered there was joyed by this indication of the Master's *siddha*hood, offering him reverential service and limitless devotion—so it is related.

At one point the Shang river was swollen with water, making it wider and more turbulent than usual. {486} The Master danced across the surface of the river, borne by the unstoppability that arises from wisdom, and by the bravery that arises from having experiential realization. A number of horse-keepers present at the time saw this feat and wondered, "Is this real or false? It must be an optical illusion." Even after they had a good look, it was exactly as it appeared. With great faith and amazement, they approached the Master. They clearly saw him walking on the water, his boots not even wet. They bowed their heads at his feet, offered many prostrations, and became inconceivably dedicated and faithful.

It is renowned that around then, while the Master was staying at Rinchen Gang in Shang, giving Dharma teachings to many *geshés*, on one occasion he generated three separate bodily manifestations. One manifestation was seen going down a perilous path alongside a cliff—it even being said that some people met him there and requested that he give them blessings and protective ribbons. Another manifestation went to Nyatsel, where a few people reverently served him. His actual body, however, had remained at Rinchen Gang giving Dharma teachings that day. {487}

Traveling by way of southern Latö, the Master went to Dingri Langkhor. While there, he recited prayers, made supplications, and finished up some other things that he wanted to do. The next morning the Master rose early, put on the accoutrements of the Heruka, and traveled to Dröpa Cave in Nyanam, where the sun never shines. He would spend that winter at Dröpa Cave.

Some monks assembled there to listen to the Dharma. The Master gave them extensive instruction in the Six Dharmas. On account of the Master's success in fostering good meditative experiences, many among those whom he instructed were able to perform the Presentation of a Dried Sheet at the time of the New Year.

Afterward, when they were holding an extensive tantric feast celebrating the sheets they had dried, the Great One issued the following command: "You cotton-clad ones, sing a song about an experience you have had!" But no one would sing. As if he were angry, the Master picked up a cup filled with rice liquor and threw it toward his students. {488} It hit the wall of the cave. Everyone thought that the cup had broken to bits. But when they looked, the pottery had not broken and the liquor had not even spilled. Everyone felt faith and amazement with respect to this indication of the Master's *siddha*hood. They took the cup as an object of worship and still have it to this day—so it is renowned.

That summer the Master went to the palace of Cakrasaṃvara, the king of snow mountains, Mount Kailash, where the noble *sthavira* Aṅgirāja still resides, surrounded by a retinue of thirteen hundred *arhat*s. While on the way there, the Master traveled day and night for five days through empty valleys devoid of people, taking very little rest. He walked unaccompanied into a pack consisting of hundreds of wolves, and into another consisting of fifty or sixty. Even when the Master was uncertain about how they might react, those dangerous animals would just sit before him in their natural state of tranquility and tameness, never entertaining any idea of harming him—so he has said. {489} Such are the powers of one who has uncontrived, loving, compassionate *bodhicitta* within his mental continuum! Such are the magical displays performed by one who has attained stability in Generation and Perfection Stage practices like the illusory body and dream yoga!

While spending that summer at Mount Kailash, the Master had amazing, inconceivable visions. He remembered the stories of many of his past lives, and foreknew his future ones. Never wavering from the completely pure state of the natural expanse, he was endowed with pure perception by which every possible phenomenon became fully disclosed to him.

Then he went again to Chubar. He remained in solitude for some time, deepening his meditation. Each night an inconceivable army of demons would appear, then try to cause trouble for him. {490} At first those ghastly apparitions made the Master feel as if all his skin was gathering at the top of his head, as if he was flying through the air, as if the ground and the mountainsides were trembling and ringing out. At times it seemed as if there were demons pouring out from within his own body. A ghoulish phantasm with fangs the size of Mount Meru appeared to eat him up. Then he had the experience of falling into a deep, dark expanse. He heard loud noises like cracks of lightning, or as if both sky and earth were shattering completely. He felt like he was grabbed by an invisible hand and thrown into the air. These are some of the indescribable, miraculous things that ocurred.

But for a preeminent *siddha* fully resolved in the wisdom that all of phenomenal existence, saṃsāra and nirvāṇa, is co-emergent with his own innate mind—how could he be frightened by or come under the sway of anything that should appear among the biasless potentiality of dependently arisen forms, which in truth neither arise nor ever cease to exist? {491} The lion is not frightened by the fox's theatrics. No matter what costume the dramatist's son may don, no matter what kind of act he may put on, his father will remain unafraid, thinking, "This is my son." In the very same manner, during this time of frightening displays put on by that inconceivable army of demons, it was the Great One's meditation that carried him through—just as a forest fire is stoked by the wind. Not falling to partiality in any way, he passed the time while remaining in a state of seeing everything as essenceless, pure from the very start.

At that time there appeared a five-colored rainbow, hanging like a curtain from the upper slope of Gang Tönting Gyelmo, the "Azure Queen Snow Mountain." The Five Long-Life Sister goddesses, borne by that rainbow, arrived in the presence of the Master. They stood in a line, holding their five lamps made from precious materials. {492} They circumambulated the Master, made offerings to him, and performed acts of reverence many times. They also made offerings at each of the signs of his *siddhis* that he had left behind. Then the five sister goddesses dissolved into rainbow light, faded into the snowy upper slope of the Queen, and disappeared completely.

After deepening his meditation at that divine abode, the Master went to Nyishang in Mön. While meditating in an isolated spot in the upper part of the valley, he was met by some locals led by a man named Tsetar—"Life Saver"—who were in the middle of hunting a deer. "Don't do that!" the Master commanded them. "Leave the deer in peace!" Not heeding him, they hurt the deer anyway. "If you do not listen to me, I will destroy you right now!" he threatened.

The hunters responded with a challenge: "If you have that kind of ability, eat this!" They handed him a bit of poisonous black aconite the size of a thumb. {493} The Great One immediately ate the black aconite, which amazed them all, moving them to complete faith. He even set them upon the way of virtuous action, which included their giving up the taking of lives.

The Master was then invited to Lajang. While staying at the home of one referred to as Lopön Jetsünpa, "Noble *Ācārya*," the Master pretended to be angry with an *ācārya* from Dzongkar named Pema. In front of the Master sat a porcelain cup filled with rice liquor. When he threw the cup at Pema's face, it circled him three times in the air, then fell to the ground. The cup was not broken and the liquor had not even spilled. They all became faithful. Everyone regarded the Master with amazement.

That winter when the Master traveled to the Kathmandu valley, the Nepalese and the Tibetans had not been getting along. The corpses of a Nepalese and a Tibetan who had been killed were left lying in the road. The Master took the two bodies to the Ramadoli charnel ground. There he cut out their thighbones, so as to make trumpets out of them. {494} Innumerable Nepalese people got together and began casting a rain of stones at him. Every part of the Master's body was hit. Eventually he became buried under a pile of stones. The people carried off his belongings, including his bodily adornments and *khaṭvāṅga* staff. After a short time, the Great One shouted *pheṭ*, stood up, and began to dance about. Everyone present became faithful. They gave back his *khaṭvāṅga*, adornments, and other things. They properly bowed in respect and offered him reverence—so he has said.

Then the Master visited the Swayambhūnāth stūpa. While performing an extensive tantric feast, the Master had visions in which he met glorious Śawaripa, master Mitrayogin, and others. They gave him extensive instructions, follow-up instructions, prophetic assurances, and so on.

Having completed those aims of his, the Master then went into the center of town. The lord of the area, referred to as the "king of Khokhom," was seated on a throne made from precious materials, surrounded by streamers and parasols, as well as people playing a limitless variety of instruments. {495} Amid that great assembly of people, with an intense fearlessness, the Great One seized the king's head, pulled him by the hair, punched him in the face, urinated on his head, and so on. Everyone was so terrified of the Master that they obeyed him as if they were serfs. They worshipped him with magnificent reverence.

At that time there was an area where a great many people had died from an epidemic. There wasn't even anyone left to dispose of the corpses. The Great One took all the bodies to a charnel ground, where he performed the transference of consciousness visualization, the "Great Oath" supplication, and other rites. As a result, rainbows sprang up from many of the corpses. After the female spirit responsible for the illness was bound by an oath to obey the Master's command, the epidemic came to an end. {496}

He went to Lapchi and stayed for some time. Then he planned to go back to Chubar. In the gorge that contains Lapchi and Chubar, between the places called Doné and Tsopé, he went down the wrong path and followed it for three days. This brought him into a forest where he came across an inconceivable variety of dangerous animals, including tigers, leopards, wild boars, jackals, black bears, brown bears—every possible type of predator. Most of them simply ran off. But others reveled and played happily before the Master's feet. He did not experience even the slightest harm—so he has said. At one point, a large snake was blocking the path ahead. With no indecision, the Master went harmlessly past it—so he has said.

In that way, through his practice that is totally victorious in all respects, the Master overwhelmed all of phenomenal existence with his glory and brought the entirety of the three realms under his control.

Then he went by stages to Tanak, where he met with the peerless master, Tsachungpa the Great. {497} In a state of delight, with their minds melded together as one, they worked extensively for the benefit of transmigrating beings. Tsachungpa taught the Master the profound path of the Six Dharmas of Nāropa based on the instructional text written by the precious *chennga* Nyernyipa. He gave him many other profound Dharma teachings as well.

Then the Master went to Zambulung, where he held a veritable feast, treating his fortunate disciples to the profound and vast Dharma. He stayed at all of the significant places in the area, including the upper and lower meditation sites, the "treasure valley," and the lakes. His meditation deepened significantly during this time.

Then he intended to go to Shang. He traveled from Zambulung all the way to Tongmön in the Shang valley in a single day. Then he went to Bara, where he gave instructions on the Mahāmudrā and the Six Dharmas to many worthy recipients. Many people performed the Presentation of a Dried Sheet. By thus making offerings of their practice and spreading the teachings of the Meditation Tradition, they further fulfilled the stainless intentions of the superior being, Barawa the Great. {498}

At one point, the protector of the realm, the great ruler [Dönyö Dorjé of the Rinpungpas] was staying at Drongpo Gang in the Shang valley. Without being noticed, the Great One proceeded there and entered the complex unhindered. Two guard dogs, named Misö and Gyangdrak—"Man-killer" and "Heard from Afar"—were tied up together. They were turned loose on the Master. With no hesitation whatsoever, he whacked the dogs with his thighbone trumpet. He continued onward, staring down everyone. Some grain had been laid out to dry, to later be ground into *tsampa*. The Master urinated all over it. Everyone remained frozen, overwhelmed by the Master's glory. They were both frightened and amazed.

Then he set out with the destination of lower Nyang. At the Ling ferry crossing, the Master encountered six or seven ruffians. They grabbed him by his earring and jostled him, which tore his ear lobe. They kept the earring. Afterward, the Master's ear was seen to be fine, with no sign whatsoever of having been ripped. {499} As the Master has said, "That which people regard as so amazing is an indication of my attainment in the practice of the illusory body."

Not long after that, the Master laid out a plan for a meditation school located at a mountain retreat in Pelnam Zhung. He named it Chöying Namkhé Dzong, "Fortress of the Expanse of Being." He stayed there for a while, giving many profound and vast Dharma teachings. The patron ruler [the lord of Gyantsé], his chief minister—who was of completely pure intention—and other people offered the Master excellent service. He set many fortunate disciples, both great and small, on the way of the essential Teachings.

Because that mountain had in the past been frequented by a pernicious spirit being, no one could successfully perform the practice of Cutting there. At night, in that area people could not even show the flame of a butter lamp or do much of anything. But ever since the Great One arrived there, there hasn't been a single word about any such disturbance. {500} He defeated many wild demons, which turned the area into a tranquil and peaceful place, an environment of virtue and auspiciousness.

One time when they were performing a large-scale ritual in Gyantsé, the Great One sent a letter to the sovereign patron of the Teachings and his nephew, announcing, "I am coming to subdue the two of you amid all the people gathered for the great ritual."

This frightened them greatly. At midnight, they sent the Master a gift and a letter of invitation. It read, "We make this request before the lord of *siddhas*, the yogin, the Madman of Ü: You are a yogin who sees reality, who has realized the falsity of appearances, and as such you are unafraid of anything. However, it would not be right for there to be any obstacle to the great virtuous rite being performed at this time. So please consider coming to bless this place in a state of peace and tranquility." The Master was welcomed at the ritual. Although the sovereign was unable to meet with the Master in person, he arranged for him to be served with inconceivable reverence. {501} The Master set many *geshés*, yogins, yoginīs, and other superior and ordinary transmigrating beings on the way to welfare. He filled them all with amazement and faith.

Then the Master returned to the Fortress of the Expanse of Being. The area surrounding that abode of accomplishments was very dry and water was scarce. So the Master shot an arrow into the air; a miraculous spring arose where it landed. By accomplishing this and other feats in plain sight, the Master gave every last person there goosebumps of faith, setting them on the path to higher rebirths and final deliverance.

An elderly householder living near there, who had been a patron of the Master, passed away. The Master went to the place high up on the mountainside where the corpse had been taken. When he performed the "Great Oath" supplication of the Kagyü, a five-colored rainbow immediately sprang up from the body, a rain of flowers fell, and so on. This brought joy to everyone.

After thus increasing the Teachings through his Dharmic activities in those areas, the Master departed for Shang. {502} Along the way, he performed the Practice of the Fierce Observance in Dramalung. The lord of the place and all of his servants got together and cast an inconceivable rain of stones at the Master, which should have wounded him. But immediately following the attack he intoned *hūṃ* and *pheṭ* and performed the dances of the nine demeanors,[43] to the amazement of all.

At that time a few monks and mendicants said to him, "You should retaliate for their hitting you."

"Being what people call a yogin," the Master began, "even when there occur what would seem to be immense challenges to my religious practice, to me they are nothing more than a pleasant chattering. How could it ever be right to purposely harm a sentient being? Repay kindness with kindness. Whatever harm is done to you—repay that with kindness as well." He never sought revenge for the attack.

In Shang, on the bank of the river, the Master encountered a monk. The monk said, "Yogin, Madman of Ü—show us an indication of your *siddha*hood today." {503} So the Master walked across the Shang river, his feet not even touching the water. With great joy, the monk said, "You are indisputably a *siddha*. It is so amazing! I come to you for refuge." The monk prostrated and cried before the Master.

That winter the Master stayed in Bara, Jak, and nearby places, as well as in upper and lower Nyang. At one point, the protector of the realm, the king of the Dharma [Dorjé Tseten of the Rinpungpa family?] and his ministers were assembled, sitting in lines, inside the Shigatsé fort. Without being noticed, the Master passed into their midst. The Master assumed a scolding look, intermittently dancing playfully about. In a state of being free from all fears, the Great One drank the cup of tea that sat before the great protector of the realm. He made a dance out of hitting things with his *khaṭvāṅga*, stomped on the tables, and so on. All were both frightened and amazed. After wisely inviting the Master to join them, they all offered him reverence, and so on. {504} Then he returned to the Fortress of the Expanse of Being.

During the monkey month of the monkey year, the Master traveled
1488 again to Zambulung. His presence amid that enormous gathering—which included most of the world's more famous *geshé*s, yogins and yoginīs, as well as ordinary people as numerous as the sands of the earth—was like that of the moon shining among the stars.[44] The Great One's physical body sparkled like crystal. He was as magnificent as an entire Mount Meru of gold. Blazing with the radiance of the sun, he overwhelmed the whole world with his glory, even the gods. He sat there, blazing with a refulgent, pellucid, placid radiance, like a stūpa made out of crystal.

During that gathering the Master set limitless fortunate disciples on the way to ripening and liberation by giving both specific and general Dharma teachings, which were profound and vast. He subdued some beings through the Practice of the Fierce Observance. Others he made joyful by imparting a lot of Dharmic advice of a tranquil and peaceful nature. {505} Others he set on the way to welfare using nothing more than his bodily demeanor or the mere sound of his melodious voice. In that way, he did the kindness of—through being seen, heard, thought of, or touched—setting every last god, human, and other transmigrating being gathered there onto the path to higher rebirths and final deliverance.

At Zambulung, the full assembly of those who had taken on the observances of yogins, assuming many different styles of dress and types of behavior, numbered about 20,000. This is not even counting the *geshé*s and ordinary monks, the chieftains and householders. Like a lotus flower growing out of but not marred by the muck of a lake, the Great One sat in the middle of that enormous assembly unblemished by the faults of saṃsāra. His body blazed with a brilliant radiance, as if it were a stainless crystal glistening with dew. Conspicuously ornamented in the accoutrements of the Heruka, it was as if he gave off an utterly captivating halo of light. {506} This made him the object of everyone's prayers. All without restriction got goosebumps of faith. In those ways the Master was responsible for bringing inconceivable benefit to transmigrating beings. While there, he also had a vision of Padmasambhava.

After that he went by stages back to the Fortress of the Expanse of Being. To the male and female meditators residing there he gave some remaining Dharma teachings, as well as commands for them to continue meditating. He gave follow-up instructions on every topic.

Then he went to Nupchölung. While staying there, he visited the Rinpung estate, where he went before the protector of the realm, the king of the Dharma, Dorjé Tseten. The Master did a succession of savage things. Nevertheless, the protector of the realm, not harboring the least bit of disbelief, could only reverently serve him. He considered the Master to be a great lord of *siddha*s, and therefore treated him with great faith.

At that time there was a glorious ruler named Küntu Zangpo [of the Rinpungpa family, father of Dorjé Tseten and Dönyö Dorjé], whose very name struck fear in every last living being. {507} Merely seeing, thinking of, or hearing about that great protector of the realm was enough to frighten people. He was staying in seclusion in Gepel. Sometimes he would go out walking around the area, accompanied by a posse of horsemen. The Great One was intent on defeating him by means of the Fierce Observance, and ended up chasing him on a number of occasions. The great protector of the realm came to consider the Master to be a lord of *siddha*s without equal. He would always try to avoid or flee from the Master. He ceased ordering people to do things like engage in disputes and initiate harmful activity. Holding the Master in respect, he paid him reverence, made offerings, and so on, on many different occasions.

The Master stayed for some time at Nubchölung, giving many Dharma teachings—some unique to the Kagyü, some held in common with the other sects. {508} At one point, a monk residing in the area died from a pox. Since it was not convenient to cremate the corpse just then, the body was temporarily buried at the charnel ground. The Master quickly went there and said, "There is a corpse here—exhume it!" No one was capable of unearthing the corpse, so the Great One did it himself. The blackened corpse he pulled out was rotten and decomposing, bluish and reeking. He tore the flesh from its face and took a handful of brains from its split-open skull. He began to eat. Everyone was frightened, and nauseated by the mere sight of it.

"Eat some of this!" he commanded the monastics. But no one could do it. Eventually one monk did give it a try, completely terrified. As soon as the brains touched the tip of his tongue, he nearly vomited, so gave up. It is renowned that after this he obtained one of the mundane *siddhis*. {509}

After staying there for a few days, the Master resumed his travels through Tsang. Having long discerned what he considered to be encouraging signs appearing in the course of his meditation, the Master went before the omniscient Śākya Chokden—the second Lord of Sages of our degenerate age, the crown jewel among five hundred, the unchanging "life pole"[45] of the Teachings, the great upholder of the venerable tradition of the Lord, the great precious *paṇḍita* who has achieved the level of stainless Great Intelligence,[46] whose qualities are difficult to describe—at the encampment of Tupten Serdokchen, the great Dharma center of Zilung. The Master received, in their entirety, the esoteric oral instructions that originated with the glorious lord of yogins Virūpa; the profound Dharma teachings of the noble fathers and sons of the Sakya sect; and the precious oral instructions for the Path and Fruit. He received the expository transmission for the root tantra of the *Hevajra Tantra*. He also received inconceivable instructions, including the *Guiding Instructions on the Madhyamaka View*. It was at the Master's request that Śākya Chokden composed the *Guiding Instructions on the Madhyamaka View*, the *Condensed Meaning of the Hevajra Tantra*, and other texts. {510} With the minds of teacher and student melded together as one, the Master departed.

At one point while the Master was staying in Nubchölung, on account of their having met before in Zambulung and other places, he went into the presence of the wheel-wielding king, the ruler Dönyö Dorjé, whose activity is totally victorious in all respects. He was staying with his son at Renda. There was a mutual understanding between patron and preceptor. In carefree amazement, Dönyö Dorjé properly offered the Master reverential service.

A few months after that, the Master traveled by stages to the Ü area, where he visited the Forest of Glorious Samantabhadra, Dakla Gampo, and other holy sites. Then he set out with the intention of visiting some of his kind lamas.

The ruler Dönyö Dorjé, protector of the realm, was staying at Lhünpo fortress in Chushül at the time. The Master planned to go there by way of the lower road. He sent most of his monks ahead to Chushül. He himself set out without delay for the fortress of Nyukla, accompanied by two of his students. {511} The two students—one called Wönpo Dorgyel, who had achieved a level of discernment equal to that of a lesser cotton-clad one, and a beginner named Namkha Zangpo—went on ahead. Outside the main gate to Nyukla, which remained barred, the two shouted and did a number of savage things. They were given some provisions and were told to go away. But they did not leave.

It was then that the Master arrived, dressed in the accoutrements of the Heruka. With no one having the slightest idea that the Master was an excellent yogin or that he was a lord of *siddhas*, they thought that he was undoubtedly an unsurpassed fraud acting like a madman.

Before the officers and leaders even had a chance to tell them what to do, fifteen or so young brigands ran out to stop the Master, intending to give him a thrashing. The Master walked without concern toward a guard dog straining at the end of its chain. {512} When the mastiff was about to latch onto the haft of his *khaṭvāṅga*, the Master made as if he were going to strike him with it. Thinking that he was about to kill the mastiff, the brigands grabbed hold of the *khaṭvāṅga*. Just as the Master was about to scold them for this, the brigands started hitting him with their own thick staffs. At each savage blow the Master would say, "I offer this to my lama! I offer this to the Buddha! I offer this to the Dharma! I offer this to the Sangha, the community of clerics!" One pounded the Master with two wooden mallets that looked like endless knots. Another smashed him with a wooden mallet used for masonry work, so large it that took two hands to lift. After pausing for a moment, out of breath, eyes shut, the Master flung his body into the dances of the nine demeanors. {513}

In addition to those three wooden mallets, the brigands pummeled him with five different staffs, including door bars, sticks for dyeing, and two short wooden broom handles. They stabbed him with knives, pikes, and other sharp weapons. Treating his body as one would a lump of dirt or a stone, without any regard or compassion whatsoever, they beat him so ferociously that one could not possibly get another hand in. The bone ornaments the Master wore made dents in the wooden implements he was hit with, in his own flesh, and so on. The attack was so disturbing that decent, conscious people could not bear to watch it, nor even to hear the loud *thwacks* that were made when he was hit. All the same, those wanting to break his ivory bangles knocked him on the wrists with innumerable staff blows. Those wanting to break his conch shell earrings hit his ears. Those who wanted to sever his Sacred Thread—a special sash made from bones—savagely beat him about the shoulders, chest, and back. {514}

At this point the people were thinking that the Master was not a human being, but might in fact be a demon or a ghoul. "If we do not make certain to kill him," they reasoned, "he might come back to eat or kill us." Thus they battered him beyond all need, without pause, so that there was no way a person could possibly survive. However, most of the people were not having any conscious thoughts of "He is this, so let's do that." Instead, they joined in putting the Great One's meditation to the test through this beating, regarding him as nothing at all.

While battering the Master in that way, they used a rope about three fathoms long to tie up his feet and drag him around. Making use of a ladder, they all worked together to hoist him up onto a story-high wall. Then they dropped him off it. They dragged him across the path below, which was covered with rubble and scree. Eventually they threw him off a steep cliff two and a half stories high. {515} His injured body, snapped like a reed, tumbled down into the rocky gorge below.

Thinking that the day's trials were finished, the Master eased his meditation somewhat. At that exact moment someone sent a mossy boulder down from above. It hit him in the ribs on his left side. Body and rock both were sent flying.

Immediately after performing those miraculous displays in plain sight of all, the Master sat up, did some yogic exercises, and exhaled the stale air, which whistled between his teeth. Then he gathered his long hair into a topknot and rested.

Everyone thought the Master had departed into tranquility. Assuming that he died on impact, there was not a single person who thought that he could be revived or that there would be no injury to his body—not among the people of excellent, average, or even lesser intellect. As soon as the Master got up from the rubble, some people ran down to where he sat. {516}

"You are an excellent yogin! Please forgive us for not recognizing that before," they said. "Given your condition, we should have an experienced physician check your pulse and the condition of your blood. Will you allow that?"

"It is true that neither the lords nor servants among you recognized who I am," the Great One answered. "But I'm not at all unwell. Showing his pulse to a physician would bring disgrace to a yogin, so I have never done so. As for medicine, I have the king of powerful medicines, which is called 'the Mahāmudrā.' If the Mahāmudrā cannot help me, no other medicine can. And if it can help me, I do not need any other medicine."

"But you cannot get up," they said. "The proper thing would be for us to carry you home on our backs and give you some hospitality. It would not be fitting for you to stay out here in the open like this." {517}

The Master responded, "I am not the sort of yogin who needs to be carried on your backs. If you carried me, it would damage my image as a realized yogin."

When they touched the Master's head, they found that his skull underneath was broken, leaving the skin as pliant as a canopy. Then the Master did some wind yoga, which, with a series of cracking sounds, made his head bulbous again—so it is related.

Then they asked, "Will you at least have some 'inner offering'?"

"I don't need anything to drink."

The people persisted: "It won't do for you to stay out in the open like this. By all means, we should carry you."

The Master got up abruptly. Like a lion getting up from its den, or like a deer beginning to frolic, he shook his body three times. Then the Master proclaimed, "Let neither lord nor servant experience anything unpleasant as a result of having made this karmic connection with me! May you all have well-being and happiness in the end and at every moment until then! {518} May you have the good fortune to find enjoyment in the holy Dharma! By the power of my making these prayers, may I and all other sentient beings achieve unsurpassed buddhahood!"

He took off with the enthusiasm of a wild horse suddenly let loose, or like a hero charging into battle. Not needing to be carried or supported or helped in any way, in the space of a single breath he traveled all the way to a town called Talam, "Horse Path." There he joined some people who were breaking and hauling rocks, and even carried some himself. He would spend the night there.

A set of bodily accoutrements and some provisions were sent to him from the fortress of Nyukla. Everyone became completely faithful, seeing the Master as an actual buddha.

The next day the Master intended to go to Lhünpo fortress in Chushül. After gracefully performing the dances of the nine demeanors, he took off running, just like a deer. Along the way he met a messenger leading a horse. They had been sent by the great ruler himself, Dönyö Dorjé, the glorious one totally victorious over every area, to invite the Master to that very same place. {519} He mounted the horse and rode to what is a truly delightful grove located at the base of the Lhünpo fortress. He stayed in Chokpu Puk, "Turret Cave." Each day the great protector of the realm would come before him. He would reverently serve the Master and make offerings of whatever was appropriate. He received the oral instructions on Singhamukha, the divine protector of the realm, along with other teachings. Then Dönyö Dorjé, the great human protector of the realm, departed for the Tsang area, while the Master remained where he was.

The great patroness of the Teachings, Sönam Zangmo, along with her son,[47] made the following accouncement from Nyukla: "Because this Master is certainly an inconceivable, preeminent *siddha*, all should confess their faults to him, make offerings, request Dharma teachings, and so on."

At that time some of us were taking it easy on the top floor of a large house in Nyukla. "What is he renowned for?" someone asked.

"The indications of the Great One's *siddha*hood are not limited to this occasion," I [Nyukla Peṇchen] explained. "He is very famous throughout the upper and lower parts of both Ü and Tsang. {520} Of the 20,000-or-so realized yogins assembled in Zambulung for the monkey month of the monkey year, not one was more amazing or illustrious than the Master.

"Although I have not seen the term 'human cutting'[48] used in the many well-spoken teachings of the Buddha or in the teachings of the learned and meditatively accomplished ones, in truth this sort of thing expresses the intentions of the sūtric and mantric systems as a whole. This practice is described in such texts as the *Condensed Perfection of Wisdom Sūtra*, where it says, 'Give up your head and limbs without any trepidation.' It is clearly described many times in the sections of the Mother tantras explaining the Practice. It is explicated at length in the *Guhyasamāja* and other Father tantras. It is also taught in tantras of the other classes, such as the *Buddhasamayoga Tantra*.

"Within the traditions of secret oral instructions, in both Pacification and Cutting the Demons, there are said to be four kinds of demons to be defeated: obstructing demons, unobstructing demons, the demon of outward displays of joy, and the demon of pride. {521} The practice of 'human cutting' pertains especially to defeating the sort of demon that causes obstructions.

"First, the Master successfully cut off any desire to remain living at home. Then he roamed through places not especially far from there, staying at charnel grounds, haunted spots, and other suitable locales. He practiced the Equalization of Taste, which is an instruction for severing unobstructing demons, which are nonhuman spirits. This resulted in realization. Once he achieved stability in his realization, he wandered to all of the important and minor places, where he successfully neutralized the obstructing demons possessing physical forms, such as other humans and the four elements.

"As a result of this kind of training, his body was transformed into that of a perfect Enjoyment Body, while his mind was transformed into the unalloyed Dharma Body—thus exhibiting the fruits of his training in the spiritual path. The Master saw each of his spiritual undertakings to its conclusion. {522} He also completed most of the Mother tantra instructions on the Secret Practice, the Public Practice, the Practice that Is Victorious in All Respects, and the All-Good Practice—however it is that they are defined. He also cultivated the illusory body, and the visualizations for the five stages of the *Guhyasamāja Tantra.*

"In the course of working to enhance his realizations, the Master used to sit facing his reflection in a mirror. He would imagine that the person he saw in the mirror was indifferent to such concerns as praise or censure, experiencing all things as the same. Once the Master had grown accustomed to that, he would actually enter into his reflection and see that the person seated before him was indifferent to praise or censure—even if expressed by Dharma brothers sitting right beside him. He thus rendered all experiences equal.

"Once he had mastered that practice, he would go into the middle of a marketplace or a town and subject himself to minor difficulties, which he made part of the path. When he had no fear of such things and went out on the road, he did the Practice of the Insane Observance. Keeping secret his lineage, clan, family, and so on, he wandered in various unfamiliar places. {523} He abided without any concern for conditions or appearances, distinctions like high or low, good or bad, praise or censure, pleasant or unpleasant to hear, pleasure or pain, expectations or apprehensions, things to be adopted or rejected, and so on—none of these; nor for hot or cold, hunger or thirst, weariness and fatigue, and so on—not one of these. Nor did he have any fear of avalanches or roofs collapsing on him, and so on; nor of fire, water, wind, and the like. Without any fear or apprehension about any of those things, he overwhelmed all with his greatness by means of his assurance in his realization of the nature of reality and his *samādhi* of the Great Illusion. Until such time as the Master manifests a rainbow, *vajra* body, that which we refer to as his 'training' is precisely this.

"For example, in the esoteric oral instructions on the deity Kṛṣṇayamāri—'the Black Slayer of the Lord of Death'—where it says 'roaming at night . . . ,' this means that you should remain in the Generation and Perfection Stage meditations on Vajrabhairava, and while staying in an isolated place, smear your naked body with the ashes of a corpse. Put on the bone ornaments. Play a hand drum and strike the dancing poses. If you train in this way, you will achieve the ability to overwhelm the nonhuman spirits of the world with your glory, and the ability to pass unhindered through walls and the like. {524} You will have forestalled minor external difficulties, including dangerous precipices, fire, water, and poison. The oral instructions say that once one has attained these abilities, he should 'do training that engages with the whole of phenomenal existence, saṃsāra and nirvāṇa, including the four elements, humans, nonhuman spirits, and so on.' This is precisely what the Master was doing.

"To perform what is called 'the Practice'—which can be 'with elaborative elements' or 'without' them—is no different from this.

"Or as Virūpa says in his text on Raktayamāri—'the Red Slayer of the Lord of Death'—without elaborations:

> Once you have torn to shreds the categorizations
> with which worldly people accord themselves,
> you will be like a sword tempered in sesame oil,
> you will act like a heroic lion.

"—and so on. Amazingly, things like this are said in every esoteric oral instruction of the Perfection Stage.

"There are some fools who do not have the wealth of great learning; very unfortunate beings whose intellects are obscured by partisan jealousy, whose mouths have been poisoned by demons. {525} They say, 'This kind of behavior is not taught. We do not know what to make of this kind of yogin. His manner of enacting the Practice does harm to the Teachings.'

"By saying such things, fools expose their own shortcomings. Knowing these to be the kind of statements that amass sin, what could be gained by responding to them? Alas, there is no end to immoral actions.

"Living and studying the Dharma were combined into one in the Master's practice. Once he achieved stability in his practice, he was able to submit himself to difficulties. What is there to strive for beyond that? What could be more amazing than someone like him? Do not think that the amazing stories of all the *mahāsiddhas* of India differ from this except in terms of their distance from us."

On account of my praising the Master in such a manner, a messenger was dispatched to invite him back to Nyukla. {526} The Great One turned his loving gaze toward us and came there. He stayed for about thirteen days, during which time he gave inconceivable profound and vast Dharma teachings. The faithful hopes of every last one of us were fulfilled.

During this time I said to the Master, "It is truly amazing that you were not injured by the savage brutality you recently endured."

"I have borne a great many difficulties with this body of mine," he told me. "Many of them were worse than what I endured the other day. This time, because I was tired and my religious practice was weakened, I was completely helpless."

Nothing is more amazing than being able to endure the difficulties visited upon our flesh and blood bodies, which result from the ripening of our past karma! There are many teachers who sit on lofty thrones, surrounded by great retinues of followers, who are seen by themselves and everyone else as like buddhas. But when they meet with difficulties as minor as a cold that lasts for a few days, or having a foot pricked by a thorn, they cannot endure it. {527} And yet immediately after the Master took such a nasty trip down that gorge full of brambles, without pausing to rest, he climbed the narrow mountain path all the way back up to Nyukla. I go for refuge to the one who is able to endure such incomparable hardships!

I suggested to the Master that even after achieving a rainbow body, a *vajra* body, such things can still be difficult to endure. He responded, "This was only a minor thing to bear. Thanks to the kindness of the peerless Dakpo Kagyü, and thanks to my experience of the Mahāmudrā, I have been able to take the whole of phenomenal existence, saṃsāra and nirvāṇa, as the enemy, not just small occurrences like this. Although I may fall into difficult situations, I am not one to be afraid."

I questioned him further: "The fact that the Master has endured great physical trials, on this and many other occasions, could in general only be because you have completed the accumulations of merit and wisdom over the course of inestimable lifetimes, and have become perfectly habituated to all of the ripening empowerments and liberating instructions of the Vajrayāna. {528} But the fact that none of the difficult circumstances you've faced could cause any damage to your body, speech, or mind—is this on account of the Generation Stage meditations? Or on account of your control over the yogic winds? Or because you have a special power that derives from your unfailing control over the yogic drops? Or because you have realized the view of the Mahāmudrā? Where does ability this come from? When you find yourself in a difficult situation, what kind of meditation do you do?"

"In general, whatever one does while maintaining the Mahāyāna attitude of *bodhicitta* will be of benefit to others," the lord of *siddha*s answered. "From the perspective of one who has not broken any of his Vajrayāna *samaya*s or vows, everything looks like the play of the gods. For one skilled in controlling the yogic winds and doing *tummo*, the bliss caused by the melting of the yogic drop pervades his entire body, so that whatever happens to him feels only like great bliss. One trained in illusory body and dream yoga realizes all appearances to be without truth. One who recognizes his lama as a buddha will see everything as being a blessing. {529} For the sake of the Dharma, you must endure hardships that could potentially hurt you. Even if heaven and earth were turned upside-down, you should not be afraid. You must achieve a sky-like realization of the Mahāmudrā. You have to achieve and to exemplify all of these things. But unless you can heal yourself by taking control of your winds, and things like that, it will be hard to endure such difficulties.

"As for me, from within a state of sky-like, fundamental awakening to the Mahāmudrā view, I have rendered all possible experiences equal. This is the reason that I have not been hurt. If one is of strong religious practice and clear understanding, even if his body is chopped into a hundred or a thousand pieces and smashed to dust, he will not feel any pain on the inside, and his external body will not be harmed—it's like swinging a sword at a rainbow, or trying to strike a sunbeam with a staff. But if one is of weak religious practice, he will feel pain and his body will be harmed. {530} So no matter what, you must be certain about your sky-like realization."

In that very way, through the inconceivable enlightened activities of his body, speech, and mind, the Master set all transmigrating beings on the way of the essential Teachings.

Presiding over an assembly including the great lords of the
infinite ocean of maṇḍalas,
plus ten million heroes and *ḍākiṇīs*,
the *vajradhara*, lord of the dance, sovereign over existence and the
tranquil beyond,
was seen by his disciples to perform magical displays with his
emanated body—
the theatrics of his wisdom in this world of reflections—
by which he overwhelms with his glory all of the amazing things
of this earth.

Divinity in the form of a conscious man,
he plays by means of perfect optical illusions,
always making for an amazing display.

Although he had transcended existence, he took rebirth within it.
Although he had become a victor himself, he engaged with the Victor's teachings.
Although he was omniscient, he crossed the ocean of learning.
Although he had achieved the four bodies, he learned from hundreds of teachers.
Although he had already taken hold of the *vajra*, still he exerted himself in practice. {531}

In the perceptions of others, he underwent spiritual training,
then proved himself invincible through miraculous feats, victorious in all respects.
His *vajra* body resplendent with the accoutrements of the charnel ground,
he performs the dances of the nine demeanors, overwhelming all of phenomenal existence with his glory,
shining above all other transmigrating beings, even the gods.

With his supreme magical displays, he took control of others' perceptions.
With the manifestations of his body, speech, and mind,
he blessed and increased the essential Teachings everywhere—
in India, Nepal, and Oḍḍiyāṇa, land of the *ḍākiṇīs*,
in Tibet, Mongolia, and beyond.

If they cast upon your body a rain of weapons
that raised a cloud of dust to blot out the sun, and made the whole earth rumble,
still you would be as if a rainbow:
unharmed and shining with the splendor of great wisdom,
amazing in the eyes of all transmigrating beings—even the gods.

Ema! To a person of discerning eye,
wealthy in the riches of faith and sincerity,
what could be more amazing than he? {532}

Such was the fourth chapter of *The Life Story of the Noble Künga Zangpo, the Glorious Preeminent* Siddha *Whose Practice Is Totally Victorious in All Respects, Called "That Which without Restriction Gives Goosebumps of Faith,"* relating the story of how by taking meditation as the essence of practice, he traversed all of the external and internal Stages and Paths and achieved every possible good quality that results from realization; of how in the perceptions of others, by means of his practice that is totally victorious in all respects, he overwhelmed all of phenomenal existence with his glory; of how all the inhabitants of the world prostrated to him, even the gods; and how, having taken on the Observance of a fierce Heruka, he conquered the armed hordes of all four types of demon.

5

Teaching

FROM NYUKLA, THE Master traveled by stages to Chushül, Sheldrong, and other places. Many individuals would come forward to serve him, make offerings, request their desired Dharma teachings, and so on. In Sheldrong, the great patron of the Teachings [Dönyö Dorjé?], together with his officers, requested Dharma teachings on topics like the Five-Parted Mahāmudrā. They treated the Master with reverence and respect. {533}

The Master then planned to go from the Sheldrong area to Kyishö. Following certain prophetic signs originating from the four-faced wisdom protector Mahākāla and from the protector of the realm, Singhamukha, he traveled from the Lünpa area to Kyimo valley. While there, the superintendents and officers performed magnificent acts of reverence, treating the Master with great respect.

Then, traveling in stages by way of the southern route, he went from Yamda to Jangkha. At Tarma, some people caused a minor disturbance. But they ended up honoring the Master with donations. Not a single person was left with any misguided thoughts about him. No one could respond to his savage behavior in any way.

The Master then traveled to Densa Til, where he met with the *mahāsattva*, the peerless Sharmepa. In the course of their happy conversations, father and son delighted one another. Sharmepa performed limitless acts of reverential service, describing the Master with words of great praise. {534} Sharmepa also gave him some remaining Dharma teachings. At this time the Master visited the skull cup of the precious great abbot [who ordained him as a monk, Sönam Tashi Gyeltsen Pelzang]. At Sapmo Drak, he made offerings before the skull cup of the lord of yogins Bangrimpa, and before the remains of the learned Dharma lord from Lhündé [Penjor Gyatso]. He performed amazing prayers, supplications, and the like. All who knew of the Master, whether they were powerful or lowly, offered inconceivable expressions of their respect for him.

Then he went by stages to Ölkha. For a few days the Master stayed at home, treating his father with great kindness. Through being seen, heard, thought of, or touched, the Master set limitless people around there, both laymen and clerics, on the way to welfare. Everyone resounded with prayers and praises for the Master.

When they were descending from the upper part of Nyangpo, the Master and his students had to traverse a narrow path between two rock faces at a spot called Dreshé. {535} A number of workers and nomadic herdsmen were thinking about killing the Master and his students. They gathered some enormous rocks on the mountainside above the defile, then sat in wait.

The Master commanded those who were accompanying him at the time, "We will walk in a line with me at the head. Let no one go in front of me!" They pressed onward in a column. The workers and herdsmen set the boulders rolling, so as to fall on the heads of the Master and his students, and also began throwing a great rain of stones. Right when they were about to be crushed under a rock, the Great One, shouting *phet*, leapt up to where the workers and herdsmen were. He stared them down and pointed threateningly at them. All of their limbs became paralyzed. They were so scared that they knew not what to do. {536} Then they prostrated and bowed respectfully at his feet—so he has said.

Some of the Master's female disciples gathered in Nyangpo to honor him. One time, a tantric feast was held in the Master's honor inside a tall building, with many female disciples making offerings and paying him reverence. Around midnight, the Master went up onto the roof in order to relieve some of his "musk"[49] outside. He tumbled off the roof and fell from a height of eight stories. But his body bore no harm whatsoever from the fall. He immediately went back inside, at which time they each paid him reverence, made dedications of merit, and so on.

After setting inestimable transmigrating beings on the way to welfare through the enlightened activities he performed in that area, the Master then went to Draksum Lung, "Three Boulder Valley." When he opened the divine door to the wondrous holy abode called Lekma, in the upper part of the valley, the entire sky became filled with a vast rainbow, as if it were draped with a multicolored canopy. {537} The air teemed with rainbows and a great rain of flowers. The whole earth became filled with pleasant sounds and odors.

As the Master visited each of the holy abodes around there, he would meditate on and make offerings to all of the maṇḍalas of deities, both external and internal. By holding inconceivable tantric feasts, he fulfilled the intentions of every last member of the assembly of Kagyü lamas, of all the peaceful and wrathful deities of the infinite maṇḍalas, and of the heroes and *ḍākiṇīs* of the body, speech, and mind. He established dependent connections for the sake of spreading the teachings of the Victor to every distant place. He did all he could to promote the welfare of every transmigrating being without exception, and to satisfy his fortunate disciples with the definitive secrets of the Vajrayāna. The number of pure visions the Master saw at those places is beyond counting. {538} He had a vision of the peerless Lord of the Śākya, surrounded by a thousand other buddhas; a vision of Vajradhara, surrounded by the eighty-four *mahāsiddhas*; of Cakrasaṃvara, Hevajra, Guhyasamāja, and of Vajravārāhī accompanied by two attendants; of Saraha, Śawaripa, Maitripa, and others; of Virūpa, Indrabhuti, and Ḍombi Heruka surrounded by seven ladies. He also had visions of Tārā, Avalokiteśvara, Mañjuśrī, Vajrapāṇi, and other deities, their number beyond counting; of Vaiśravaṇa and the eight horse-masters, the four-armed wisdom protector Mahākāla, Kākamukha—the "Raven-Faced One"—and others. In short, he saw earth and sky as teeming with the infinite bodies of deities. With the heaps of offerings he projected like Samantabhadra, the Master amazed all of the world's inhabitants, even the gods. Amid all of that, a physical Dharma throne appeared for the Master to sit upon. He gave a teaching that boiled down to their very essence the instructions on the Mahāmudrā and the Six Dharmas. He also taught things like the *dohās*, and made extensive prayers and good wishes. {539}

This is only a small part of the amazing story of the things that occurred. There are other texts providing written descriptions of those places, so if one wants more detail, one may look at them.

After in that way setting inestimable transmigrating beings on the path to purity in Nyangpo, Longpo, and all the other places in upper and lower Kongpo, the Master traveled to the Drikung area, by way of Nyangpo.

At Drikung Til he met the Dharma lord of Drikung,[50] along with his brother. With due respect, they arranged a seat for him, paid him reverence, and so on. But without returning the favor by prostrating or making an offering or anything, the Master just lounged on his cushion, holding onto his knee. He spoke perfectly, extolling the precious Kagyü, exhorting the need to uphold the Teachings, and so on. In their amazement and faith, everyone expressed a succession of praises.

Then the Master and his retinue traveled by stages through Utö and lower Penyül. In those places he set many fortunate disciples on the way to ripening and liberation. {540} He treated many transmigrating beings with kindness, setting them on the way to welfare through being seen, heard, thought of, or touched. Whenever he met a malicious person while traveling on the roads between those places, he would make a demonstration that generated amazement and fear in everyone. Those unruly people did not cause the Master the slightest bit of trouble.

In Dechen he met the protector of the realm, the ruler Tsokyé Dorjé [of the Rinpung family]. With the proper show of respect, the Master was welcomed there, offered a seat, paid reverence, was seen off when leaving, and so on. During their meeting the two had conversations about the Dharma and other topics. There was a mutual understanding between patron and preceptor, and a timely coming together of good things.

Then the Master went to Lhasa. In the presence of the Jowo statue, he made supplications and recited prayers to his complete satisfaction. He gave instructions and follow-up teachings to many assemblies of *geshé*s and other people, through which they all received the particular Dharmas they wanted. Every last one of those people worked to reverently serve and make limitless offerings to the Master.

At that time, a powerful and troublesome spirit being was residing in the trunk of a large tree in front of the engraved ceremonial stone pillar.[51] {541} The Master shot an arrow into the tree and said, "Let this tree be a vessel for the glorious four-faced protector!" Amazingly, after that nobody could bear to even touch the tree anymore. People made offerings before the arrow, and so on.

The Master traveled from one place to the next. He was served by people from Neudzong and other estates. When the Master was in lower Nye, Dharma lord Drakjorpa came to meet him. Drakjorpa had some pure visions, including one in which he saw the Master's body as extremely large. He became completely faithful, requested Dharma teachings, and so on. Then the Master went to Sheldrong, upper and lower Geré, and other places. At Sinpori, "Ghoul Mountain," he encountered his tutelary deity Cakrasaṃvara, and others.

Next he went to Nyukla, where he stayed for a few days giving profound and vast instructions to many assemblies of both *geshé*s and ordinary people. {542}

The Master then stayed for a long period at a hermitage associated with Yöl Rinchen Ling. During this time he imparted to me [Nyukla Peṇchen] and others extensive instructions on many different topics.

These included the Six Dharmas, the Mahāmudrā, the *Four-Fold Scroll of Marpa*, the Equalization of Taste, and the Seven-Day *Tummo*. Some of us had before then been staying with the master of wisdom and love, the ally of the teachings, *ācārya* Minyak Rapjampa. To many of these people, the Master gave the reading transmission for lord Milarepa's *Collected Songs*, along with the *Dohā Trilogy*.

The Master and I spent a few months together, as teacher and student, at Nyukla. During this time he was served in every appropriate manner. A *khaṭvāṅga* dubbed "Blazing Auspicious Light" was made and offered to him, along with some other things.

Then the great secretary—who had indefatigable faith in the teachings of the precious Kagyü and in the individuals who uphold them—invited the Master to Kharak fortress. The great secretary offered inconceivable reverential service to the Master. He received limitless Dharma teachings on topics like the Six Dharmas and the Mahāmudrā. His faith in the Master had no end, like the ocean. The great secretary made an offering of a Dharma estate called Tarpa Ling, "Liberation Park." {543} There the Master established a new monastery in the form of a school for meditation and so forth.

At the lower part of the valley is a place called Zangtel Puk, "Transparency Cave." The Master stayed there for a while, giving many profound instructions, including the Mahāmudrā of Co-emergent Union, to many local mendicants and *geshés*, and to the great secretary and his relations. At the moment when the Master was giving the introduction to the nature of the mind, the sky became filled with rainbows and he himself appeared to project a halo of light. When the Master was going to Zangtel Puk for the very first time, he went on ahead of everyone and scaled completely unhindered a rock face more than a story high, without using a ladder or anything, which no one else could manage to climb. He performed some amazing, inconceivable displays, like generating four bodily manifestations at the same time. While the Master was staying at Zangtel Puk, the entire snowy neck of Kharak Mountain, the goddess, was adorned with rainbows and the like.

One time the Master went to the eastern valley of Nyangkhöl. {544} He was riding an excellent horse from Tashigang, headed for a monastery called Lawateng. The night was so dark that the man leading the horse could not even see the ground in front of him. When they came to the edge of a gorge about five stories tall, the Master and his horse fell right into it. Through the force of the Master's compassion, the horse was able to hold on, but the Master himself fell. His left thigh smashed against the corner of a rock at the bottom of the gorge. Some of his things were destroyed, like his deer antler horn and the bells that hung from his bone ornaments. But the Master himself was not injured in the least. Upon arriving unharmed at Lawateng monastery, he performed a dance and gave some Dharma teachings.

In that way the Master spent five or six months in the area of Nyukla and Kharak, fostering benefit to transmigrating beings and initiating a tradition dedicated to definitive meaning of the Teachings.

At that time the omniscient Karmapa was in the process of establishing in Yöl a seminary for the study of the philosophy of the precious Kagyü. It contained a monastic college dedicated to the Karma Kagyü. {545} Out of their unsurpassed devotion to the Master, all of the monks received general Dharma instructions, supplicated him, and so on. They praised him with perfect devotion.

At some point during this time, the Master's ornamented *ḍamaru* drum fell from his horse. They searched for it with no success. The Master said, "My *ḍamaru* has been bundled up in some cloth and placed on a shelf. If I announced that it has been lost, someone would bring me a replica that looks just like the original. In time, my *ḍamaru* will return to me." After a little over a year, an ornamented *ḍamaru* was found on a shelf inside the home of a "tax person," bundled up in a cloth, just as the Master had said. The man returned the *ḍamaru* to the Master with a newfound faith in his clairvoyance.

One time, while performing the sort of hostile behavior he did during that period, the Master encountered a brigand. {546} He removed the sword from the brigand's belt, leaving the scabbard and grabbing the blade with his bare hands. He immediately bent the sword over his knee and tied it into a knot. Everyone was amazed. People got goosebumps of faith just hearing about it.

Then the Master went by stages to the Tsang area. At Norbu Ling in Nyemo, the one who embodies inconceivable good qualities, the patron of the precious Teachings, the superintendent of Rinchentsé, along with his nephew, performed limitless reverential service. The Master gave many profound and vast Dharma teachings on the Mahāmudrā and other topics. With patron's and preceptor's minds melded together as one, they presided over a feast of every possible Dharmic and material thing.

The superintendent had an excellent horse, which kicked the Master hard two times and stamped on him repeatedly with its hooves. {547} It was a frightening sight, making everyone wonder, "How will he fare this time?" But the Master bore nothing whatsoever resembling an injury. Everyone regarded him as something amazing on account of this feat. His fame spread to all.

The Master went to Droyetak fortress, where he met the great protector of the realm, Dönyö Dorjé. Then he proceeded to Dreyül Dzongkar. At the great Dharma center of Kyemö Tsel, he visited the precious silver reliquary, before which he offered prayers and supplications. He met with the Dharma lord of the three realms, Jamyang.[52] All being of like mind, the resident and visiting *ācāryas* happily made offerings and paid the Master all due reverence and respect. For his part, the Master offered long-life prayers before Dharma lord Jamyang and sponsored a reverential tea service for the monks. Many of the monks and *geshés*, both old and young, received Dharma teachings from the Master, and so on. {548} They all described him with inconceivably great praise and reverence.

Then the Master went to Nupchölung and other places, where he cared for many disciples, whether they were superior or ordinary in their respective mental capacities.

At one point the Master was at Bumtso Dong, taking medicinal baths. His health declined somewhat, so he stayed inside for a few days, resting in meditation. In every direction there was great talk saying that the Master had departed into tranquility. His students living in the area gathered there, including both *geshés* and mendicants. People congregated from every direction, bringing with them heaps of different materials to use for offerings. From many different places, high and low, people came leading horses, mules, and other animals, with the purpose of taking relics of the Master back with them. At this time the Master got up, performed a dance, and spoke with his melodious *vajra* voice, thus putting an end to all of their speculation. {549} He then imparted limitless supportive advice to the people gathered there, which gave all without restriction goosebumps of faith. The banner of the Master's fame spread far and wide.

Traveling through Tsang, he went back and forth between upper and lower Shang, lower Nyang, and other places. All of the patrons he had connections with paid him due reverence and respect, requested Dharma teachings, and so on. Out of their dedicated and faithful zeal, all of the people, both great and small, bowed in respect to and served the Master. He nourished his followers with whatever Dharma teachings they wanted. Through his purposeful enlightened activity, he set on the way to welfare every last person he came into contact with.

At the Tupten Serdokchen Dharma center in Zilung, the Master went before the victorious lord, the omniscient spiritual friend, the great *paṇḍita*, the lord of the Dharma, Śākya Chokden. Father and son reveled in conversations about the Dharma. By paying reverence and respect through the giving of both Dharmic and material things, the Master delighted and satisfied everyone at the monastery, whether resident or visiting. {550}

Then at Tanak he went before the lord of *siddhas*, the victor Tsachungpa. The Master worshipped him with a heap of offerings like Samantabhadra.

With father's and son's minds melded together as one, they engaged in conversation. Upon hearing the melodious sound of the *siddha*'s secret words of definitive meaning, the Teachings that express essential meanings became clear to the Master—as clear as things are to a young adult in the prime of his life.

Then out of his indefatigable faith, the patron and proponent of the Teachings, the officer [the lord of Kharak] paid the Master reverence, received Dharma teachings from him, and so on, in a particularly thorough manner. Back at Tarpa Ling in Sheldrong, which the Master had established in the form of a school for meditation, the patron served all of the *ācāryas* in whatever ways they needed. With unsurpassed devotion, he established conditions that allowed for the wheel of enlightened activity to turn freely. The officer had a severe illness at that time, but gradually got better. An inconceivable number of local *geshés* and mendicants gathered there. {551} When the Master cast upon them a great rain of profound and vast teachings of definitive meaning, it was as if they had found the very life of the essential Teachings. The teachings of the precious Kagyü were burnished to a perfect sheen.

One day during that time, the Master was meditating in one of the monastery's residences. A *geshé* from Ngari came in and, not seeing the Master, thought he was not there, and so turned around to leave. The Master rose from his *samādhi* and said something, which made the *geshé* turn back and see him there. Moved by an inconceivable faith, the *geshé* offered some incense and prostrated. About this instance the Master has said, "I had forced the yogic winds and my consciousness into my central channel and entered a non-referential meditation—that is why he didn't see me." Around that time, a mendicant from Tsibri, which is in Latö Gyel, saw the Master's body as transparent, with the color of beryl. It is related that on another occasion, a monk from Nenying saw the Master's body as perfectly white, like a snow mountain. {552}

On one occasion, without getting off his horse, the Master rode unhindered through the doorway of the home of a practitioner of the Old Mantra system, the Nyingma. He passed straight through the lintel. The *ngakpas*[53] took up various weapons and hit the Master's body, causing him inconceivable troubles. But he did not bear the slightest injury. By performing an amazing dance, he overwhelmed them with his glory.

In that way, through his enlightened activity—by being seen, heard, thought of, or touched—the Master set inestimable transmigrators in all of the upper and lower parts of the Tsang region on the way to ripening and liberation, and increased the teachings of the Meditation Tradition without partiality or bias.

The Master went by stages to the Yakdé area, by way of Chölung, Kyitsel, and other places. Lords and commoners reverently served him in ways that were appropriate to each. The Master gave the specific profound and vast Dharma teachings they all wanted, and so on. {553}

Then he went by stages to Nyemo. A feast of Dharma was held for the people, foremost among them being the superintendent himself. The Master was worshipped with inconceivable acts of reverential service. Many *geshés* from monasteries in higher and lower places, including Rugönsar monastery, requested the Dharma teachings they wanted and extensively paid reverence and made offerings to the Master.

Then the Master went to Kharak. After staying for a while near the excellent waters of Kharak, he went to the Yamdrok area. At Taklung monastery he gave to many assemblies of *geshés* and ordinary people limitless Dharma teachings of definitive meaning, profound instructions, *dohās*, and so on, in accordance with their individual wishes. He established every last worthy being in the essential Teachings. The teachings of the Kagyü blossomed like a thousand-petaled lotus in the sun.

During this time, many people saw the Master walk across the Turquoise Lake in Yamdrok, with his feet not even touching the water. {554} This gave them all without restriction goosebumps of faith. Melodious praises of his supreme awesomeness spread in every direction. The superintendents of Taklung, Nakartsé, and other districts properly served and respected the Master. All of the people gathered in their faith made inconceivable offerings and reverence.

After staying around there for some time, the Master went again to Kharak. Like Samantabhadra projecting a heap of offerings, he used all of the things he had in his possession to sponsor tea, food, and alms for the inhabitants of Densa Til, and of all of the monasteries in higher and lower places, including Kyitsel, Zilung, and Tashi Lhünpo.

At the precious abode housing the skull cup of the peerless Dharma lord Drakchokpa, the Master performed an extensive ritual. Inconceivable assemblies of *geshés*, mendicants, and ordinary people gathered there in their faith. He satisfied them all with an extensive feast of both Dharmic and material things. {555}

Then the Master—the unchanging "life pole," the unslackening victory banner, the wellspring for the spread and increase of the teachings of the precious Kagyü—sat upon the throne adorned with lions, with his legs crossed in the fearless *vajra* posture. With the banner declaring his victory over all opposition visible in every place, for all time, the Master remains there to this day, as the lone means of bringing welfare to every last being in the whole world, the gods included. For as long as saṃsāra exists, may he remain as the refuge and protector of transmigrating beings!

I prostrate to the one who exhibits
a limitless succession of unstoppable actions,
sending many transmigrating beings to celestial states
by means of a hundred amazing dances, the magical displays of
his wisdom.

Just like tiny bugs looking at minute particles,
in a hundred overblown ways people mistakenly praise
those with incomplete learning and short-lived realization. {556}
How then can they fail to bow before this noble one—
the lord of the Dharma who protects all of us in existence and the
tranquil beyond,
the protector who has been awakened since before any of the
buddhas,
his body, the magical display of a dramatist's wisdom-illusion,
the sole possessor of eyes that see the essential reality?

Such was the fifth chapter of *The Life Story of the Noble Künga Zangpo, the Glorious Preeminent* Siddha *Whose Practice Is Totally Victorious in All Respects, Called "That Which without Restriction Gives Goosebumps of Faith,"* relating the story of how he turned the wheel of the profound and vast Dharma for many superior and ordinary transmigrating beings.

THE VICTORS OF the ten directions and their sons, all speaking in unison, could not fully relate the entire life story of our protector—the one who embodies all the wisdom, love, and abilities of all the buddhas of the three times; the guide to the essential meaning, who achieved the supreme *siddhi* of the Mahāmudrā in one life and one body; who overwhelms all of phenomenal existence and its inhabitants, saṃsāra and nirvāṇa, with the glory of his practice that is totally victorious in all respects—the overpowering, preeminent *siddha*. {557} In light of this fact, how could I myself have the capacity to express his complete life story? I have merely described things as far as I understand them. In order to not be too verbose, I have only written a small part of his amazing story in this brief biography, called *That Which without Restriction Gives Goosebumps of Faith,* which is now complete.

Whoever hears this elixir for the ears will get goosebumps of faith;
for the fortunate ones striving to become lords of yogins and *vajra*-holders, it is the supreme lamp of advanced instructions.
This marvelous new story, unprecedented in the world, is an ever-expanding feast of wonders. {558}
Since this supreme life story of the lord of *siddhas* is a delight to the ears of everyone, even the gods, you should adhere closely to it.

This rough account, expressed with dedication,
of the activities of the lord of heroes, victorious in all respects,
is not blemished by the faults of superimposition or negation,
and thus has no wrongdoing within it.

May the divine *gaṇḍi* gong of my virtuous effort here
be heard throughout the realms of existence,
definitively setting limitless conscious beings
on the way opened by the great heroic Sage!

Lifetime after lifetime, may I be watched over
by an authentic spiritual guide,
and thereby attain an expansive eye for the Dharma
and a speedy liberation from the ocean of existence!

As for this *Life Story of the Noble Künga Zangpo, Madman of Ü, Glorious Holy Lama, the Preeminent* Siddha *Whose Activity Is Totally Victorious in All Respects, Called "That Which without Restriction Gives Goosebumps of Faith,"* very many *geshés* and realized lords of yogins who have learned under the Master urged me again and again to write it. {559} Most important, the Master himself commanded me again and again to write it. I consented, unable to disobey his command. And so I have written this account, leaving things just as they were related to me from the mouth of the Master, the *mahāsiddha* himself. I supplemented this with things that were told to me by some of the Master's reliable disciples. I have described things exactly as I understand them personally.

These days there are some unfortunate people who have fallen under the powerful influence of false views, counterfeit logic, and sectarian hatred, who will not accept some of these stories. Even some faithful people may have doubts. Based on the indications of the Master's *siddhis* that I myself have seen firsthand, there is no need for the slightest doubt or skepticism. I, who vouch that there are no two ways of thinking about this text, who has written with the purest intentions, have received the entire Dharma cycle of the precious Kagyü from the one who is of the nature of Buddha Siṃhanāda, yet to arrive, the seventh wearer of the Black Hat crown, the invincible Karmapa, Chödrak Gyatso; from the one who is of the nature of the Tathāgata Ratnāṅga, the fourth wearer of the Red Hat crown, Chökyi Drakpa Yeshé Pelzangpo; from the great one from the Taklung plain, the precious learned and meditatively accomplished one, Ngaki Wangpo; and from the precious realized one, Kyapsé Jampel Gyatso. {560}

This was composed by the monk following in the tradition of the glo-
1494 rious Śākya, Ngawang Drakpa Pelzangpo, in the wood-male-tiger year, which is referred to as "Totally Pleasing," while the moon was waxing in the second month, inside my meditation cell in the cool, pleasant grove of the third floor of the Celestial Palace. Mangalam.

[Printing colophon to the 1494 edition:]

Svasti.

The patron for this printing was Tamdrin Tseten.
By the virtue generated through this endeavor, may the teachings
of the Kagyü be made to spread
and may the Madman of Ü have a long life!
In all of our many lifetimes,
let us be born in the presence of the Madman of Ü,
so that we may always drink the nectar of his speech.
After we have achieved perfection in learning, contemplation,
and meditation,
let us work for the benefit of sentient beings, who are endless
like the sky!

The woodblocks were carved by Tseten Dorjé, Pönpa Tak, Dargyé, and Ngawang Lekpa. We also ensured the correctness of the writing. May all sentient beings of the six transmigrations, in particular our mothers and fathers, be reborn in the presence of the Madman of Ü!

Mangalam. May it be auspicious.

PART II

From the Life Story of the Noble Künga Zangpo, Called "That Which without Restriction Gives Goosebumps of Faith," the Second Part, Which Is Called "The Drum Beat Adorning His Enlightened Activity"

by Lhatong Lotsāwa Shényen Namgyel, 1537

6

Further Activities

Once the still-developing pods, the accumulations of merit and wisdom,
had ripened in the garden of the immortal teachings of the Sage,
the supreme *siddha* became a victor—
Nārāyaṇā subduing each of the three realms with a single step.[54]

There are countless chariots, countless precious life stories
about those possessing the jewel of a non-partisan intellect—
it is this one, written in parts, pulled by the rope of pure-intentioned analysis,
that you should take into your heart.

BY THE WOOD-FEMALE-RABBIT year, when he had reached the age of
thirty-eight, the noble preeminent *siddha*—the single one to whom the 1495
gods and all other transmigrating beings bow—had achieved perfection in experiential realization. {563} Through his actions he had the ability to set superior and ordinary disciples on the way of the essential Teachings.

The Master was traveling in the direction of Tsari, the great abode of glorious Cakrasaṃvara. He was accompanied by many of his heart sons, including the realized one from Yargyap, and Ritrö Wangchuk, who looked after the treasury of the Master's enlightened activity.

At that time the Master's father, Özang Sega—who was naturally of restrained passions, his continuum completely ripened through his past generosity and compassion—was taken by a serious illness. {564} The Noble One received a request that he and his students should come quickly. When they arrived at Drangyül Ölkha, it was clear that his father was soon to give up the compositional factors of embodied life. The Master knew that no medical treatment or religious rite would be of any help.

After his father's passing, the Master and his students performed the "Great Oath" of the Kagyü as well as the transference of consciousness visualization. There appeared inestimable amazing signs, including the corpse's skull lifting up, and the sky becoming filled with rainbow light.

After one week they cremated the body in the maṇḍala for the Purification of Lower Rebirths and performed other post-mortem rites, by which they generated vast benefit for the deceased. Then, after commanding his younger brother Dorjé[55] to enter the way of the Dharma, the Master departed.

As he was leaving the area, one of the Great Noble One's nephews requested that he expel an obstructing spirit from a certain water mill, and then consecrate it. {565} With an excited look, the Master shot an arrow that penetrated halfway into the lintel of the water mill. Then he made extensive good wishes, prayers, and the like. On account of the Master's establishing dependent connections for his nephew to become rich in sons, wealth, and so on in this lifetime, in time that came about—so it is renowned.

Then the Master went to the Ölkha estate. Although he did many hostile things as part of his Practice of the Fierce Observance, the people there gave up their unfaithfulness in body, speech, and mind, and bowed at his feet. They satisfied him with heaps of reverential offerings. Then, out of indefatigable and stable faith, the local officer, lord of men, offered to provide for the Master's upkeep for one month. The teacher and his students stayed at Gampo Cave, on the snowy neck of Ölkha.

After turning the vast wheel of the Dharma there, the Master intended to go to the Dakpo area. Along the way he stopped at Samten Ling monastery. When he began to perform the Practice of the Fierce Observance, the monks cast a rain of weapons at him, including daggers, knives, arrows, staffs, and stones. {566} But just like long ago when the evildoer Māra tried to cause harm to the Lord of Sages, the Master did not bear any injury. Then, in a state of excitement, laughing with an audible "Ah la la!" the Master galloped on his horse down a long, narrow passage between rock faces, called Ramchung Dzago—so narrow that it was like passing through the birth canal all over again.

The Master went straight to Raptang in the Dakpo area. There a certain patroness who was wealthy in both faith and dispensable things offered him a vessel full of "inner offerings." Then, prostrating and making many prayers, she requested of him, "You should impart to me a *siddhi* for accumulating sons and wealth." So the great lord of the families urinated in the household's crockery, performed a costumed dance with his mind in a blissful and luminous state of non-conceptuality, sang *vajra* songs with his voice like the great roar of Brahmā, and so on. He capped off this amazing play of body, speech, and mind by making prayers and good wishes. He thus fulfilled the patroness's wishes completely. {567} Thanks to the Master's compassion, she later became flush with offspring, wealth, and livestock, and remains so to this day—so it is said.

Then he went to Gampo Nenang, and to upper and lower Dakpo. In those places he set disciples on the path to ripening and liberation.

The Master went to the great abode of Tsari while the Summer Offerings were being performed. At that time the Tsangpo river was so swollen with water that people dreaded to even look at it, as if it were a reflection of something frightening. Thinking that his doing so would be of vast benefit to the Teachings and to sentient beings, the holy Noble One forded the river unhindered on horseback.

Then, by way of the Labar area, the Master traveled in stages to the foothills of upper Tsari, to the palace of the Mahāmudrā, the abode of the authentic mother, Pangchung Urgyen Ling. {568} He was soon invited to a ritual called "Offering the Skull Cup of Alcohol to the Mother," as part of the great offering to Naktsangpa, "Black Brahmā." He picked up the Authentic Small Maroon Skull Cup and filled it with "inner offerings of nectar." Then he announced, "When something precious is held by its rightful owner, no one has reason to object."

He fiercely scolded the other attendees at length, which agitated them greatly. With a fierce, unpleasant roar, hermits numbering many dozens hit the vital parts of the Master's body with many crude weapons, including daggers, knives, and spears. One *sthavira* hit the Master's head many times with an axe, which broke open his skull. His brains began to leak out all over. It was so gruesome that anyone having any discernment whatsoever could not bear to watch. The monks who were serving as the Master's attendants were distraught, not knowing what to do. But after holding in a vase breath and resting in *samādhi* for a moment, the Great One turned even more brilliant and radiant than before. {569} "You don't need to be sad!" he told them. Then he sang *vajra* songs about topics like the utter unity of appearances and emptiness.

As a result of the Master's doing such supremely amazing and marvelous things, the hermits, the Jozang people, and the female disciples who were gathered in the area—numbering many tens of thousands in total—all unanimously supplicated him, paid him reverence, made offerings, and so on. Their treatment of him rivaled the enjoyments of the gods themselves. In the time that followed, innumerable people recited dedications and prayers, requested Dharma teachings, and so on. By knowing the different thoughts and latencies of each of those people, the Master was able to satisfy them all with teachings that were suited to their individual intellects. He thus performed miraculous feats of body, speech, and mind while staying at that holy place. It was as if the amazement and wonder of the supreme Mahāmudrā, profounder than profound, had taken bodily form in him.

Traveling in stages by way of areas east of there, the Master went to Nyel. {570} The meritorious sovereign, the Dharma king Tashi Dargyé, the singular sentinel honoring the Teachings and the great holy persons who uphold them, enjoying his domain just as the *nāga* Laksorpa enjoys the earth, invited the Master to the great Lhünpo Palace. It was like Sītā welcoming someone to the Brahmaloka heaven. Tashi Dargyé worshipped the Master with all appropriate forms of reverence. He made a wide range of offerings, the foremost of which was an excellent horse.

Then the Master planned to go to the Forest of Glorious Samantabhadra and Densa Til by way of Yartö. In the great superintendent's offering chapel there was a clay statue of a goddess who tends to be very easily offended. Doing the Practice of the Observance, the Master plucked off the ceremonial silk scarves that had been draped over the goddess, knocked over the *tormas*, and so on. The Master presented a challenging affront to the administrator Samdrup Dechen by deprecating him, scolding him with all manner of criticism, and other harsh treatment. The lord and his servants were enraged. {571} They blocked the road like a division of crack troops making ready for battle. They cast a fierce rain of various weapons upon him. An arrow hit the Master in the back with such force that its tip protruded from his chest more than the length of a finger. Uninjured, he proceeded to Rechung Cave, where he remained for some time.

Then the Master directed his steps toward Nedong, the heart of the Land of Snows, the exalted place where the religious and secular systems of law come together. The Master provided for a great general merit-making service to be performed by the hermits of the three holy sites surrounding Densa Til. He went to a flower garden in Nedong, according himself well during his stay. By sponsoring tea services and *gaṇacakras*, and by offering tea, silks, and other things, he satisfied the inhabitants of those places with enjoyments to rival those seen long ago during the Complete Age, the Kṛtayuga, when people by their very nature pursued the Dharma, wealth, their desires, and their well-being simultaneously.[56] Then, by turning the wheel of the profound and vast Dharma, he completely ripened the continuums of many tens of thousands of people, made up mainly of locals. He gave the gift of the profound Dharma to impoverished people shackled by their clinging to existence. {572} Having the ability to grant whatever anyone wanted, he was like a second wish-fulfilling tree[57]—so it is renowned.

Then the Master went to Densa Til. He met with the lord of learned and meditatively accomplished ones, the noble Sharmepa. The Master fashioned all that he had with him into a cloud of offerings. With their minds melded together as one, the Master, the sovereign *mahāvajradhara*—with the blossoming water lily of his mouth and the beguiling ruby stamen of his tongue producing his melodious Brahmā voice—told the stories of what had happened to him at Tsari, Samdé, and other places. This caused noble Sharmepa to exclaim, "A yogin who can revive himself after being killed, who has attained mastery over appearances—you are what they call a divinely emanated being!" Sharmepa put his palms together at his heart, inestimably delighted. The lord of *siddhas* offered long-life prayers and the like before Sharmepa.

Then the Master and his students went by way of Ön to Gyama, the buddha realm blessed by the noble Great Compassionate One, Avalokiteśvara.[58] At Rinchen Gang and other places, to many *geshés* whose mental continuums were filled to capacity with the trainings of discipline, *samādhi*, and discernment, who were rich with the wealth of learning, the Master gave inestimable profound instructions on the Mahāmudrā of Coemergent Union, the *dohās*, the Secret Practice of India, the Seven-Day *Tummo*, the laying-bare instructions, the life instructions, and so on. {573}

At one point, without his attendants or anyone else accompanying him, the Master went unhindered into the building that houses the throne at Gyama. The administrator Lekdenpa, king of the Dharma, who had attained a great glorious sovereignty, delighted the Master by serving him with every appropriate form of reverence.

At that same place the Master had a conversation with the great abbot of Drakmar, he of infinite learning, the clarifier of the Teachings, Künga Tsepel. There were some important and difficult points concerning the secret meanings of things pertaining to the Vajrayāna about which the abbot was uncertain. The Master resolved all of the abbot's uncertainties, thus keeping unblemished the teachings of the Buddha. At that time the Master sang *vajra* songs that sprang from his own mind. The songs incorporated images that gave illustrative examples suitable for different types of people. In the wake of all this, the administrator himself supplicated the Master. {574} The great abbot of Drakmar then handed the Master a scroll on which a series of questions were written—about which tantras the Six Dharmas are based on, their order, the *a*-stroke, how long a vase breath should be held in, its beneficial effects, and so on. The Master gave correct answers and explanations for each question. He set his disciples in that area on the path of Dharmic auspiciousness.

The Master went by stages to Tsünmo Tsel. While crossing the Tsangpo river in a large coracle made from animal hides, he performed a *kumbhaka* or vase breath, forcing the winds of the *rasanā* and the *lalanā* into his central channel. The coracle became stuck in place for a long time, moving neither forward nor backward. Then he let a burst of air from his nose and the coracle shot like an arrow over to the north side of the Tsangpo.

Then he went by stages to the blue Ya lake in Penyül, where he stayed for about a year. While staying in retreat, he turned the vast wheel of the Dharma for his worthy disciples—so it is renowned. {575}

Embodying the bliss of blazing, of dripping, of melting, and the
co-emergent bliss,
his likeness frolics throughout the three realms,
does a dance reflecting an instantaneous transference of
consciousness—
the lord of *siddhas*, the chariot traveling the path of Secret Mantra.
Is it so amazing that you, glorious one, should be said
to have achieved coronation into the state of a mighty *vajradhara*?

You are a beautiful lotus, inspiring faith
when seen by the rheumy eyes of beings wandering this realm of
existence.
While seated in meditation, you move a single petal:
a dance that conveys the tattered fabric of existence.
It is said that you, Noble One, protect the teachings of the Sage;
I consider you an optical illusion embodying Gautama's compassion.

On one occasion the Master passed unhindered through the walls of his residence, his body not impeded in any way. This and many other miraculous feats were clearly seen by those present when they occurred, including lama Gendün Tashi and lama Daöpa.

During that time, on the fifteenth of the month, when the moon was completely full, the sovereign *mahāvajradhara* sat on a seat with his legs crossed in the *vajra* posture. {576} While pointing threateningly at the moon with his left hand, he commanded, "Until I, Künzang, the Madman of Ü, get up from this seat, you, moon, shall not go anywhere!" He took in a vase breath and rested in *samādhi* for some time. The moon remained unmoving in the middle of the sky, like an elephant bound by a tether. Then in a single instant he blew the wind from his nose, snapped his fingers, and stood up, at which time the moon flew toward the western mountains like a mighty *garuḍa*.[59]

At that time the Master taught the Mahāmudrā, the Six Dharmas, the *dohās*, the Secret Practice of India, Cutting, and other things. He expressed these teachings with his body, through his costumed performance of the dances of the nine demeanors, and with his speech, the sound of the divine *gaṇḍi* gong. All the while his mind did not diverge from his awareness of the nature of the spontaneously existent Mahāmudrā, and so on. {577} With the ceaseless play of his body, speech, and mind he caused the blooming of the water lilies of his disciples' intellects.

As soon as the Master broke the seal of his retreat, the great secretary Sangyé Gyeltsen, a lamp elucidating the teachings of the Sage, invited him to Lungshö Trakha. The great secretary delighted the Master with generosity, service, and with his own personal religious practice. He offered reasons that the Master should impart to him the very secret oral instruction of the *Tiger Encountering the Lion*, an unsurpassed Vajrayāna teaching. The sovereign *mahāvajradhara* happily assured him that he would.

To the great secretary and the leading monks—the foremost of whom was the great pillar supporting the Teachings, Targyé Chödzepa—the Master gave the Mahāmudrā, the Six Dharmas, the *Dohā Trilogy*, the *Six Treasuries*, the *Glorious Unpolluted Tantra*, and more. The Master gave Targyé Chödzepa many of the particular Dharma teachings that he wanted. With the flower of his speech, the Master gave him the following encouragement: "I am so lowly that if you threw me into a fire, I would not give off an aroma. If you threw me in water, I wouldn't even make a *plunk*. But no one is happier than I, for you have an expansive intellect. There is a mutual understanding between the two of us. {578} From among my greater sons, you will be the primary holder of my transmission." The Master gave Targyé Chödzepa the name Drikung Rechen, "Great Cotton-Clad One of Drikung." The Master also recited extensive prayers and good wishes.

After spreading the teachings of the profound Vajrayāna in all of the places around Reting monastery in upper Uru—the abode blessed as a second Densely Arrayed Akaniṣṭha heaven by glorious Atīśa and his spiritual sons—in the sheep year the Master went to Kya-lhuk Cave. While he 1499 spent the winter in that holy place, there assembled many people requesting the Dharma. He gave them the Mahāmudrā of Co-emergent Union. He gave the experiential instructions on the Six Dharmas, as transmitted by Barawa, to his greater heart sons—including Chertong Repa, Medro Rapjampa, Tapa Chöjé, Nyangpo Rechung, Nyelpa Jatang, Dechen Repa, Ewaṃ Rechen, and Namkha Lekpa, a fully ordained monk from Gyama.

In the month of the *māgha* constellation in the Kālacakra system, or the horse month in the Chinese, when the earth was covered with a blanket of snow, it was time to give embodied beings afflicted by the feeling of coldness a glorious new garment to wear: the cold itself. {579} Inside an extremely cold cave, those training in the Six Dharmas performed the Presentation of a Dried Sheet. There were various indications of the warmth generated by their *tummo*. Outside, the frozen Tsangpo river melted, the ground thawed, and so on. In the perceptions of some disciples, the Master was seen to perform inconceivably amazing miracles, such as manifesting four bodies at the same time. He gave the instructions in their entirety over the course of three months. The result was that the beginners learned how to maintain their religious practice, while the more mature practitioners saw great improvement in their meditation, progressing in terms of experiential realization. After the Master concluded such a fruitful year of teaching, the female disciples who had come from distant places all went their separate ways. Meanwhile the teacher and a subset of his students departed to circle through Ja, Drikung, Densa Til, and other places. {580}

At one point, the Master took the community surrounding the *mahāsiddha* Gendün Pel [Minyak Rapjampa?] into his protection by gracing them with a visit, as the *mahāsiddha* had requested him to do long before. To about two hundred lay and monastic students of the Dharma, he gave instructions including the text on the Mahāmudrā, *Dispelling the Darkness of Ignorance*, the *dohās*, the Secret Practice of India, the Five-Parted Single Sitting, and Cutting. To a subset headed by the *mahāsiddha* Gendün Pel, the Master gave, as experiential instructions, the Six Dharmas as transmitted by Barawa, the *Four-Fold Scroll of Marpa*, the life instructions, and more.

During that visit there was an occasion when the Master drank a lot of "inner offerings" of liquor and whatnot, then began to act as if intoxicated. In front of him was a cup filled with liquor. The cup somehow circled above his head, then smashed against the earthen wall of his residence. But the cup did not break and the "nectar" did not even spill. He was seen to do this and many other things that proved his total mastery over other people's perceptions and thoughts.

Over the course of three months, the Master gave instructions, reading transmissions, and the like in their entirety. He seemed to be extremely delighted with the *mahāsiddha* Gendün Pel. "You uphold and protect the teachings of the Kagyü in general," the Master said. {581} "In particular, you teach in an unbroken manner the empowerments, reading transmissions, and esoteric oral instructions of the eighty *siddhas*. I am the granddaddy of the eighty *siddhas*! Include me when you do prostrations, invitations, and the like that are addressed to them!" He made all of the people of upper and lower Medro turn away from the poisons of sensory perceptions, then enter into the profound path to total liberation.

By stages he went as invited to the Gyangom estate. They made magnificent reverential service and offerings to the Master. In turn, he gave them assurances that they would become rich with sons and material things.

In the monkey year, the Master went to the Charnel Ground of the Nāga
Queen. At that time there arrived an inestimable number of his greater 1500
heart sons, each a master of realization. Among them were more than ten learned and meditatively accomplished ones, including Drikung Rechen and Rapjampa Yönten Rinchen, who is rich in many good qualities resulting from knowledge of scripture and from realization. There were thirteen whose bodies were filled with the bliss-heat of *tummo*, including Üpa Rechung, "the Lesser Cotton-clad One of Ü." There were Sakya Chöjung, Ölkha Chöjung, and others. {582} It is said that this gathering was a manifestation of the grandeur of the Master's enlightened activity.

At one point, out of their irreversible faith, the commander of thousands [Tashi Dargyé?] and his wife and retinue invited the mighty sovereign *vajradhara* to the Ja estate. He tasted the nectar of the Master's speech and became his main patron from that time onward.[60]

At that time the Master gave his mendicant heart sons Dharma teachings on the Mahāmudrā, the Six Dharmas, and other topics. He satisfied them by giving things that were appropriate for each, including charm boxes, clothing, and the *Vajra Verses on the Aural Tantra*. Then he dispatched them to important holy sites to work for the benefit of transmigrating beings.

Traveling by way of Zholung Tsokha and other places, the Master went by stages to Zhokpu Jomo-nying. While he was staying there, the great lord of the families said, "Long ago I assumed responsibility for benefiting all transmigrating beings. As the task of helping transmigrators has taken longer than expected, I have not yet transformed my body of material substance into a rainbow body." {583}

Another time he made the following announcement: "Now for a few years I will renounce all distractions and only do practice."

While he was staying in retreat, doing nothing but meditate, at one point the earth spirit Zhoklha Chukpo developed complete respect for the Master and arrived before him. The deity said, "I request that you stay here. I will serve you and carry out your enlightened activity." So the Master imparted to him some vows, including having him take refuge in the Three Jewels[61] and generate the mind of *bodhicitta*. The Master verbally assured that he would stay.

Due to various factors like his bathing in the waters at that holy place, the Master seemed to become physically unwell. "Let's go to Lhasa," he said, "both to visit and for a change in water."

After first sending his heart son Sakya Chöjung to the Kham area to benefit transmigrating beings, the Master traveled swiftly and directly to the Lhasa area with a subset of his students. Mounted on a horse called Trinkyi Shukchen Norbu Yangdong—"Strength of the Clouds, Broad Jewel Blaze"—he galloped unhindered through the very crowded and narrow southern entrance to the Barkor and arrived at the open area within. {584}

With a great wave of completely unsullied fortune, the Master provided for the faces of the two Jowo Śākyamūṇi statues [in the Jokhang and Ramoché temples] to be repainted with gold. He made offerings of butter lamps, ceremonial silk scarves of the five colors, and more. He also spread the Teachings, both in general and all of the individual ones. He made completely pure prayers about equating his very life with religious practice, that all sentient beings should achieve the state of a *vajradhara*, and so on.

Then at one point when he was staying at Galo Cave, the Master had a vision of an isolated and auspicious abode conducive to virtue and concentration, which was in accordance with the prophetic commands of his lama and the *ḍākiṇīs*, and with the clarified perceptions he had seen during meditation. It was a palace of glorious Cakrasaṃvara, where *ḍākiṇīs* and Dharma protectors naturally congregated. The mountain behind the site looked as if draped with a veil of white silk, while the mountain before it was laid out like a golden maṇḍala. The lesser mountains looked like they were bowing in the direction of the holy site, their palms joined in respect. The valley itself was like an unperishing blue lotus flower, lying completely open. The various streams containing water possessed of the eight good qualities[62] ran without interruption and were beautified by melodious sounds and necklaces of white bubbles. {585} The ground there was beautiful, as if the petals of a blooming lotus—or an *indranīla dukūla*, a vestment of sparkling blue-green sapphire. The sky above looked like it was overlaid with a ruby hoop enclosing a thousand golden spokes. The mountains facing the site appeared to be overlaid with the eight auspicious signs,[63] made of gold from the Jambunāth river, and topped with beryl. By merely going to that abode, many hundreds of different *samādhis* would be established within one's mind. The amazing layout of the place seemed to be the work of a single maker.

Delighted at the prospect of visiting the great holy site that had appeared to him thus, and knowing that if he directed his lotus feet there it would result in limitless benefit to the Teachings and to sentient beings, the Master set about going to Tsimar Pel mountain.

He commanded his attendant Dechen Repa, "Since I am going to equate my very life with religious practice in this abode, you must use whatever means necessary to make this monastery ours." {586}

Dechen Repa then asked, "Wouldn't it be better if we, teacher and students, stayed in whatever mountains, as we did in the past?"

"We will benefit the sentient beings of this realm through the four types of enlightened activity," the Master declared. "In particular, we will establish a shining example for the teachings of the Meditation Tradition. So do as I have said!"

The attendant obeyed the command of his holy lama. He sought control over the monastery through various means. Thanks to conditions established through blessings that had been given, and to dependent connections that had been created in the past, in the dog year, on the morning 1502
of the fifteenth day of the eleventh month according to the Mongolian, Hor system, the sovereign *mahāvajradhara* was invited into the residence at the great abode of Tsimar Pel, which was like a second Densely Arrayed Akaniṣṭha heaven. His heart's wish was completely fulfilled.

The magician of existence and the tranquil beyond, who is like the
single performer behind the countless amazing things in the
infinite realms,
the lord of *siddhas*, the glorious Heruka—
may you plant your lotus feet at Tsimar Pel mountain! {587}

When, by performing a hundred wisdom dances,
the sovereign *vajradhara* laid out the Akaniṣṭha he enjoyed,
he did so for the viewing pleasure of limitless transmigrating
beings—
his watchful gaze had been cast upon this realm of existence!

From the excellent crystal vase of your mind,
filled with the nectar of Nāropa's esoteric oral instructions,
you bestow that essential gift to countless worthy peacocks,
holding nothing back from them.

When the jewel, the raindrop of your fame,
has fallen through the vast sky over the Land of Snows,
the jasmine garland of the Secret Mantra way
will blossom in the garden of learned and accomplished ones.

The sovereign *vajradhara*, the lord of all the families, at the very center of the world and its inhabitants, made the following pronouncement in a state of delight:

"I have maintained the Practice of the Observance throughout the Land of Snows.
Even if a rain of weapons were cast upon my *vajra* body,
it would be like trying to strike a rainbow with a staff—
so how could I be subject to any harm at all? {588}
I have established karmic connections with all beings, superior and ordinary.
To benefit all the future members of the Meditation Tradition,
I will equate my very life with practice in this prophesized holy place!"

Such was the sixth chapter of *The Life Story of the Noble Künga Zangpo, Called "That Which without Restriction Gives Goosebumps of Faith,"* relating the story of how the Master maintained the Practice of the Observance throughout the entire Land of Snows, and established karmic connections with all beings, both superior and ordinary.

7

Triumph over Saṃsāra

THEN THE SOVEREIGN *mahāvajradhara* said, "I will now devote myself mainly to practice, so let no one else stay near this place." His retinue vacated the area.

While the Master was staying in utter solitude like a rhinoceros, at one point a few unruly beings, overcome with a jealousy that was caused by malevolent curses, raised a dispute over the site of Tsimar Pel. Many divisions of troops arrived there. But, indifferent to the eight worldly concerns, taking whatever arose as part of the path, he remained meditating in a sky-like *samādhi*. {589} Because of this, whatever torments they tried to inflict on him were as harmless as a bat's wing brushing against an indestructible mountain.

After that the Master went into a very strict retreat. He subsisted on parts of the *sewa* plant,[64] and on essences that he extracted from flowers. There was a boulder the size of a yak, which was lying on the path that went around his residence. On one occasion, he excitedly picked it up, carried it in front of him for some distance, then dropped it in a better spot. A handprint was left in the solid rock. Today the rock remains there on the side of that mountain, as a physical means enabling worthy beings to accumulate merit. It is seen as symbolizing the solidified mass of ideation accumulated since beginningless time, having been hacked at by the pickaxe of wisdom.

One time, a mountainside visible from Tsimar Pel was struck by lightning, which initiated a perilous rockslide. {590} The Master blew a burst of wind from his nose, pointed at the rocks with a threatening *mudrā*, and commanded, "You stay right where you are!" Those rocks have remained there on that sheer mountainside to this very day. These indications of the relationship between our thoughts and our perceptions, performed by the

Master, are beyond the compass of description. However, they can be partially understood by sentient beings who are sufficiently fortunate.

In the snake year, the Master's heart son, the great *paṇḍita* of Chokro,
1509 Rinchen Samten, came from the Tsang area to visit him, accompanied by about two hundred of his own students. They offered many precious things, including gold, silver, coral, and amber, as well as a shawl, a charm box, a cushion, and many garments made from cotton and other materials. Father and son communicated through the window to his sealed retreat. With their minds melded together as one, the Master resolved whatever uncertainties the great *paṇḍita* had, and imparted limitless instructions to him.

The Master told the *paṇḍita*, "Even if heaven and earth were turned upside-down, I would not leave this place to go anywhere. {591} And because of your great idleness, you will not come back here after this. So it will be difficult for us, father and son, to meet again. I charge you with composing a commentary on the *Dohā Trilogy*, and a ritual arrangement for guru *pūjā* that accords with intentions of the *siddha* Lingrepa. Furthermore, achieve vast benefit for the teachings of the Buddha and for sentient beings through the three activities of the learned—teaching, debating, and writing!" The Master gave him some gifts, including a deerskin rug, a charm box, and porcelain cups. The great *paṇḍita* and his students offered long-life prayers and the like, then went back to Tsang.

In the fire-female-snake year[65], the learned and meditatively accom-
1510 plished one, adorned with the flowing vestments of monastic discipline, the great *paṇḍita* of Nyukla, Ngawang Drakpa Pelzangpo, made extensive offerings and prayers, including before the two Jowo Śākyamuni statues in Lhasa. Then he traveled to Tsimar Pel to meet with the sovereign *mahāvajradhara*. {592}

Thanks to the phenomenon of dependently arisen connections, the two were able to meet. Because the father was rich in compassion, and the son was rich in faith, they stayed together for three days, their minds melded together as one. The Master was delighted. He gave a prophetic command stating that Ngawang Drakpa—that miraculous form of Avalokiteśvara—possessed a special mandate for the instructions of the peerless Dakpo Kagyü, including the Mahāmudrā, the Six Dharmas, the *dohā*s, and the Secret Practice of India. The Master instructed him, "You should make printings of the *Collected Songs* and the *Life* of noble Milarepa, the *Dohā Trilogy*, the *Secret Practice of India*, and other texts. Faultlessly protect the teachings of the Buddha in general, and in particular the teachings of the peerless Dakpo Kagyü."

During this meeting the Master also instructed him, "You must do things to extend your life span." He made many other announcements that indicated his knowledge of the future.

Before Ngawang Drakpa and his students departed, the Master gave them many things that they desired, including cushions, charm boxes, clothing, bowls, and other items that he had blessed. {593} The Master also recited prayers, good wishes, and the like. With his religious and worldly interests both satisfied, the great *paṇḍita*, lord Ngawang Drakpa, went back to Nyukla. He and his servants were laden with a splendor that could rival the divine grove that contains the wish-fulfilling tree of the gods.

Another time, lord Gönpo Gyeltsen—possessing an expansive eye that knows all of the religious and political sciences—came from his great seat at glorious Drikung, accompanied by many servants. They made offerings of tea, clothing, silk, gold, silver, and various types of garments—which, taken together, were like Indra's heap of amulets, or like the emerald earth itself. This completely delighted the holy Noble One. The Master spoke on longevity practices, protecting against and turning back obstacles, and so on, pouring nectar into the cupped hands of the faithful. He gave them objects that he had blessed, including knotted *vajra* protection cords and charm boxes. Then the Master gave Gönpo Gyeltsen the title of "Dharma King Who Makes the Whole World Tremble." {594} The Master said, "Because you and Dharma lord Künga Rinchen need to have good bodily health for the sake of the Teachings in general, as well as for certain particular ones, I will not cast you out of my circle of protection." He made other felicitous announcements as well. Then Gönpo Gyeltsen returned to Drikung.

On another occasion, at Tupten Serdokchen, before the lord of learned and meditatively accomplished ones, the *paṇḍita* Śākya Chokden—who is unmatched in the Land of Snows for the way he fosters the teachings of the Victor through teaching, debating, writing, and the other activities of the learned, all performed with his expansive eye that knows the whole collection of the Kangyur, the translated words of the Victor, as well as the entire textual tradition of the Six Ornaments[66]—the Master arranged for inestimable offerings to be made, including a long-life cushion marked with a crossed *vajra*, tea, clothing, and silk. Using only five *nyaks*[67] of tea leaves, a batch of tea was made for the whole assembly of about a thousand monks. The tea turned out to be strong and delicious, which the whole assembly regarded with amazement. {595}

In the sheep year, the Master's heart son Sakya Chöjung returned to
his presence after meting out the nectar of the profound Vajrayāna in 1511

places throughout Kham. He offered the Master material things without end, including gold, turquoise, pearls, clothing, and silk. With their minds melded together as one, the Master filled the vase of his student's mind with a nectar that can never be surpassed.

When requesting permission to travel to the Tsang area to visit his mother, Sakya Chöjung offered into the hands of the Master an empty skull cup lined with silver.

The Master then announced, "Because the image of the son's skull being handed to the father has occurred, the dependent connections between us have been somewhat disrupted. Since you have been in the Kham area for so long, it is important that you pay a visit your mother. But if you go, do not go to Lhasa. And if you insist on going to Lhasa, do not stay there for a full day."

Sakya Chöjung and his students departed, going without hindrance into the presence of the Jowo statue. {596} When he performed the Practice of the Observance, all the people of Lhasa gathered and cast a rain of weapons. Some butchers hacked at him with their blades. As a result, he gathered up his miraculous forms and entered into the path of the Truth of the Cessation of Suffering.[68]

When they were in the process of cremating Sakya Chöjung's corpse, the noble holy Master emanated himself in the form of a white vulture. He soared gracefully through the sky, circled the crematory hearth, and so on. Everyone there was amazed by this and the many other indications of the Master's total mastery over people's perceptions—so it is renowned.

Another time, the abbot of Drikung, the divine emanation, the superior being Künga Gyeltsen,[69] arrived to visit the Master with five or so of his students. They brought an offering of some *tsimar* extracts.[70] The Master gave them some instructions, satisfying them with the unsurpassed nectar of his speech. He also gave assurances that those individuals would be of vast benefit to the Teachings and to sentient beings.

For the past ten years or so, the Master had stayed in a strict retreat, showing the maṇḍala of his body no more than a few times. {597} Only teaching in private on a handful of occasions, he did not give extensive instructions or reading transmissions or anything. He did not interact with the people staying in the residences next to or nearby his own, and was served by only two or three attendants.

But now he declared: "Many of my sons working for the benefit of the Teachings and of sentient beings have succumbed to difficult circumstances and passed away. These include Sakya Chöjung, Üpa Rechung, and Chertong Repa. Therefore, I must appoint other sons to maintain my transmission, to serve as their replacements. I will now give many profound and vast Dharma instructions, the foremost being the *Tiger Encountering the Lion*."

This announcement resounded in every distant place. Many worthy beings from the three regions of Ü, Tsang, and Kham gathered at Tsimar Pel to taste the nectar of the Master's speech. {598}

When the Master had reached the age of fifty-five, on the eighth day of
the fifth month of the monkey year—on the day of the memorial offering for 1512
noble Drakchokpa Ratnabhadra, when the alignment of the planets and stars was particularly favorable—he began giving a great many teachings to an assembly of about five hundred. Those teachings included the Mahāmudrā of Co-emergent Union; the Five-Parted Single Sitting; the *Dohā Trilogy*; the *Six Treasuries*; the Secret Practice of India, in its greater and lesser forms; the root symbol; the great laying-bare instruction on Cutting; the life instructions; *Finding Ease in the Nature of Mind*; the minor *dohās* composed by Virūpa, Tilopa, Śawaripa, Nāropa, and other *siddhas*; the laying-bare instructions; the *Hevajra Tantra*; the Dharmas of Ngok; the *Jewel Ornament Commentary*; the great commentary by Nāropa; the *Valid Understanding of the Authentic Word*; and the commentary *Sun of the Little Collection*.

At that time his principal Dharma students or great sons included Wonré Sönam Namgyel, Nyima Rapjampa, Nyida Rapjampa, and Sönam Wangchuk; Taksher Repa, the renunciant from Balok, Gonak Chödzé, Jikmé Repa, Sengé Repa, the realized one from Renga, and Sönam Gyeltsen, the realized one from Kharnak. {599} To them the Master gave a different set of numerous instructions, including the Seven-Day *Tummo* as transmitted by glorious Galo; the Six Dharmas as transmitted by Barawa, with all of their ancillaries; the Aural Transmission of Rechungpa; the Aural Transmission of Ngendzongpa; the *Four-Fold Scroll* of noble Marpa—and lastly the instructions on the glorious four-armed wisdom protector Mahākāla, with a retinue of five, a retinue of four, and a retinue of two. He gave these teachings over the course of four months.

An extensive *gaṇacakra* was laid out to celebrate the end of the Dharma teachings. The Master gave gifts that were appropriate for each student. He commanded that Wonré Sönam Namgyel and his students should pledge to meditate for three years at Adrak Khung. They assented and departed.

The Master directed Jikmé Repa and his students and Dharma brothers to raise prayer flags and hold feast offerings at a number of great abodes, including the snowy enclave of Mount Kailash, Lake Manasarovar,

Lapchi, Chubar, the Swayambhūnāth stūpa, as well as at Drakar Taso and the rest of the Six Fortresses of noble Laughing Vajra. {600} They were to have painted with gold the statues, miraculous footprints, and other holy objects housed at those sites. They were also to erect a statue of the Master himself. With pledges to remain in *samādhi* for a period of three years, he sent them off.

He sent ten of his disciples, including Sengé Repa and the realized one from Renga, to the Kham area, along with their respective students. He dispatched Taksher Repa with a command to practice at the excellent holy sites in Drikung and Ölkha.

To everyone else, he said, "You should all go and meditate in different holy sites. I too will remain in meditation." Then he went back into retreat.

That year many new monks arrived at Tsimar Pel, including Wönpo Dorgyel, Künga Nyima, and Rikdzin Nyima. Shortly after this the Master sent Nyida Rapjampa to Kham, for the benefit of transmigrating beings.

During the summer Dharma teaching session, the nephew of the ascetic Tarpa Gyeltsen—who is a miraculous form of the noble Great Compassionate One, Avalokiteśvara—came from the area of Uma Drakar along with many of his students. {601} Even though those upholding the fundamentals of the training who gathered there in their faith were great in number, the Master satisfied each of them with teachings that suited their individual intellects.

The secret yogin Künga Lekpa, Madman of the Drukpa, also arrived during that time. He offered inestimable heaps of offerings, as well as a supplication to the Aural Transmission that he had composed. This delighted the Master. The Master gave him cycles of Dharma teachings of profound meaning, which fulfilled Künga Lekpa's wishes. Then he departed with the gifts he had been given.

Another time, Döndrupa, the superintendent of Nyukpa, arrived accompanied by his servants. He made inestimable offerings, the foremost of which were clothing and cushions. With the nectar of his speech, the Master gave him the ripening instructions for the Aural Transmission of Rechungpa. The Master made extensive pronouncements about how the superintendent had been his student in a previous lifetime. {602} When he was getting ready to leave, the Master gave him some gifts, including a charm box. He reassured the superintendent by saying, "It will be difficult for you to come back here again and again, so you should get the instructions that I have transmitted to Rinchen Samten of Chokro." Then they departed.

Not long after this, the Master satisfied many learned and meditatively accomplished ones—the foremost of whom was the renunciant from Doring, Dharma lord Künga Nyima, along with his students—by giving them many profound and vast Dharma teachings, including the Mahāmudrā of Co-emergent Union, the Five-Parted, and the Six Dharmas as transmitted by Barawa.

During the next summer Dharma teaching, the Master gave the Mahāmudrā of Co-emergent Union, the Five-Parted, the Aural Transmission of Rechungpa, and other teachings to the "Dharma-door keeper" of Drikung, lord Penjor Drakpa, along with his students, as well as many mendicants.

While the Master was turning the unsurpassed wheel of the profound Dharma, Tapa Chöjé arrived with some of his students. The Master said, "I am delighted that you have come. Stay here for a few years. Papa will give you all his oral instructions." {603} The Master gave him the name Künzang Gönpo Rinchen. It is said that he became an excellent student who upheld the Master's transmission.

From the sky, the mouth of the noble lord of *siddhas*—
the mighty *vajradhara*, successor to a long-standing tradition—
the thunder of the Aural Transmission is intoned without hurry,
which drives the peacocks, his worthy students, mad with joy.

Here in this place encircled by snow mountains,
the inexhaustible treasury of the north,
the lord of the family, mighty Jambhala,
dispenses the wares of virtue from his own vast fortune.

Because of his play amid the endless emptiness,
the mountain which pervades the three realms has crumbled.
In this degenerate age, the virtue of this lord of *siddhas*
is like a bolt of lightning in the night sky.

If not for the sun of the Noble One's exposition,
propelled across the sky of the Kagyü
by the wind of his miraculous feats,
wouldn't this realm of existence be enveloped by darkness? {604}

In the dog year, in the first month of the Hor system, on a day when
the alignment of the planets and stars was particularly favorable, the holy 1514

nephew of the Master, who had been living in Ölkha, was caught by the hook of the noble *mahāvajradhara*'s compassion and came before him at Tsimar Pel mountain. The aroma of his requisite and inestimable devotion was pleasing to the bee of the Master's mind. Not even the bliss felt upon achieving the First Stage[71] could compare to that which was born in him at that time. With his mouth like a verdant divine lotus flower, his teeth like the light of the moon falling on a lake of milk, the Master gave assurances to the boy, saying that this meeting was like the nephew of the victor Jikten Sumgön arriving before him at Drikung Til.

With inestimable delight, the Master consulted with the Victor and his sons. At that astrologically favorable time when he was thirteen years old, the boy exchanged his clothing for the robes of a monk. {605} Knowing that he would bring vast benefit to the teachings of the Buddha, the Master gave him the name Künzang Nyida Pembar—"Totally Good, Blazing with the Glory of the Sun and the Moon." The Master tossed some consecratory grain and handed the boy a white conch shell draped with ribbons. When he blew the shell while facing each of the four directions, it made a very loud sound. The Master said that this created a good dependent connection. The Master promised not to cast him out of his loving gaze, and so on.

During the winter Dharma teaching that year, the Master gave extensive instruction in the Mahāmudrā and the Six Dharmas to the veritable ocean of followers who were gathered there, the foremost of whom was the lord of learned ones, Bum Rapjampa.

From this time onward, there was a perpetual stream of visitors arriving to see the Master. There could be up to five hundred at a given time.

On one occasion, the commander of Ling came from Kham to visit the Master, accompanied by his servants. The great official made inestimable offerings of things like tea, clothing, and silk. The Master satisfied him with Dharma teachings, blessed objects, and so on. {606} Then he gave him the new name of Lingré Nyida Öbar.

Another time, Tilmarwa of Bodhgaya, the great cotton-clad ascetic from India, came with his students to visit the Master. He offered the Master a conch shell that can call the eighty *siddha*s to assemble. The noble Master happily blew the conch in each of the four directions. Then the Master gave each of the thousand and eight mendicants a new name, all of which included Dungkar, "White Conch."

During that winter teaching session, the Master told his nephew Künzang Nyida Pembar to train in the *Hevajra Tantra*, the *dohā*s, and so on. He did as he was directed.

At one point, for the purposes of spreading the teachings of the Kagyü and prolonging his own life, the Master sent Dzongkar Rechen, Künga Nyingpo, Chakchenpa Saraha, and others to hold tea services and raise prayer flags at a few monasteries in upper Tsang, including Tropu. They were to have statues of the Master raised at Śrī Bariko and Chumik Ngombum. {607} At Śrī Samten Ling, tea for an assembly of about a hundred was made from only a very small parcel of tea leaves. The tea turned out to be strong and delicious, which amazed everyone—so it is renowned.

Then Sengé Repa and his students returned from Kham. They offered the Master a measure of brilliant Chinese fabric, as well as clothing, silk, tea, and so on. They were like the treasures of the heavenly Alakāvatī realm. Sengé Repa requested many profound oral instructions specifically. The Master gave the prophetic command that he should benefit transmigrating beings in the Kyishö area and sent him on his way.

One time when an attendant came into the Master's residence to bring him some water, it appeared that he was not there. For a few days nothing happened. Some people said that perhaps the Master had gone to the Charnel Ground of the Nāga Queen and passed away. Others said it seemed as if he had passed away inside his residence. Stories like these spread all over. {608} Back at his monastery, people wondered if he had abandoned his physical body for a rainbow body. The truth was that the Master had forced his yogic winds and consciousness into his central channel and had entered a *samādhi*.

Not long after that, there arose a conflict between Ü and Tsang. This greatly saddened the Noble One. He said that many innocent sentient beings had died, and because of their negative associations, had been reborn in hell. With those beings in mind, he put all of the objects in his possession toward the production of virtue. He repeatedly made prayers for the spread of universal compassion, and so on.

Shortly after this, the king of Lowo Möntang, who is sustained by his massive virtue, sent offerings that are beyond the compass of description. These included a letter prefaced by melodious words of praise, about five hundred large pearls, and a deerskin rug. For his part, the Master sent back a decree, which established a good dependent connection between them. {609}

One time the precious one—an emanation of the victor Avalokiteśvara, the Great Compassionate One—came from Changlung into the presence of the Master, accompanied by many of his students. He offered long-life prayers, sponsored a tea service and alms for the community, and made offerings that are beyond comprehension. Delighted, the noble Master satisfied him with many Dharma teachings. Then the Master spoke to him about needing to maintain the transmission of Niguma, gave a cushion blessed for long life, and so on, thereby establishing many avenues of dependent connection between them.

The Dharma king Ngawang Namgyel [a cousin of Dönyö Dorjé, at this time acting as head of the Rinpung regime] sent a letter that praised the Master as a "lord of *yogins*," and so on, along with some offerings.

At another point, Ritrö Wangchuk, the master of his enlightened activity, arrived before the Master. He fashioned a heap of offerings from all of the things that he had in his possession. He also made extensive prayers. {610} The Master gave him Dharma teachings with their profound critical points, and made prophetic commands, such as, "You will benefit transmigrating beings in the Yarlung area." After Ritrö Wangchuk departed, he became *tishrī*, the lama of the great emperor.[72] He was renowned for being of great activity—so it is said.

Lopa Chennga [Ngawang Chödrak Gyeltsen], adorned with great glory in clan and family status, and Dharma lord Rinchen Jampa Chönyipa, the learned and meditatively accomplished one, came to visit the Master, accompanied by many of their respective students. The Master gave them many Dharma teachings, including the Mahāmudrā of Co-emergent Union. He told them how they should assiduously uphold and protect the teachings of the Buddha, saying, "You should teach the Dharmas that papa has transmitted to you!" He prayed that they should have long lives, that their activities should increase, and so on.

Another time, the one occupying the throne of the Pakmodrupa, who lovingly upholds the teachings of the Buddha from his position of power over both worldly and religious affairs [*gongma* Ngawang Tashi Drakpa[73]], sent a letter and some offerings. The letter praised the Master with such titles as "lord of yogins," "preeminent *siddha*," and "Madman of Ü, king of the Dharma." {611} He also made prayers for the Master's long life, and so on. In return, the Master sent some blessed objects, including a knotted *vajra* cord, along with some prayers. This strengthened their relationship as patron and preceptor.

When the army of Kyishö was on its way to upper Ur, Apo Söpa, the superintendent rich in heroism, paid the Master a visit, accompanied by some of his servants. The superintendent made inestimable offerings. Upon tasting the nectar of the Master's speech, he attained indefatigable faith. He offered a ceremonial silk scarf, as pure white as his intentions, with "Good, happy day" inscribed on it.

Shortly after that, the protector, the superintendent of Shakpa, came to visit the Master. He received a few profound instructions, including the *Dohā Trilogy*. They conversed at inestimable length about holy places and other topics. Their individual wishes were fulfilled. {612} The superintendent offered a ceremonial scarf for the sake of establishing a dependent connection between them. He attained irreversible faith in the Master.

Another time, in the course of events, some soldiers ended up coming in through the Master's roof!

Some high-ranking military officers had come to visit the Master, to make prayers and so forth. On account of this, there arose the danger that some people from Chiru Taktsé[74] and other places—not taking into account the Master's true intentions, and pulled into unruliness and deceit by the bridle of bad karma, and by the hook of grasping at self—might arrive at Tsimar Pel and cause trouble for him. Some faithful people informed the Master about this. In response, the sovereign *mahāvajradhara* announced, "I, the son of the glorious Pakmodrupa, have taken the whole of phenomenal existence as my enemy. Even if heaven and earth were turned upside-down, I would not leave this place for anywhere."

To five or so members of his retinue, including his nephew and successor, Künzang Nyida Pembar, the Master issued the following command: "No matter what harm the other side inflicts, do nothing to retaliate. Let them do as they please." {613}

On the twenty-fifth day of the ninth month in the Hor system, when most of the monks had departed to do the autumn begging rounds, a great many troops—both laymen and monks—surrounded the Master's residence. In accordance with their individual degrees of merit, they cast a great rain of arrows and stones, or hacked at the walls of the residence with bars and other implements. After they destroyed the middle of the three levels of awnings, a few soldiers came in through the roof of the Master's residence carrying various weapons, stalking him like cutthroats.

When they got a full view of him, the great hero was wearing the eight accoutrements of the Heruka, posed majestically on the great fearless lion throne, staring into space. Unable to attack him, they prostrated, asked for his blessing, and so on. Nevertheless, because their minds were oppressed by craving, they carried off all his belongings. {614}

The Master immediately went onto the roof of his residence. He was even more exquisitely radiant than before, shining with the brilliance of ten million suns. With his voice like Brahmā's *gaṇḍi* gong, he proclaimed,

"When extreme difficulties like this arise, if you do not know how to make them part of the path, you will struggle with obstacles. So come!"

When everyone had gathered before the Master, he told them, "Don't look so dejected and miserable. A yogin will face uncountable challenges of this sort! We have no shortage of things to eat and drink." Next to the Master was a basket containing a handful of soft cheese that was left over. He spit once upon the cheese. When he passed the dish around, each person got about a handful of cheese. Everyone was amazed—so it is renowned.

At the end of the day, the sun, wrapped in the red glow of sunset, went off to the feast in Godānīya, the western continent. {615} Darkness fell like a great rain sent down by the beautiful, immortal goddesses. The moon, protector of the night, rose in the sky. At that time, in their individual homes the unruly-minded guilty parties clearly saw a range of inauspicious signs. They were pursued by a great fear and knew not what to do.

When the orb of the sun arose in the east, bringing its warming vapors, a few of those people who still had their wits about them came to return the Master's belongings.

When the Master's attendants told him for what reason those people had come, he said, "Because I understand the perfection of generosity, I had already designated those things to be given away. But do take back my *khaṭvāṅga*, 'Blazing Auspicious Light,' because it is associated with a *samaya* vow. And take back my *dzomo*,[75] out of compassion for her." He did not accept anything else.

As it says in scripture:

> He who remains meditating on reality
> shows the unbearable hordes of demons to be
> apparitions.[76]

In that very manner, even when the Master was attacked by armies of nonhuman spirits during the night, or by armies of embodied beings during the day, he could not be shaken. Such is the way of one who has achieved perfection in *vajra*-like *samādhi*. {616}

Oh mighty *garuḍa*, possessing the sharp talons of meditative equanimity,
roaming the sky of the Sage's teachings with wings spread wide:
guide us down the path of profundity during this degenerate age.

There are other learned and accomplished *garuḍa*s in India and Tibet
whose heroism makes the hearts of the *nāga*s and demons
rise up in their throats—
but their life stories aren't as amazing to behold,
lacking the theatrics of the Glorious One.

The compassion of mighty Vajradhara,
in the form of his sparkling body—the king of all wish-fulfilling
jewels!
Who can tally the amount of virtue that the people of the snowy
mountains
must have had in order to purchase it?

Under the Bodhi tree of the son of the Gautamas,
the armies of demons were laid down to sleep.
Shooting the five arrows, oh Noble One,
you have finally finished them off. {617}

Such was the seventh chapter of *The Life Story of the Noble Künga Zangpo, Madman of Ü, the Lord of* Siddhas, *Called "That Which without Restriction Gives Goosebumps of Faith,"* relating the story of how, because he was able to remain unwaveringly within the profound meaning, he was not subject to external or internal causes of harm, and how his realization made him victorious on the battlefield of saṃsāra.

8

Further Practice and Teaching

IN THE EARTH-MALE-TIGER year, after making it through that inaus-
1518 picious year marked by obstacles, the Master turned sixty-one. Then his enjoyments began to brim like a lake in summer. Stories about him had reached every distant place, as if carried by messengers. His patrons and leading disciples offered him a continuous stream of material enjoyments, like the jewels that issue from the throat of the magical mongoose possessed by the god Vaiśravaṇa, the Lord of Treasure—so it is renowned.

The renunciant Ngawang Döndrup Namgyel—who, with his supremely expansive eye knowing both worldly and religious ways, watches over the Teachings and the great persons who uphold them; the one who had been held most dear by the great *paṇḍita* of Nyukla, Ngawang Drakpa—along with his brother, received word from the Master that his community was in need of *tsampa*. {618} So the two brothers [nephews of Nyukla Peṇchen?] made free use of their wealth in both faith and dispensable things, and the renunciant himself arrived at Tsimar Pel to offer about a hundred *khels*[77] of *tsampa*, as well as inestimable other things. In return, the Master satisfied him with prayers, Dharma teachings, and the like. Ngawang Döndrup Namgyel attained indefatigable faith in the Master and became very dedicated to the students who held his transmission—so it is renowned.

Another time, lord Künga Namgyel, the great heart son of the *vidyādhara* Pema Lingpa, came to visit the Master, accompanied by his students. He tasted the nectar of the Master's speech and was given the name Nyentrö Rechen, "the Great Cotton-Clad One of Haunted Places."

Not long after that, master Durtröpa—"Charnel Ground One"—came from Kongpo with about a hundred of his students. After making inestimable offerings and receiving profound Dharma teachings, they departed for Tsang.

Then the learned and meditatively accomplished one, *paṇḍita* Dorjé Gyelpo, came with his students. It was like when the *ṛṣi* Sūryaratha, "Chariot of the Sun," came long ago from the kingdom of Shambhala to the Land of Snows in order to spread the unsurpassed secrets contained in the glorious *Kālacakra Tantra*, the scripture on original buddhahood. {619} The *paṇḍita* made inconceivable offerings to the Master. In the course of their conversations about the holy Dharma and other topics, they established dependent connections that would result in vast benefit to the teachings of the Buddha. The peacock, having pure intentioned faith, was joyed by the camphor of profound Dharma teachings. The bliss he experienced was beyond even that of a whole swarm of adolescent bees who arrive in a grove of lotus flowers and become intoxicated by the scent. Then he departed.

After winter had arrived, one day the Master said, "Last night in my dream, a large statue of Vajrapāṇi located in Tsang somewhere appeared to be destroyed. It would seem that an affliction has befallen a holder of my transmission."

Not long after this, some people arrived to request prayers for the learned and meditatively accomplished one from Chokro [Rinchen Samten], who had passed into another realm. The Master appeared saddened and remained in thought for a moment. "My son has not taken rebirth," he then declared. "He remains in a pure realm." {620}

Then it resounded that the Master had made the following announcement: "To appoint replacements for the prominent sons of mine who have passed away, worthy beings should now come be near papa!"

Serious students of the Dharma gathered at Tsimar Pel. During the Dharma teaching that followed, when the Master was discussing the histories of the members of his lineage in the course of teaching Lazik Repa's instructional text on the Mahāmudrā, *Dispelling the Darkness of Ignorance*, he said, "My lama, the noble Drakchokpa Ratnabhadra, was Cakrasaṃvara. Chuworipa was Tilopa. Sönam Zangpo was Nāropa. Tsachungpa Yönten Penjung was Padampa Sangyé. The lamas who have preceded me in this lineage were all *siddhas*, not ordinary people."

During the main part of the teaching, Serma Rapjampa and Gangkar Rechen were having a conversation about whether or not one who has achieved buddhahood sees appearances, whether or not ideations are in fact the Dharma Body, and other topics.

To set matters straight, the Master informed them, "After achieving the level of buddhahood, one still has perceptions. Once you become enlightened from the usual way of experiencing appearances as variegated and uneven, everything will appear to you as infinite buddha bodies and buddha realms. {621} This is what is meant by the expression, 'a buddha's perceptions of brilliance.'"

He continued, "As for whether or not ideations are actually the Dharma Body, there are systems that do and systems that do not accept this. As they say in the tradition of glorious Pakmodrupa and his sons:

> 'Clouds and fog arise from the sky, dissolve back into the sky, have the same nature as sky.
>
> I bow to you who came from the sky.
> Like the sky, have no attachment.
> Father sky, father sky!
> My name is Infinite Sky.'"

Thanks to the gestures he made with his hands, the things that he said, and the many other forms of his play, everyone's understanding became totally clear.

From among the greater assembly, to about a hundred mendicants who had renounced their lives—including Gangkar Rechen Loden Dorjé and Nyida Drukdrak Śākya Chöpel, the Rapjampa of upper Tsang—the Master gave the Six Dharmas as transmitted by Barawa, in the manner of experiential instructions. Speaking to them through the window to his retreat, he corrected their respective understandings of the yogic exercises and other practices. {622} For background Dharma instructions he gave the *dohā*s and other teachings. After completing the Dharma teaching, the Master sent those disciples to the great abode of Tsari with commands to do practices involving Vajradhara, Saraha, and others. He gave each of his greater sons gifts of material things. He dispatched most of them with commands to practice in different holy places.

To a subset of disciples who remained at Tsimar Pel, including his heart sons and his spiritual heir apparent, the Master gave the *Great All-Perfect Yard*, with all of its ancillaries. He also gave many oral instructions relating to the Aural Transmission that they had not received before. There were wondrous signs that appeared externally during that time. When the Master was having his own magnificent visions, he would make different pronouncements, saying things like, "I am the granddaddy of the eighty *siddha*s, and thus I remain surrounded by those *siddha*s."

Present was Nyida Pembar, who, among all the students who had become learned in the Golden Dharmas of the Shangpa Kagyü[78] and many other teachings, had become distinguished as "the Rapjampa of upper Tsang." The Master also gave him some gifts, which included a charm box. {623} Then the Rapjampa went to Dorjé Dzongkha to practice.

At that time, Danün Dorjé, having fulfilled his pledge to practice, came before the Master accompanied by his students. He made inestimable offerings and fulfilled the wishes of the holy one.

In the snake year, Dzongkar Rechen finished receiving the Master's oral instructions. For the benefit of transmigrating beings, the Master sent him 1521
to some amazing places, including China's Wutai Shan, "the Five Peaked Mountain," and Emei Shan, "Posing Elephant Mountain"; the Fragrant City; and the Palace That is Pleasing to Behold.[79]

It was at this same time that the *siddha* from India known as Jaharbhi arrived at Tsimar Pel. He had become immortal on account of his mastery over both perceptions and thoughts. He offered the Master some pleasantries, saying things like, "Even in India there is no guru greater than you." He offered a charm box carved from stone. *Ācāryas* living in Tibet say that this yogin is none other than the one known in Tibet as Mitrayogin. {624} The lama Jaharbhi is currently renowned in both India and Tibet. As a *siddha* doing practices on Cakrasaṃvara, who has achieved the *siddhi* of an immortal rainbow body, he makes the hearts of the *tīrthikas* rise up in their throats—so it is said.

The assembly that gathered during the horse year was enormous.
The Master gave general instructions on the Mahāmudrā and the Six 1522
Dharmas. Administrator Zurkhang Sharpa and superintendent Mönkyiné came to meet the Master during this time, and made inestimable offerings. They gave him an offering of three bricks of tea on behalf of the king of the Dharma, the great *gongma* [Ngawang Tashi Drakpa?], the emperor who was rich in authority and power thanks to his heavenly mandate. The Master was delighted. In return, the Master sent the *gongma* a letter adorned with a seal and some prayers, along with some blessed objects for gifts. The Master gave Dharma teachings that satisfied everyone, from lords to servants, who came to meet him.

During that time, Apo, from Tsari Yöndrel, came bearing the skull cup of the hero, the lord of the dance [Drakchokpa?], accompanied by his students. When he handed the skull cup filled with alcohol to the great lord of the families, the sky became filled with rainbows, a rain of divine white lotus flowers fell, and so on. {625} The Master offered heaps of things to the skull cup. He gifted Apo and his students with an inestimable endowment.

It was also during this time that Serma Rapjampa and his students returned to the presence of the Master, having fulfilled their pledges to practice. With inestimable delight, the Master gave him some gifts. With the moonlight of his compassion, the Master caused the water lily of his student's intellect to blossom.

Serma Rapjampa asked the Master, "Has my lama, the one from Chokro, taken rebirth?"

As the Master informed him, "He and the one from Nyukla are now in a pure realm and will not take rebirth." He said many other things as well.

On another occasion there arrived from the king of Santika and the king of Mön, Trangpo Dar,[80] offerings so vast that enumeration cannot do them justice. The foremost among them was some brocade clothing that was special in many respects, including having a seamless weave—so it is renowned. {626}

The commander of Yargyap had possessed a great sovereignty, like a king truly wielding the wheel of power. But because of the ripening of some past karma, and on account of some shady dealings and other factors, he ended up losing his reign.

At that time he went before the Master. He had become totally fed up with the world. This caused him to develop inestimable dedication and deference with respect to the Master. Now having no other use for his ancestral wealth, he offered many things to the Master. The Master told the commander many stories about the past, saying things like, "This has happened because such is the nature of saṃsāra." The Master also gave him assurances about the future. The commander departed after receiving Dharma teachings, blessed objects, and so forth.

After that, the king of Ngari Gungtang—whose stainless ancestry begins with the luminous gods; their Dharmic sovereignty, their lineage, clan, and family having not degenerated from the time of the Three Dharma Kings down to the present—sent a request for prayers for the continuation of his lineage, along with a letter prefaced by words of praise, a copy of the *Collected Sayings of the King*, a deerskin rug, and limitless other things. {627} The Master was truly delighted by this. To establish the necessary dependent connections, he sent back a ceremonial silk scarf of stainless white, and three arrows. He said that after the boy was born, he should be named Tri Künzang Nyida Drak.

The ruler did as he had been instructed and got the desired result. He then projected inestimable heaps of offerings for the Master—so it is renowned.

It is recorded that in succession the administrators of Taklung and Horkhang, the lord of Gyelchen Tsé in Penyül, and others, all sent letters and offerings. Some of them also came to visit the Master, making their extensive offerings in person.

On one occasion, the Master's heart son, Drikung Rechen, came to visit. He offered never-ending material things, as well as prayers for the Master's long life. When the Rechen departed, his demeanor suggested that he himself foreknew what the future would hold. {628}

It was not long after this that, one day, the Master realized that people were on their way to request prayers for that very same disciple, who had passed into another realm. The Master broke from his meditation. Right when he was in the middle of asking, "What people or news have arrived? This morning, I perceived my body's channels and *cakras* to be collapsing, after which my perceptions concerning this life all but disappeared"—just then the people coming to request prayers arrived.

The Master announced, "This morning the Rechen has done the transference of consciousness. It is similar to how the realized one Tsachungpa[81] transferred his consciousness into the heart of the *siddha* Urgyenpa." Then he recited limitless prayers on behalf of his heart son.

The winter Dharma teaching of the monkey year was attended by about five hundred mendicants, the foremost of whom was Ḍāki Rechen. The 1524
Master gave them extensive instructions and reading transmissions for the Mahāmudrā, the Six Dharmas, and so on. When the Dharma teachings were finished, he dispatched most of them with commands to practice in various holy places.

During the following year's winter Dharma teaching, the Master gave the Mahāmudrā, *Dispelling the Darkness of Ignorance*, and other teachings, all in the manner of experiential instructions. He gave these teachings to many *geshés* learned in the repositories of conventional knowledge—including Bum Rapjampa Gendün Nyima from Tsang, Rapjampa Tönpa Yarkhur from Kham, and Gendün Pel, the Rapjampa of Minyak—and to a good many mendicants who had become perfected in terms of experiential realization, including lama Dzarangpa and his students. {629}

During the main part of the teaching, the Master is noted to have said, "This time, the Dharma students are trustworthy and have kept their *samaya* vows pure. When I impart the introduction to the nature of the mind that is the *Tiger Encountering the Lion*, the lamas of the Kagyü will surely be smiling." For background Dharma instructions he gave things like the *dohās*. Then the teachings were brought to a close and the Master sent his more prominent disciples to Tsari and other places.

In the time after that, the Master continued to give the Mahāmudrā, the Six Dharmas, and the many other Dharma teachings that were requested by all the Dharma lords—both resident and visiting, including the throne-holders of various Kagyü monasteries—who gathered at Tsimar Pel in their faith, bringing their disciples along with them. He fulfilled the hopes of all his students who arrived before him from distant places. The Master's actual activities are beyond the compass of description. For fear of being too verbose, I will give only a rough summary here: {630}

Nyida Rapjampa came from Kham with his students and his retinue. At that same time, Dharma lord Döndrup arrived from upper Tsang with his students. The offerings they made are beyond the compass of description. The Master gave them oral instructions, which completely and utterly fulfilled their wishes. Then he satisfied them with the giving of blessed objects and other gifts. Then they left their separate ways.

On another occasion there arrived from Drikung Til a letter relating their need for a consecration ritual for a new stūpa in the auspicious many-doored style. The letter included words of praise, calling the Master things like "the 'life pole' of the teachings of the Kagyü," and "precious Dharma lord from Ü." The letter was accompanied by a perfect ceremonial scarf and many other pure offerings. The Master was delighted. He donned the eight accoutrements of the Heruka. Then he sang the "Great Oath" in a loud voice, made inestimable prayers, and so on.

During that year's spring Dharma teaching, the Master gave many profound and vast teachings, including the Aural Transmission of Rechungpa, to an assembly of about four hundred. The foremost among them were ten or so great lamas, including Khamsum Zilnönpa. {631} At the conclusion of the teachings, Nyida Rapjampa of upper Tsang and some others departed, having taken pledges to practice for three years at glorious Tsari.

During the period between Dharma teachings, Matibhadra, the Rapjampa of Changra—who is preeminent in the exposition of scripture and reasoning, a trailblazer in the conventional sciences, a guide to the authentic path—had come from Tupten Serdokchen monastery to Penyül for the sake of the Dharma, accompanied by about two hundred students. They came to meet the Master. While the Master was meeting with the Rapjampa and each of his students individually over the course of three days, satisfying their wishes for the Dharma, the visitors in turn satisfied the monks of Tsimar Pel with reverential treatment.

When the group was getting ready to leave Tsimar Pel, about forty *geshés*, the foremost of whom was the Rapjampa himself, came to the window of the Master's retreat. He gave them all names that included titles like "Repa." Then the Master gave limitless gifts to the group as a whole and to the Dharma lord specifically.

"They say that in the upper part of Tibet," the Master related, "the most famous one is you, the Rapjampa of Changra. {632} In the lower part, the most famous is the Rapjampa of Minyak. In the middle, the most famous is the great *paṇḍita* of Nyukla. Since the other two have passed away, you must pass on many of the Dharma teachings that I, the father, have transmitted to you. Ensure that you are of great benefit to the teachings of the Buddha!" Then they departed.

At one point, the victorious lord Mikyö Dorjé—the miraculous form of lord Siṃhanāda; the eighth bodily manifestation of the roar of the glorious, invincible Karmapas—sent the Master a letter asking about some difficult aspects of the Vajrayāna. The letter came accompanied by a rosary made of *manahu*.[82] It included the following words: "Lord of yogins, Madman of Ü, who has dispelled ignorance by means of his reflexive awareness; who, because of his control over the channels, drops and winds, is not subject to any harm that could be caused by the four elements; who has realized the falsity of appearances—please set sentient beings of the five degenerations[83] on the path of the Vajrayāna!" {633}

Beaming with the largest possible smile on his face, the Master spoke about the contents of that letter. Based on what he said, a response preceded by a *vajra* garland of pleasantries was written and sent off.

Oh the glory of a crystal vase consisting of the Victor's will,
and filled with the nectar of his fine explanations—
besides you, who in the world today possesses
the sweet nectar of the tradition initiated by mighty Vajradhara?

Who but you, oh sovereign lord of *siddhas*,
holds the magical crown jewel of the *nāgas*, the teachings of the Sage?

The drum sound of your fame maintains
that even the Karmapa himself—magician of existence and the
tranquil beyond,
the victorious lord guiding the transmigrators of China and Tibet—
has paid honor to the Noble One.
But how could I or anyone else find the deluded words to describe
something with the loveliness of an exotic girl with a lotus tucked
behind her ear?

During that winter's teachings, the Dharma lord of Yargyap, his students, Medro Rapjampa, and others all came to visit the Master. They set out inestimable heaps of offerings. {634} Not long after that, Dzongkar Rechen returned from his work of benefiting the transmigrating beings of China. He delighted the Master with offerings that included an image carved from black agarwood, tea, cloth, silk, and ceremonial scarves. It is said to have been like when Sumāgadhā pleased the Lord of Sages and his retinue in the city of Puṇḍravardhana.

Künga Nyishar came back from Kham, at which time he made extensive offerings, the foremost of which was a whitish turquoise one *to*[84] in size. He also sponsored a tea service and distributed clothing and silk to the general assembly, provided for a *gaṇacakra*, and so on. It is said to have been like when the Śākya king and his retinue invited the Buddha to the city of Śākya.

I have heard that lama Künga Nyingpo also set out offerings of a similar scope on this occasion.

The Master then dispatched Dzongkar Rechen and his students to the holy places of lower China, where they were to blow the assembly-calling conch, make offerings, and so on. He sent his attendant Rikdzin Nyima and his students to Kham in order to benefit transmigrating beings. He sent Sakya Dükar Rechen and his students to China's Wutai Shan and other places. {635} Meanwhile, lama Künga Nyingpo and his students went to Kham.

On one occasion, the reincarnation of Gampopa [the Second Pawo, Tsuklak Trengwa] came with his students to visit the Master. When he was received at the window to the Master's sealed retreat, the Master said that it was like when Gampopa Daö Zhönnu, "Youthful Moonlight,"[85] first went before noble Milarepa. He said things such as

"The milk of the white lion of the east
is certainly potent!
Only Indra, 'Lord of the Gods,' can drink it . . ."

After welcoming the boy in that way, they cut his hair. The Master gave him all the profound Dharma teachings that he needed, including the *tummo* practice as transmitted by glorious Galo. After finishing the instructions, the Master gave the boy a deerskin rug, a mother-of-pearl ladle, a horn made from an antler, and other things, thereby establishing many avenues of dependent connection between them. Carrying those objects, and bearing within his heart the honey of great respect for the Master, the young Pawo went back to Dakpo in the Kongpo area.

After spring had arrived, the Master sent his nephew Künzang Nyida Pembar and some others to the great abode of Tsari to deliver gifts of gold. {636}

At that time, some people wielding spears came to stir up trouble for the Master, but they were pacified by the splendor of his great compassion. Afterward, they offered confessions and gave the great gift of their respect—so I have heard.

Around that time the Master extensively taught the Mahāmudrā and the Six Dharmas to some students, including Chödzé and Rapjampa Ngawang, who both hail from Döl Tashi Pelgang. He fulfilled everyone's wishes by imparting whatever Dharma teachings they wanted—so it is renowned.

Although during that time there was a huge number of people who arrived at Tsimar Pel to request Dharma teachings and visit the Master, because he knew their individual thoughts and latencies, he was able to satisfy the peacock of each person's intellect by giving him just the right teaching—so it is renowned.

Upon Künzang Nyida Pembar's return from the great abode of Tsari, the Master informed his nephew, "From now on you will have to act as caretaker for the monastery and the things contained within it, lead the assembly in its prayers, and so on. {637} You must take on greater responsibilities, both general and specific." The nephew did as instructed.

In the earth-female-ox year, Künzang Nyida Pembar sponsored tea
services and distributed alms, offered butter lamps, and so forth. This 1529
was done in order to fulfill the intentions of past masters, to increase the Teachings, and to prolong the life of the Master. Before the skull of Dharma lord Drakchokpa at Densa Til, they offered tall prayer flags in the five colors, an endowment for butter lamps, and a *zho*[86] of gold. At places like Gachil they made offerings including ceremonial silk scarves and butter lamps. The foremost of the offerings made at this time were garments to be worn by the statues of the great abbot Śāntarakṣita, *ācārya* Padmasambhava, and the Dharma king Trisong Detsen [at Densa Til].[87]

The general assembly [of Densa Til] was lauded with offerings, which included seventy *zho* of gold, ceremonial scarves, Chinese bells, and alms for the community. In the same manner, at Drikung Til monastery, offerings of ceremonial scarves and butter lamps were made before the silver reliquary, before the auspicious many-doored stūpa, and elsewhere. The offerings and alms that were given to the precious Dharma lord, the general assembly of Drikung Til, and the others, are beyond the compass of description. {638}

Offerings the likes of which the intellects of ordinary people cannot fathom were made at the great abodes of Tsari, Lake Manasarovar, Mount Kailash, Jālandhara, and Bikché mountain, at Lapchi, Chubar, and the rest of the Six Fortresses of Milarepa, in Lhasa, at Ramoché, Tsel Gungtang, and Drak Yerpa. This included the offering of ceremonial scarves, liquid gold to be applied to the statues, the setting out of feast offerings and *gaṇacakras*, sponsoring tea service and alms—whatever was appropriate for each place. During this time, tea services were given at a hundred and eight different monasteries, along with alms for the individual members of those communities, and donations to those communities in general. For the five hundred or so members of the assembly at the Tsimar Pel meditation school, a tea service and a *gaṇacakra* were held for them. Each member was also furnished with one *zho* of gold. The many people who were then only visiting Tsimar Pel also had their individual wishes fulfilled in whichever way was most fitting.

At one point the *ācārya* of Tangsak came to visit the Master with about thirty of his students. In ways both worldly and religious, the Master fulfilled all the individual wishes of the teacher and his students.

The administrator came from Khartsé with some of his servants during that time. {639} They made inestimable offerings, the foremost of which was a roll of cloth. The Master was delighted and sang some songs. In the course of the Master's imparting the life instructions, the Five-Parted Single Sitting, and other teachings, they tasted the nectar of his speech and saw the remarkable displays of his bodily demeanor. After attaining indefatigable faith, they departed. The administrator became a patron of the Teachings—so it is renowned.

Because Ngodro Rapjam Khyenrap Namgyel—the most beautiful ornament in all of Kham, the throne-holder of the Karma monastic college—had extolled the Master to him, the king of Jangsadam [in present-day Yunnan province] sent him a letter. The letter included words of praise, such as calling the Master, "the apotheosis of the intentions of all the *sūtras* and tantras, who reposes in an uncontrived meditative equanimity that perceives all the phenomena of existence, saṃsāra and nirvāṇa, in their sky-like reality, as they have been since the very beginning..." There also arrived a brick of green tea, a roll of cloth, and other material offerings. {640}

On one occasion during that time, the administrator of Gomdé Nangpa, Sönam Zangpo, came with about five hundred servants bearing inestimable offerings. With his great love, the Master gave them many instructions of the profound path, including the Mahāmudrā of Co-emergent Union. The Master gave the administrator the name of Dharma lord Nyida Pembar—"blazing with the splendor of the sun and the moon"—as well as extensive gifts.

During that time, Chözang Nyida Drukdrak, the Rechen of upper Nyang,[88] returned from fulfilling his pledge to practice at Tsari, arriving in the presence of the Master accompanied by his students. The Master gave many prophecies concerning the Rechen's past and future, then sent him away again.

Throughout this period, many individuals arrived at Tsimar Pel to have their heads shaved. One of these was Künzang Selwé Nyingpo from Shigatsé.

During the winter Dharma teachings of the iron-female-rabbit year, the Master gave detailed and extensive instructions on the Six Dharmas 1531 and other topics to many Dharma students, including the ascetic Tarpa Nyima Rechen.

At that time the learned and meditatively accomplished Gangkar Rechen, Namkha Sönam Penjor, came to visit the Master, accompanied by many of his students. {641} They made limitless offerings of clothing and other things. The Master answered the Rechen's questions at notable length. After the Master gave him some commands and gifts, the foremost of which was a white conch, they departed.

Then it was heard all around that the Master had made the following announcement: "If you want to meet with papa, come this year! I do not know if we will be able to continue meeting again and again."

Following this announcement, a huge number of people came to visit the Master. The number of people who offered tea services and *gaṇacakras* is beyond counting.

With his knowledge of the future, the Master made many pronouncements about how certain people would in time grow fed up with the world and renounce it. He did this in order to motivate those individuals who hold on to things as permanent, he said.

That year they renovated various features of Tsimar Pel, including the southern and northern assembly halls, the awnings, and the thrones of the monastery's past masters.

The Master gave many coded teachings, saying things like, "The fortress's construction work, Dharma thrones, and so on have all turned out very nicely. But it seems that this fort commander won't be staying..."

The Master's nephew and heir apparent wondered, "This year the Master is making many announcements that are unlike any he has made in the past. Is he going to pass into another realm?" {642}

Once the great being had commenced that year's summer teaching session and a huge assembly had gathered, he declared, "The essence of all the Teachings and all the treatises is this..." Then he gave oral instructions on the Secret Practice of India.

Later, just when he was about to get to the oral instructions on the Four Mistakes,[89] the Master announced, "Let's end the teaching here." He then told many stories about how certain people had grown fed up with the world and had renounced it, and about the specific years and months when certain lamas had passed away. This was undoubtedly a sign that the Master—himself a testament to the combined merit of embodied beings—was going to expire.

To those who possessed greater merit, the Master transmitted many announcements through the medium of coded teachings. Meanwhile he exhorted the general assembly, "From the age of forty-six to the age of seventy-five, I have stayed in this very place. Because of the inestimable Dharma teachings I have imparted to you, you have all reached great heights. {643} But the lama cannot be there in every way all of the time. Each of you must generate determination." Then the Master went into retreat.

At that time they were in the process of building a golden statue of the Sage about a story tall at Tupten Kyetsel in Lhünrap. The Master received a letter telling of how they needed someone to perform a consecration ritual, how they needed blessed objects, and so on. The letter was accompanied by pastries and other offerings. The Master sent them some blessed objects, the foremost of which was his own charm box. Then he did things like toss consecratory grain. On account of his actions, on the day when they consecrated the new statue of the Protector, the sky was perfectly clear, a rain of flowers fell, and such like.

> Even the great hero Nāropa must dance along
> when he sees the performance of the lord of *siddhas*.
> As the actions of the Noble One show,
> the Aural Transmission and the *ḍākiṇīs*' sanction have again
> been obtained.

If one experienced for just a moment
the kingly state of seeing the truth of reality—
knowing past and future, all that remains concealed to others—
one would think that the very fabric of existence had been torn
apart. {644}

Do not fear the flocks of ducks with small intellects
who float across the vast ocean of the three vehicles,
which is all contained within the cupped hands of the *ṛṣi*
Agastya[90]—
for what you see is only an amazing illusion.

The lama to the gods, who uses the scalpel of the central channel
to reopen eyes rendered useless by blindness:
if you want to see clearly again,
come visit the doctor of the authentic path.

Such was the eighth chapter of *The Life Story of the Noble Künga Zangpo, Called "That Which without Restriction Gives Goosebumps of Faith,"* relating the story of how, while equating his very life with religious practice, he turned the Dharma wheel of the Vajrayāna and set all beings, both superior and ordinary, on the path to ripening and liberation.

9

Death

THE MASTER REMAINED in a very strict retreat, not granting an audience to anyone, neither high nor low. Although it had been his intention to perform the miraculous feat of the rainbow body, he instead decided to leave behind material objects that would enable his students to accumulate merit, in the form of bodily relics the size of mustard seeds. {645} He therefore refrained from performing the miracle of the rainbow body.

In the middle month of autumn, in the water-male-dragon year, on the
1532 day of the full moon, which was also the anniversary of the Buddha's descent from heaven,[91] the Master instructed his heir apparent and nephew, Künzang Nyida Pembar, to come before him. Seated on the great throne of the fearless lion, he gracefully performed the dances of the nine demeanors. Pointing threateningly at his nephew's heart, the Master gave the first part of his last testament, which was about the need to uphold and protect the Teachings, both particular ones and in general—and especially about the need to foster them at the meditation school of Tsimar Pel.

Then he gave the middle part of his last testament, saying: "You yourself take care of the ornaments of Nāropa, the conch shell that assembles the eighty *siddhas*, my *khaṭvāṅga*, 'Blazing Auspicious Light,' my statue of noble [Drakchokpa] Ratnabhadra, and my books. Since it is now time for you to serve as my replacement, you must assume the burden of the Teachings. Do not do lots of unnecessary things, but remain in meditation." {646}

Then he gave the final part of his last testament, saying, "Since today is a holiday, keep the butter lamps burning all night. Set out inestimable offerings. You, my students, should not be sad that I am going to the Akaniṣṭha pureland. My destiny to train discpiles in this realm is complete."

The Master made *mudrās* representing the five types of offerings, which indicated that at that moment he was seeing many buddhas and bodhisattvas.

During the first watch of the night, when the moon had come into view over the mountains in the east, like a lamp beckoning to the sovereign lord of *siddhas*, the Master sat with his legs crossed in the *vajra* posture, his hands in equipoise, staring straight ahead. By assuming that unspeaking bodily demeanor, the Master concluded his teaching of the Dharma. Then, to motivate those who hold on to things as permanent, he laid down on the bed of the Truth of the Cessation of Suffering. {647}

In Kuśinagara long ago,
after setting his last disciples on the way to truth,
the Lord of Sages passed joyfully into nirvāṇa.
Today his successor has displayed the very same.

He who reaches down to those fallen into saṃsāra,
the precious chariot to carry these travelers on their journey,
the precious medicine for those whose lives are in danger—
today when you lay down on the bed of the Truth of Cessation,
it was as if a black horde had risen against the teachings of the Sage.

You obliterate all of the terrors of existence, a wish-fulfilling tree
with no precedent—
oh why did you abandon this realm of your disciples
and let your body dissolve into the expanse of reality?

Without you, lamp to the Kagyü teachings,
who will illuminate the authentic path?
Who will protect us, your faithful sons,
now that even you, with your great love, have forsaken us?

Without you, oh lord of *siddhas*, oh tree who grants
all the wishes of the embodied beings who have fallen into this desert
wasteland,
who will give the cooling shade of the authentic path of wisdom
to those suffering in the heat of saṃsāra? {648}

At that time the sky over Tsimar Pel was filled with rainbows of an unbounded variety of colors. The air became choked up with the great rain of divine white *uptala* flowers that fell from the sky. There fell flowers of the *tamala* tree, of the *sahakāra*, the mango, and others, in blue, green, yellow, white, and red—not to mention the many flowers that remain uncategorizable in terms of their type and color. In the space above the Master's residence, a hundred and eight crystal stūpas radiated many different colors of light. The gods struck their great drum and thunder was heard below on earth. Everything became pervaded by a magnificent odor that had never been smelled before, medicinal plants burst into bloom, and much more. Sky and earth were filled with amazing, inconceivable signs. Certain of the signs that appeared at that time, though, like earthquakes and shooting stars, arose in accordance with the collective deficiency of virtue among sentient beings.

The casket that enclosed the blessed corpse was bedecked with his Six Ornaments and placed inside a tent of lovely silk brocade. {649} The monks who assembled at the meditation school began to recite supplications in unison, make offerings, and so on, without sleeping, never tiring. Everyone in the mourning room cried an unending stream of tears. People were saying, "If you repeatedly beat on the drum of your breast with the mallets of your hands, through the compassion of the sovereign lord of *siddhas*—who is the essence of all the buddhas—a special *samādhi* will be born in your continuum. While in it, your and the lama's minds are inseparable."

Then, without their sending messengers or informing people that the Noble One had gone to another realm, the heralds of the gods and the demons descended from the sky to inform people in every distant place of the news that the *siddha* Künga Zangpo, the Madman of Ü, had passed away.

On account of this, the Master's more prominent disciples and his patrons, from powerful to lowly, all gathered at the great meditation school of Tsimar Pel. They brought with them inestimable materials for making offerings beside the Master's body. {650}

After two weeks, on the morning of the day of the new moon, they set out a heap of offerings that surpassed what any analogy can describe. When the nine-deity maṇḍala of glorious Hevajra was constructed and the corpse offered into it, the body was cremated in a fire of wisdom, red in color, like an eight-petaled lotus. The smoke turned into a rainbow and filled the limitless sky. From the cremation fire came the sounds of *tamburas*, *piwangs*, drums, flutes, and other instruments. This was followed by a roar pronouncing the vowels and consonants of the alphabet. The whole sky was covered in rainbow light, as if draped with a canopy. There arrived an inestimable number of alluring goddesses, lined up like packets of powder strung together, holding parasols, victory banners, and pendants—so it is related.

At that time two lotus flowers, each the size of a shield, like the flowers of the wish-fulfilling tree, circled the crematory hearth clockwise as they fell to the ground. {651} A few witnesses who had purer karma saw the crematory hearth as encircled by the Eight Sugatas,[92] with the Master sitting in the middle. Others saw the Master sitting astride a white lioness, pointing threateningly, surrounded by a halo of rainbow light, or in some other form.

For two weeks after that, the Master's students performed guru *pūjā*, meditations on and offerings to Vajravārāhī, all-seeing Vairocana, and other deities.

Then on the fifteenth of the month, the astrologically favorable day when the waxing moon had become full, all of the Master's students and patrons unanimously invited his great nephew to take over as his successor. They threw flowers, expressed good wishes, and so forth, at which time various amazing and marvelous things occurred. People saw the sky become filled with rainbow light, and heard the sound of thunder. For the sake of the Dharma, Künzang Nyida Pembar assented to their request. It was certain that he would be a great upholder of the Master's tradition.

When they were close to finishing the post-mortem rites, at Densa Til and the Forest of Glorious Samantabhadra they offered a *zho* of gold to support the continuous burning of butter lamps and incense before the skull of noble [Drakchokpa] Ratnabhadra. {652} Before the statues of the great abbot Śāntarakṣita, *ācārya* Padmasambhava, and the Dharma king Trisong Detsen, they laid out offerings that were appropriate for each. The monks of the general assembly were given inestimable things, including alms, yellow shawls and undershirts, porcelain cups with sleeves, and cymbals. They were all delighted.

Before the silver reliquary at Drikung Til they made offerings of butter lamps, ceremonial silk scarves, incense, and so on, as they had in the past. Offerings were made before the Dharma lord, the foremost of which were a shawl and an undershirt. The general assembly of monks was furnished with armor, helmets, and the like.

At Taklung, ceremonial scarves and the rest of the seven types of offerings were placed before the Dharma lord. Alms were given to the general assembly.

Tea services and alms were furnished for the inhabitants of a hundred and eight monasteries in total, including Trabkha, Ewaṃ, Lo monastery, Gyama, Rinchen Gang, Gomo Langtang, Tangsak, Changlung Chöding, and Riwo Ganden.

Back at Tsimar Pel, those who had performed the meditations and offering rituals received to their complete satisfaction blessed objects like charm boxes, valuables like *dzomo*, and other material things. {653} Tea services and alms were provided for the general assembly, honoring them in every appropriate manner.

After four weeks the precious crematory hearth was opened. Blessed objects that accorded with the merit of the Master's disciples were brought out. First there was the Master's complete skull, with his jaw still attached. It was brilliant, like refined gold, and covered with inestimable images of deities, including white Tārā and the glorious four-armed protector, Mahākāla. There were five-colored relics,[93] two-colored relics, and ones of other sorts, as numerous as the sands of the River Ganga. It seems that the Master's body had somehow turned itself. It was now covered with the images of inestimable deities. The Master's tongue and other bits of his body were recovered, unburnt and fully intact.[94] The amazing things that appeared on this occasion exceed what can be enumerated—so it is renowned.

After this the Master's more prominent disciples, under the leadership of the throne-holder, had the intention of erecting a reliquary made from precious materials, paid for exclusively with good religious merit. {654} Everything they needed fell to them like rain. The mistress of Serkhang,[95] who was possessed of the necklace of an illustrious familial lineage, strung together with merit, took primary responsibility for the undertaking. As a result, the silver reliquary was completed after about a year and a half. That wish-fulfilling jewel was brought to Tsimar Pel on a favorable day during a waxing phase of the moon, along with a heap of offerings.

As for then filling the reliquary, five of the Master's five-colored relics, along with some of his hair, fingernails, and teeth were placed inside the sun and moon ornaments atop the stūpa. Inside the *dharmacakras*, the rings atop the stūpa, were placed the divine images that arose from the Master's bones, relics of the victorious lord [the Third] Karmapa Rangjung Dorjé, of Jetsün Drakpa, and of noble Sakya Paṇḍita, as well as *dhāraṇis* of the higher tantra classes. Into the pediment were placed a book that had belonged to the Master and which was associated with one of his *samaya* vows, along with every possible type of blessed object and all manner of *dhāraṇis* of the Yoga Tantra class. {655} The Master's complete skull was put inside the main bulbous part of the stūpa. *Dhāraṇis* derived from all four classes of tantras, as well as blessed objects, *yakṣa* wheels, and other things were also put inside. This was all carried out in accordance with the *Consecration Tantra* and the *Tantra for the Accomplishment of the Single Hero*.

When they were consecrating the reliquary, after the more prominent disciples and the other monks had completed the preparatory stages and had begun the main part of the ritual, they threw flowers, expressed good wishes, and so on. At that time the sky became filled with rainbow light, there were the sounds of various divine instruments being played, and so forth—so it is renowned.

That amazing assemblage of objects remains there at the Master's seat, the glorious, supreme meditation school of Tsimar Pel, as a material support enabling the sentient beings of this degenerate age to accumulate merit.

Such was the ninth chapter of *The Life Story of Künga Zangpo, the Madman of Ü, the Preeminent* Siddha *Whose Practice Is Totally Victorious in All Respects, Called "That Which without Restriction Gives Goosebumps of Faith,"* relating the story of how the Master's body dissolved into the expanse of reality, and how the many supreme blessed objects he emanated were then placed inside a repository. {656}

THE LIFE STORY of the holy Noble One, limitless by its nature, is beyond what can be expressed by the words of all the Victors of the ten directions. Nevertheless, the omniscient Peṇchen of Nyukla, Ngawang Drakpa Pelzangpo, told a small part of that amazing story, covering up to when the Master was thirty-seven years old. As for this part of the life story relating the years after that, an initial version was composed by the Master's beloved nephew, Künzang Nyida Pembar, who has seen the very face of the Mahāmudrā of profound meaning. Based on that—and having obtained the assurance of the second Victor of the degenerate age, glorious Karma Trinlepa Choklé Namgyel, the *paṇḍita* of Dakpo in the east; and having received from Yülgyel fortress [in Nyukla] the command that I should do so—I, Shényen Namgyel, a monk of noble descent, began composing this text at Tekchen fortress during the auspicious waxing part of the month, and finished not long thereafter, in the fire-female-bird year, when I was 1537
twenty-six years old. {657}

Upon seeing the moon, this amazing life story,
the water lilies, the hearts of all the learned ones,
are made to blossom.
Does any other story have a single drop of such amazing nectar?

There are hundreds of *pratyekabuddha*s dressed in saffron robes,
intoxicated by arrogance, grasping at self,
imagining that they have accumulated merit and wisdom over
many eons.

Those who want to abandon the Hīnayāna
and stand atop the golden mountain of the superior way
should prostrate to the lineage of the glorious one—
who spread the wings of the profound path
and soared across the sky that is the ten Stages to
enlightenment. {658}

Ngawang Khyenpé Pel,[96] the scion revitalizing the venerable Dharma
tradition of Atīśa—
who brought the jewel of the holy Dharma from the Land of the
Noble Ones, a veritable island of jewels,
burnished it atop the lion-faced victory banner of Reting temple,
and thus caused a great ambrosial rain of the teachings of the Sage
in this land of *Bhoṭa*—
he gave a biography of the lord of *siddha*s
to all the beings of the world:
a wish-fulfilling jewel snatched from the king of the *nāga*s.

But the lake of my pure intention to
string together the rest of this amazing story
was still brimming.
So drink to contentment with cupped hands, without bias,
from this part of the life story, the nectar that streams from that lake.

You who shine with the light of jewels;
who were bowed to by glorious Mikyö Dorjé,
the victorious lord Karmapa,
whose emanations fill all the innumerable worlds; {659}
you whose brilliance overcomes
every dark corner of existence and the tranquil beyond:
the moonbeams of your words
are drunk in by the lily of the heart,
which then overflows with the nectar of your life story,
giving goosebumps of faith, without restriction, to all.

By whatever virtue is created in planting this garden,
may the essential Teachings be made to increase,
everywhere, always, without degenerating!
By whatever virtue has been obtained by the light
of the full wisdom moon of the heart of the Madman of Ü,
may the teachings of the Sage increase!

Wise Śiva lets down his hair,
the marvelous sovereign River Ganga,
so that it may refresh the oceans,
the minds of the cunning gods.
Intending for this story, even more amazing than that one,
to appear in many places simultaneously—
like the moon reflected in innumerable waters at once—
woodblocks for its printing have been made.

Funding for the writing and carving
was again readily supplied from the Yülgyel fortress
of the ruler Tamdrin Tseten, {660}
who is unrivaled in knowledge or in wealth.

The text was edited by Lochen Künchö, who is learned in language,
written out by *tülku* Ngawang Lekpa,
then carved, just as written, by three skilled in that craft.
The sponsor holding the great seat of Tsimar Pel,
Tsari Rechen, Sarahapa,[97] and everyone else who contributed
  to this—
may they all attain supreme omniscience!

Epilogue

THE MADMAN OF Ü'S LEGACY

IN 1494 A small team was entrusted with Nyukla Peṇchen's handwritten manuscript of the first part of the *Life of the Madman of Ü*, tasked with creating the physical means for its mass reproduction. They carved the text of the biography—a reversed, mirror image of the text, carved in relief—into a series of fifty-one double-sided blocks of wood. The finished product was a set of wooden stamps that could be used again and again to print copies of the text. An initial run of the biography was printed, after which the woodblocks would have been stored away until such time as they were needed again. The primary sponsor of this undertaking was Tamdrin Tseten, a lord who was based in Nyukla.

Forty-three years later another team was assembled (including at least one member of the original crew) to carve woodblocks for the second, shorter part of the *Life*. Tamdrin Tseten again possessed the means and the desire to sponsor the undertaking. This generous lord was likely a relative of Nyukla Peṇchen.

The colophons to the two parts of the biography portray the individuals involved with these two projects as being motivated by pious aspirations. For one, they recognize the significance of the printed biography as a vehicle for the ongoing dissemination of Buddhism itself. They also frame their efforts in creating the woodblocks as an act of devotion to the Madman of Ü, and to the Kagyü sect he represents. They express a hope that the biography will enliven peoples' religious faith, which will benefit both them and the religion they serve. All of this is described using the language of "merit" (*dge ba*). They piously dedicate all of their work on the project to the generation of merit, to be applied toward achieving these various goals.

The creation of these woodblocks must be seen as the foundational act for the most enduring and stable component of the Madman of Ü's legacy.

This text is *the* record of the great yogin, the foremost repository of information about his life. We do not know how many copies of the biography were created from these two sets of woodblocks, or, after their respective inaugural print runs, when. Records suggest that in the early twentieth century it was possible to have a new copy of the biography made at a printing house south of Lhasa.[98] Whether or not the text has been available for new printings continuously over the past five centuries remains unclear. Even if there were periods during which it was not possible to get a new copy of the *Life* printed, old copies were in circulation, although perhaps in small number relative to other *printed* texts.

Even after the woodblocks were made, individuals would continue to write out copies of the *Life* by hand. One such copyist appended the following note to the end of work: "I, Tsewang Penjor, wrote out this text in order to purify myself of sins and obscurations; to return the kindness of my loving father and mother; and to benefit the sentient beings in all six realms of rebirth."[99] In many other instances, copying the text manually would have been motivated by sheer necessity.

The Life of the Madman of Ü, however, is by no means the only vehicle for Künga Zangpo's legacy. He appears as a character in the religious biographies of many other Kagyüpa ascetics. Although the Madman of Tsang is nowhere mentioned in the *Life of the Madman of Ü*, the Madman of Ü appears a number of times in one of the three biographies of the Madman of Tsang. It is even written that their students on a few occasions got into physical altercations with one another, resulting in a number of violent deaths. The Madman of Ü is also encountered a handful of times in the *Life* of Drakpa Tayé (1469–1531), another exceptional yogin of the Kagyü.[100]

The four-volume *Miscellaneous Writings* of Drukpa Künlé, Madman of the Drukpa (who visited Künga Zangpo at Tsimar Pel in 1512 or 1513) provide a record of his interactions with and his opinions about the Madman of Ü.[101]

Another reflection of the Madman of Ü's legacy is provided by the autobiography of his contemporary, the Nyingma treasure revealer Pema Lingpa (1450–1521). Pema Lingpa relates a dream that he had in 1499, in which some disciples of the Madman of Ü and the Madman of Tsang arrived before him and did some "crazy" (*smyon*) things with their hats.[102] Ever since his initial rise to prominence, the Madman of Ü has lived alongside the Madman of Tsang in the imaginations of other Tibetans.

The great yogin is also memorialized in many histories of the Kagyü. Sangyé Darpo, a grand-disciple of the Madman of Tsang, mentions the Madman of Ü a handful of times in his text, *History of the Kagyü:*

The Combined Luster of a Heap of Jewels. Writing in the 1540s, Sangyé Darpo mentions the Madman of Ü, along with the Madman of Tsang, as among the "*siddha* yogins" (*grub pa thob pa'i rnal 'byor pa*) who trained under Shara Rapjampa Sangyé Sengé (1427–1470). (Shara Rapjampa is not mentioned by name in the *Life of the Madman of Ü*.) Sangyé Darpo also lists the Madman of Ü as a member of the lineage descended from Götsangpa Gönpo Dorjé (1189–1258); as a disciple of Chuworipa; and as a guru to many.[103] In 1575, Pema Karpo (1527–1592), the fourth of the Drukchen incarnation lineage, mentions the Madman of Ü as a member of the cluster of lineages known as the "Upper branch of the Drukpa [Kagyü]" (*stod 'brug*). A twentieth-century Tibetan historian of the Kagyü lists him among the Middle branch (*bar 'brug*).[104]

Texts of this style are primarily concerned with relating the histories of particular lineages; many convey nothing more about the Madman of Ü than where he was located in the history of the Kagyü—a point about which the texts do not necessarily agree.

The *Life* informs us that further information on the Madman of Ü's activities can be found in texts relating the histories of particular holy sites that he visited (127). One example is a pilgrim's guidebook to Dakla Gampo monastery and the surrounding retreat centers, written in 1617 by the twenty-first abbot of Dakla Gampo monastery, Gampopa Mipam Chökyi Wangchuk Trinlé Namgyal Pelzangpo (1589–1633). The travel guide states that during the time he spent in the area, the Madman of Ü pointed out new ways of viewing the divine nature of the local environs (*zhal gzigs mang du phye*). (The text also tells of how the Madman of Tsang ascended the mountain behind Dakla Gampo monastery, had visions of a maṇḍala of skeletons, and in one cave saw the sixty-two deity Cakrasaṃvara maṇḍala.)[105]

In a similar fashion, a guidebook for the great pilgrimage site of Mount Kailash, written in 1896, asserts that just outside the famous Cave of Miracles (*rdzu sprul phug*, so named because of the amazing feats Milarepa is said to have performed there), there is a marking in solid rock that is actually a footprint left behind by the Madman of Ü. The Madman of Tsang is also associated with the Cave of Miracles.[106] The information about the Madman of Ü preserved in these texts reflects local oral traditions, offering a partial snapshot of the locals' understanding of the history of the place. (A history of the Drakar Taso meditation site written in the eighteenth century tells of the Madman of Ü's time there, but this account, by contrast, is drawn directly from the *Life of the Madman of Ü*.)[107] The short tales told about the Madman of Ü in these guidebooks are concerned primarily with the miraculous and faith-inspiring feats he performed in each place, which subsequently became part of local legend.

The printed version of the *Life* comprises the stable and enduring core of the Madman of Ü's legacy. The other textual sources in which the Madman of Ü is mentioned tend to perpetuate a general awareness that he once existed, but often say little or nothing more about him.

The vast majority of Tibetans who have come to know anything about the Madman of Ü over the past five hundred years did so without seeing a single one of these texts, for the most potent and vibrant aspect of the great yogin's legacy has always been popular oral lore. These stories—told, heard, and retold across many generations—have only a tenuous relationship with the *Life* or the other written literature just described (the exception being guidebooks to holy places, which are in many instances written accounts of *oral* literature). Most of these stories would have been associated with particular sites; pilgrims and visitors to those places might take some anecdote about the unpredictable yogin back home with them. The extracanonical lore of the Madman of Ü covers the Tibetan cultural world in an uneven patchwork.

Unfortunately, since beginning my research on the Madman of Ü and his legacy, I have not had the opportunity to conduct ethnographic research investigating what memories of the Madman of Ü still persist within the Tibet Autonomous Region. The limited evidence at my disposal, however, suggests that the fabric of Tibetan popular oral culture still bears some mark of the yogin. I cannot offer a comprehensive picture of the Madman of Ü's legacy among Tibetans today, but the few glimpses we see are edifying.

There are two stones curiously embedded in the surface of a wooden pillar inside the Jokhang temple complex in Lhasa. Some Tibetans have traditionally maintained that these two stones became lodged in the pillar after being thrown by the Madman of Ü and the Madman of Tsang.[108]

In 1966, the revered Bhutanese Buddhist master commonly referred to as Geshé Chapu—but who is known more formally as the sixty-ninth Jé Khenpo of the Drukpa—composed a new biography of Drukpa Künlé, based on both earlier textual sources and current oral traditions. According to this biography, on one occasion Drukpa Künlé, the Madman of Ü, and the Madman of Tsang traveled together to Tsari. While there, the Madman of Ü left a footprint on a rock and the Madman of Tsang made a handprint. Drukpa Künle then declared, "Even my dog has that kind of power!" and pressed his hunting dog's leg into the solid rock, leaving a paw print. Geshé Chapu states that these three marks could still be seen at Tsari at the time of his writing.[109] (Stories of enlightened yogins are often structured around the trope of a contest, which can add drama to—and a reason behind—displays of superhuman capabilities.) Here Geshé Chapu is in all likelihood making record of a tale then current among Bhutanese, and probably Tibetan people as well, in Tsari and other places in the southeastern part of the Tibetan cultural world.

One final example: While doing fieldwork on the "holy madmen" in 2009, I visited Phyang monastery, of the Drikung Kagyü, in Ladakh. In the course of my conversation with the abbot, he informed me that the monastery had, among their collection of holy items, the skull of the Madman of Ü. The abbot described the skull as having on it a "self-arisen" (*rang byung*) image of the goddess Vajravārāhī, perhaps one inch in size. Allowing me to see the skull was unfortunately out of the question, for its great specialness (*dmigs gsal*) determines that it should be brought out only rarely, on special occasions. The current inhabitants of the monastery ventured no guess as to when or how the skull may have come to be there, other than to say that perhaps it arrived by way of Mount Kailash.[110] (One of the Madman of Ü's stated reasons for not performing the miracle of the rainbow body was so that blessed, potent, useful objects such as these could be left behind.)

The fact that the inhabitants of this monastery believe that they have the skull of the Madman of Ü in their possession—whether it is his actual skull or not—shows that some of the extracanonical lore about the Madman of Ü reaches all the way to the far western extent of the Tibetan cultural world. Although the current inhabitants of the monastery do not seem to know anything specific about the Madman of Ü, he nevertheless continues to have a place among the pantheon of respected Kagyüpa masters from long ago.

This is only the tip of the iceberg. In the five hundred years since his death, scores, perhaps hundreds of different stories about the Madman of Ü have gone into circulation. The majority of them would have originated in central and western Tibet. These tales were remembered, told, and heard by people living in places throughout much of the Tibetan cultural world. He was remembered especially at holy sites (where holy people, and stories about them, tend to gather), in the heart of Lhasa, and in the rugged mountainous regions along the present-day border with Nepal. I cannot speculate about how much is remembered of Künga Zangpo in his home village of Ölkha.

The Madman of Ü lives on in the imaginations of the Tibetan people. This is in part because of his biography, but mainly thanks to stories associated with particular places and objects. Although this more popular, folk understanding of the Madman of Ü may presently constitute the most broad-based aspect of Künga Zangpo's legacy, it is also the most fragile. While the biography will last for centuries to come, the Madman of Ü's legacy in the oral tradition may someday, before many more generations have passed, become yet another example of the impermanence of phenomena, as the network of Tibetan people, places, and stories—the vessel of the Madman of Ü's popular legacy—sadly, has been irrevocably dismantled by forces external to itself.

Notes

INTRODUCTION

1. The degree to which Kyepo Dar was able to participate in this marriage (sexually and otherwise) would have been largely dictated by his older brothers. Early in the biography (60) it is said that Künga Zangpo was the youngest of five brothers. Later, there is mention of his meeting with his "younger brother" (*gcung po*) named Dorjé, at Ölkha (140). It could be the case that Künga Zangpo was not in fact the youngest of the brothers, or that the word *gcung po* here does not literally mean "younger brother," but perhaps a younger relative, such as a nephew. No sisters of Kyepo Dar are mentioned in the biography, which does not necessarily mean that he did not have any.
2. The term *rten cing 'brel bar 'byung ba*, "dependently arisen," the equivalent of the Sanskrit *pratītyasamutpāda*, is used in Buddhist philosophy to describe the empty nature of things: things do not exist independently of other phenomena, but dependently. The fact that things are "dependently arisen" means that there are "connections" between them. These two different meanings of the term *rten 'brel*—as referring to "dependent arising" and to the system of signs and connections between occurences—are very much related, perhaps as two sides of the same coin.
3. In dubbing his nephew with this name, the Madman of Ü combined two parts of his own name, Künga and Zangpo (*kun dga', bzang po*), to make Künzang (*kun bzang*). This is a common practice among Tibetan Buddhist masters.
4. Dpa' bo gtsug lag phreng ba (1504–1564/6), *Chos 'byung mkhas pa'i dga' ston* (Beijing: Mi rigs dpe skrun khang, 2006), 592.12–593.8. This biography would be repeated in Situ Peṇchen and Belo Tsewang Künkhyap's eightheenth-century history, *Garland of Biographies of the Karma Kamtsang*: Si tu paN chen chos kyi 'byung gnas (1699/1700–1774) and 'Be lo tshe dbang kun khyab, *Bsgrub brgyud karma kaM tshang brgyud pa rin po che'i rnam par thar pa rab 'byams nor bu zla ba chu shel gyi phreng ba* (New Delhi: D. Gyaltshan and Kesang Legshay, 1972), 1:648.3–649.3.

5. 'Brug pa kun legs, *'Brug pa kun legs kyi rnam thar* (Beijing: Bod ljongs mi dmangs dpe skrun khang, 2005), 161.18–162.12; R. A. Stein, *Vie et chants de 'Brug-pa Kun-legs le yogin* (Paris: G.-P. Maisonneuve et Larose, 1972), 262–3. See also 'Brug pa kun legs, 50.12–51.12, Stein, 102–103; 'Brug pa kun legs, 251.13–253.20, Stein, 395–9; 'Brug pa kun legs, 415.10–416.21, 423.11–16, 440.7–441.6, and starting at 456.7.
6. By contrast, the 1973 printing of the first half of the biography, mislabeled as the yogin's *Collected Songs* (*mgur 'bum*), is rife with inaccuracies, exemplifying just how wrong things can go in the scribal process.
7. Tashi Namgyal's "The Three Divine Madmen," in English and Chinese, first appeared in *The Dragon*, a periodical of International Drukpa Publications (Spring/Summer 2002): 40–52; the English was reprinted in the volume *The Dragon Yogis: A Collection of Selected Biographies and Teachings of the Drukpa Lineage Masters*, 41–9 (Gurgaon: Drukpa Publications, 2009). Franz-Karl Ehrhard, "The Holy Madman of dBus and His Relationships with Tibetan Rulers of the 15th and 16th Centuries," in *Geschichten und Geschichte: Historiographie und Hagiographie in der asiatischen Religionsgeschichte*, ed. Peter Schalk, 219–46 (Uppsala: Uppsala University Library, 2010).

   In the spring of 1999, Tami Okawa, a student at the University of California, Berkeley, participating in the School for International Training's Tibetan Studies program, produced a translation of the second part of the *Life*, with the help of two monks residing in Kathmandu, identified as Lama Thardal and Lochoe. The work was never published and I did not draw from it in producing my translation, but the intrepid team deserves recognition for their contribution to our collective project.

CHAPTER 1

8. Sarasvatī, the Indian goddess of composition, the arts, music, and learning, is invoked to grant her blessing to the text that follows.
9. In Buddhist cosmology, Mount Meru is the center of the world, and believed to be indestructible.
10. The endless knot is one of the "eight auspicious symbols," described in note 63.
11. The *dge bcu*, which characterize a good place to live, are the following: pastures, both adjacent and located nearby; land, for both building on and farming; water, for both drinking and irrigation; stones, for both masonry and making millstones; and wood, for both construction and fuel.
12. *skyes bu chen po'i mtshan dang ldan pa.* It is believed that individuals possessed of or destined for spiritual greatness possess certain physical characteristics, such as images of conch shells or *cakras* on his palms and the soles of his feet; partially webbed fingers and toes; smooth skin; a radiant complexion; and so on. These are the major and minor marks referenced in the verse that follows.

13. Franz-Karl Ehrhard identifies this figure as Götruk Repa (*rgod phrug ras pa*, 1363–1447), "The Holy Madman of dBus," 222.
14. I have been unable to find a list ennumerating what are here referred to as the *ngal dub cu*.
15. This likely refers to Taktsé fortress (*stag rtse rdzong*), which was located in Ölkha.

CHAPTER 2

16. This is Barawa Gyeltsen Pelzang (*'ba' ra ba rgyal mtshan dpal bzang*, 1310–1391).
17. *dge tshul*. Künga Zangpo never took the "full" monastic ordination of a *dge slong*. Nevertheless, the novice vows he took at this time would have been generally regarded as a lifelong commitment.
18. An ordination ceremony is conducted by a "preceptor" (*mkhan po*; in Sanskrit, *upādhyaya*), who imparts the actual vows the new monk or nun will adhere to; and an *ācārya* (*slob dpon*), a "master" who is expert in the *Vinaya*—the body of literature that lays out the rules and regulations for the monastic life. A quorum of monks must be on hand to serve as witnesses.
19. Here Machik Lapdrön is referred to by the title *spyod yul ma*, which is a mistake for *gcod yul ma*. This is evidence of the fact that the homophonous (in the central Tibetan dialect) *gcod*—Cutting—and *spyod*—the Practice—were often conflated at this time. See note 48.
20. This text, titled *Dpal na ro'i chos drug gi khrid yig bde chen gsal ba'i 'od zer stong ldan*, is discussed in an article by Marta Sernesi, "A Manual on Nāropa's Six Yogas by sPyan snga Nyer gnyis pa (1386–1434): Tucci Tibetan Collection 1359," *Indo-Iranian Journal* 53 (2010): 121–63. Indeed, this article discusses many of Nyernyipa's works that were studied by Künga Zangpo. The young Kyepo Dar is said to have studied a text called *Brilliant Rays That Open the Eyes* (*mig 'byed 'od stong*), which likely refers to a text by this same author. This is a history of the Kagyü, written at Tsetang in 1418.
21. I have yet to come across such a text.

CHAPTER 3

22. The *mtha' bzhi* are four common ways of thinking about things: as existing, not existing, both existing and not existing, and as neither existing nor not existing. These are said to be "extreme" and mistaken because they are not in line with the truth of emptiness, which ultimately renders phenomena outside of all such absolute and delimited saṃsāric categories.
23. The "four bodies" of buddhahood (*sku bzhi*) are the three *kāyas*, as explained in the Introduction, plus a fourth: the *svabhavakāya* or *svabhavikakāya* (in Tibetan, *ngo bo nyid kyi sku*), the "essential nature" body. This can be said to refer to the emptiness of buddha mind (which necessarily exists in tandem with its wisdom); or to the totality of the "three bodies."

24. The *ye shes lnga* are five types of true knowing: mirror-like wisdom, equality wisdom, individually discriminating wisdom, all-accomplishing wisdom, and *dharmadhātu* or "expanse of being" wisdom. The ultimate wisdom of the buddhas is singular in nature.
25. The *skyabs gsum* are the same as the Three Jewels (*dkon mchog gsum*): the Buddha, the Dharma, and the *sangha* or monastic community.
26. The Buddha taught that saṃsāra is composed of three spheres of existence or realms (*tridhātu, khams gsum*), which are the Desire Realm, the Form Realm, and the Formless Realm. Lesser sentient beings occupy the Desire Realm, which is material and coarse; gods and the consciousnesses of practitioners in certain states of concentration occupy the Form Realm, which is semi-material; and consciousnesses experiencing even higher states of concentration occupy the Formless Realm, in which there is no materiality whatsoever. Alternatively, it may be the case that this and/or other references to the "three realms" (*khams gsum*) in the *Life* are intended to mean the realm of the gods, the earthly realm, and the underworld.
27. The *phrin las [rnam] bzhi* are pacifying, enriching, magnetizing, and destroying.
28. Becoming attached to the bliss, luminosity, or non-conceptuality that one has experienced is said to cause one to be reborn in, respectively, the Desire Realm, the Form Realm, and the Formless Realm. Meditators resting in one of the four levels of concentration (*bsam gtan bzhi*) will go to the Form or Formless realm.
29. The Tsachungpa referenced here was a disciple of the famous Tibetan *siddha* Urgyenpa Rinchen Pel (*u rgyan pa rin chen dpal*, 1229/30–1309), discussed in *The Holy Madmen of Tibet*, 224–5. Later in his life, Künga Zangpo will encounter a different man known as Tsachungpa: the Shangpa Kagyü master Khyenrap Yönten Penjung.
30. The Attainment of Appearance (*snang ba thob pa*) refers to understanding the illusoriness of all the categories by which external and internal phenomena are described, which is an early step in a practitioner's development as a bodhisattva.

    The Five Eyes (*spyan lnga*) are the physical eye, the divine eye, the eye of discernment, the eye of the Dharma, and the eye of wisdom (or the eye of a buddha).

    The six types of higher perception (*mngon par shes pa drug*) are clairvoyance, clairaudience, mind reading, remembering one's own and others' former existences, the ability to perform miracles, and the knowledge by which all afflictions are eliminated.

CHAPTER 4

31. In *The Holy Madmen of Tibet*, 39, I translate this reference to the *gnas gsum*, mistakenly, as "the three realms" (intending the Desire, Form, and Formless realms of saṃsāra). I have since corrected my understanding of the passage. All other passages from the *Life* translated in *The Holy Madmen of Tibet* match the current translation.

32. I have left a few words out of my translation, since neither I nor anyone I consulted was able to make definitive sense of them: *dam tshig gi rdzas gza' bsrungs la sogs pa bsten par mdzad*. The 1494 printing reads the same, 17a2. Read in its existing form, the line might be taken as saying that the *samaya*-bound implements Künga Zangpo adopted were connected to a protector deity like Rāhula. It may be that some words are missing from the text, or that *gza' bsrungs* is mistakenly used in place of *bza' btung*. For more on this passage and the tantric garb it describes, see Chapter 2 of *The Holy Madmen of Tibet*.
33. The *yi ge drug pa'i bro brdung* would seem to be a dance relating to the six-syllable mantra of Avalokiteśvara.
34. *lam lnga lam gsum gyi dbang gsan pa'i tshe* ... I have been unable to determine what the *lam lnga lam gsum* here refers to. The 1494 edition, at 21a5, reads the same.
35. The *yan lag bdun pa* are prostrating, making offerings, confessing one's failings, rejoicing in the virtues of others, requesting for the wheel of the Dharma to be turned, requesting one to not pass into nirvāṇa, and dedicating to others the merit one has generated.
36. The "messengers" (*pho nya*; Sanskrit, *dūta*) referred to here are low-level tantric gods or goddesses, similar to *ḍākiṇīs* and heroes. While the field-born (*zhing skyes*) messengers exist naturally, the mantra-born (*sngags skyes*) arise from oaths spoken by tantric ritualists.
37. The *snang ba gsum* here mentioned may refer to the white, red, and black appearances that arise as one enters the *bardo*, which are connected to increasingly subtle states of mind; or perhaps to the three types of perception: impure, mixed, and pure.
38. The *snang* [*ba*] *bzhi* refer to four stages of perceiving the highest reality. They are ennumerated (with some variation) as: (1) *chos nyid mngon sum gyi snang ba*, when one first sees reality directly; (2) *nyams snang gong 'phel gyi snang ba*, when the experience of that perception is further developed; (3) *rig pa tshad phebs kyi snang ba*, when one's awareness reaches its fullest possible extent; and (4) *chos nyid du 'dzin pa zad pa'i snang ba*, when one transcends grasping to the highest reality.
39. *dbyings 'khor lo gsum gyi dngos grub*. I am uncertain what this refers to. The 1494 edition, at 25a1, gives the same reading.
40. The four demons or *māras* (*bdud bzhi*) are those of the aggregates, the basic afflictions, the Lord of Death, and the son of the gods.

    I am uncertain what the four liberations (*rnam par thar pa bzhi*) here refer to. Liberation is more typically enumerated as eightfold (*rnam par thar pa brgyad*). There are also the "four doors to liberation" (*rnam par thar pa sgo bzhi*).

    The four immeasurables (*tshad med pa bzhi*) are loving kindness, compassion, joy, and equanimity.
41. It seems that *jo bzang* refers to a certain population, perhaps an ethnic group, based in the vicinity of Tsari.

42. The Sanskrit *sthavira* (in Tibetan, *gnas brtan*), "elder," is a respectful way of referring to an older monk of virtuous conduct.
43. The *gar gyi nyams dgu* are the modes through which wrathful deities express themselves, and are especially associated with the Heruka.
44. A special event in honor of Padmasambhava was held at Zambulung every twelve years, in each monkey year.
45. The *srog shing* is the wooden dowel inserted into a statue, running from the top of the image's head to its base.
46. Attaining the *dri med legs pa'i blo gros* marks the reaching of the ninth Stage (of ten) in one's development as a bodhisattva.
47. This may refer to Nyukla Peṇchen and his mother. The patroness mentioned at the end of the biography as the "mistress of Serkhang" (*gser khang*) is the mother of Nyukla Peṇchen (a daughter of Norbu Zangpo, *nor bu bzang po*, of the Rinpungpa family; aunt of Dönyö Dorjé). I have been unable to confirm whether or not she was known by the name of Sönam Zangmo. On this genealogy, see *The Holy Madmen of Tibet*, 277–8.
48. *mi gcod gtong ba.* In this passage, Nyukla Peṇchen uses two terms somewhat indescriminately: *gcod* and *spyod*. The two words are pronounced the same way in the central Tibetan dialect, "*chö*," which has long been a major cause of confusion.

    In the context of describing the ascetic behavior of the Madman of Ü, *gcod* refers to the meditative practice of Cutting. *Spyod*, meanwhile, refers to the advanced tantric practice of *caryā*, "the Practice" (often referred to as *brtul zhugs spyod pa, vratacaryā*, the Practice of the Observance). Nyukla Peṇchen, like many Tibetans, has conflated the two practices with one another, mistakenly seeing the two terms as referring to a single practice, rather than two separate ones, with different origins and parallel histories of descent. Another instance of this problem is indicated in note 19.

    For more on this issue and the murky historical relationship between these two practices, see Chapter 2 of *The Holy Madmen of Tibet*.

CHAPTER 5

49. Here *gla rtsi* serves as a coded, perhaps more respectful way to say that he had to urinate.
50. This is likely Gyelwang Künga Rinchen (*rgyal dbang kun dga' rin chen*, 1475–1527), the sixteenth throneholder of Drikung Til, who is referred to later in the *Life* as Künga Gyeltsen. I thank Terence Barrett for the suggestion.
51. This likely refers to the famous stone pillar or stele (*rdo rings* or *rdo ring*) erected outside the Jokhang temple in 821 or 822. Inscribed in both Tibetan and Chinese, it marks the peace agreement that was established between the king Tri Relpachen and the Chinese emperor.

52. This likely refers to Jamyang Chöjé Künga Chözang (*'jam dbyangs chos rje kun dga' chos bzang*, 1433–1503), who served as abbot of Kyemö Tsel monastery from the early 1480s.
53. Literally meaning "mantrika," the *ngakpa* (*sngags pa*) was a lay ritual specialist, usually of the Nyingma. This status was traditionally passed down from father to son.

CHAPTER 6

54. According to Indian mythology, Viṣṇu (also known as Nārāyaṇā; in Tibetan, *sred med bu*) once incarnated as a dwarf who was miraculously able to cross all of existence—the heavens, earth, and the underworld—in just three steps, thus tricking and defeating the demon lord Bali.
55. *gcung po rdo rje*. See note 1.
56. According to formulations of time prevalent in Tibet, an eon or *kalpa* (*skal pa*) is composed of four distinct eras: the Complete Age (*rdzogs ldan gyi dus*), the Three-Facet Age (*gsum ldan gyi dus*), the Two-Facet Age (*gnyis ldan gyi dus*), and the Age of Strife. During the first, individuals have no trouble maintaining simultaneous commitments to the Dharma, to wealth, desire, and well-being. In the Three-Facet Age, they only manage to maintain commitments to three. We currently live in the Age of Strife (*rtsod ldan gyi dus*; in Sanskrit, *kaliyuga*), when people can only pursue one of the four.

    There is a separate, somewhat overlapping term: *snyigs dus*, translated in this book as "degenerate age." In the more technical context of Buddhist cosmology, this refers to a specific phase within the Age of Strife. However, the term *snyigs dus* is commonly used by Tibetans, both in writing and in conversation, to locate us generally within this same cosmology of global periods of improvement and decline, as popularly understood, in the latter, worse half of a *kalpa*.
57. Traditional Buddhist cosmology maintains that there is a wish-fulfilling tree on the summit of Mount Meru, within the realm of the gods. The demigods jealously make war with the gods over this tree.
58. This refers to the fact that Gyama was the birthplace of the great king Songtsen Gampo, said to have been an incarnation of Avalokiteśvara.
59. The *garuḍa* is a mythical bird-like creature with a humanoid body. They are mortal enemies of the *nāgas*.
60. The indentification of this person as Tashi Dargyé would seem to be contradicted by the fact that he died in 1499. Perhaps this is a reference to his successor. Or there could be a mistake in the chronology of events given by the text.
61. The Three Jewels, in which Buddhists place their trust and faith, are the Buddha, the Dharma, and the *sangha*, the community of monks and nuns.
62. The very best kind of water is characterized by the *yan lag brgyad*, which are the qualities of being cool, tasty, light, soft, clear, odorless, easy on the throat, and not upsetting to the stomach.

63. The *bkra shis rtags brgyad* are the parasol, golden fish, vase, lotus, conch, endless knot, victory banner, and wheel.

CHAPTER 7

64. The *sewa* (*se ba*) plant has been identified as the *Rosa omeiensis* or the *Rosa sericea* (one subtype of which is the winged thorn rose).
65. The text is mistaken about the year, as the fire-snake years nearest to this are 1497 and 1557; 1510 is an iron-male-horse year.
66. The six great masters or "jewels" (*rgyan drug*) of the Madhyamaka school in India: Nāgārjuna, Āryadeva, Asaṅga, Vasubandhu, Dignāga, and Dharmakīrti.
67. It is difficult to say how much a *nyak* (spelled *nyag*) would have been at this time, but it is a small measure of weight, similar to an "ounce."
68. The Truth of the Cessation of Suffering (*'gog pa'i bden pa*) is the second of the Buddha's Four Noble Truths, which states the possibility of nirvāṇa.
69. See note 50.
70. The *tsimar* (*rtsi dmar*) is a medicinal herb, a type of *Corydalis*. The name of the Madman of Ü's monastery, Tsimar Pel (*rtsi dmar dpal*), may also related to this plant. There is also a protector deity knows as Tsi Marpo or Tsi'u Marpo (*rtsi dmar po, rtsi'u dmar po*).
71. The first of the ten Stages *in one's development as a bodhisattva is referred to as the Extremely Joyous (pramudita, rab tu dga' ba)*.
72. *ti shrI gong ma chen po'i bla ma*. It is unclear whether this is meant to refer to the emperor of China or to the Pakmodru *gongma*. Because he was headed to Yarlung, which contains the seat of the Pakmodru government, the latter possibility seems more likely.
73. Ngawang Tashi Drakpa (1488–1563/64) assumed the throne of the *gongma*, in Nedong, in 1499. He was selected by the Rinpungpas, who were then controlling central Tibet, and was married to a daughter of Dönyö Dorjé. He oversaw the Pakmodru regime as it reasserted itself vis-à-vis the Rinpungpas beginning in 1509. See Chapter 4 of *The Holy Madmen of Tibet*.
74. Chiru Taktsé is in Penyül, on the northern side of the Kyichu river.
75. A *dzomo* (*mdzo mo*) is a female yak–cow crossbreed.
76. *gang tshe chos nyid don la mnyam par sus bzhag pa/ de tshe bdud sogs mi bzod cho 'phrul sna tshogs ston*. These lines appear in *Shes rab kyi pha rol tu phyin pa gcod kyi gzhung dang man ngag mtha' dag gi yang bcud zab don thugs kyi snying po*, which is attributed to Machik Lapdrön. This text is contained in the *Gdams ngag mdzod*, compiled by Jamgön Kongtrul Lodrö Tayé (*'jam mgon kong sprul blo gros mtha' yas*, 1813–1899), vol. 14 (*pha*), 18.3–4 (9b3–4) (Delhi: Shechen Publications, 1999). Here in the *Life*, 615.6, the word *gzhag* is given in place of *bzhag*.

CHAPTER 8

77. The *khel* (spelled *khal*) is a measure of volume. One *khel* of grain weighs about thirty pounds.
78. The *shangs pa'i gser chos* include the Six Dharmas of Niguma (*ni gu chos drug*); the Amulet-box Mahāmudrā (*phyag chen ga'u ma*); incorporating appearances, sounds, and thoughts into the path (*lam khyer rnam gsum*); the teachings on the red and white forms of Khecarī (*mkha' spyod dkar dmar*); and the teachings on immortality and infallability (*'chi med chugs med*).
79. These four places are referred to as *ri bo rtse lnga, glang chen 'gying ri, spos dang ldan pa'i grong khyer,* and *pho brang lta na sdug*. The first two are well-known holy sites in China.
80. Santika and Mön were independent minor kingdoms, ethnically non-Tibetan, partially Buddhist, in what is present-day Yunnan Province. To Tibetans, these were foreign polities.
81. This is not Tsachungpa Yönten Penjung, but the disciple of Urgyenpa, who lived generations earlier. See note 29.
82. A type of stone.
83. The *snyigs ma lnga* are the degenerations of views, afflictive emotions, the bodies and intellects of sentient beings, their life spans, and of the time itself.
84. One *mtho* (pronounced similar to the English "toe") is said to be about the span from the tip of one's thumb to the tip of the middle finger when both fingers are extended.
85. The name Daö Zhönnu derives from the fact that Gampopa is said to have been a reincarnation of one of the Buddha's disciples, who went by the name of Candraprabhakumāra (*zla 'od gzhon nu* in Tibetan).
86. A *zho*, which is one tenth of a *srang*, is a very small unit of weight.
87. Here and elsewhere in the *Life*, these three figures are referred to simply as "the three: the abbot, the *ācārya*, and the Dharma king" (*mkhan slob chos gsum*).
88. On 166 he is referred to as Nyida Drukdrak Śākya Chöpel, the Rapjampa of upper Tsang.
89. The *log bzhi* are mistaking what is impermanent for permanent; mistaking what is easy for difficult; mistaking non-self for self; and mistaking the pleasant for the unpleasant.
90. In Indian mythology, the sage or *ṛṣi* Agastya (*snying stobs ri byi*) once swallowed all the world's oceans at Viṣṇu's request, in order to root out and defeat the demons who had taken refuge in the waters.

CHAPTER 9

91. The *lha babs* [*kyi*] *dus chen*, which commemorates the future Siddhartha Gautama's descending from heaven and entering his mother's womb, is still recognized and celebrated today.

92. The "Eight Sugatas" or "Eight Medicine Buddhas" ([*sman bla*] *bde gshegs brgyad*) are Śākyamūṇi (*shAkya thub pa*); Bhaiṣajyaguru (*sman gyi bla ma*); Abhijñārāja (*mngon mkhyen rgyal po*); Dharmakīrtisāgaraghoṣa (*chos bsgrags rgya mtsho'i dbyangs*); Aśokottamaśrī (*mya ngan med mchog dpal*); Suvarṇabhadravimalaratnaprabhāsa (*gser bzang dri med rin chen snang ba*); Śabdaghoṣarāja (*sgra dbyangs rgyal po*); Suparikīrtitanāmaśrī (*mtshan legs yongs bsgrags dpal*).
93. *Ring bsrel* (in Sanskrit, *śarīraṃ*) are small, pearl-like objects produced in the process of cremating a holy being.
94. This and the preceding sentence of my translation are a tentative rendering of the Tibetan. In the 1972 edition, at 653.5 the troublesome passage reads: *gdung log dang dung lcags chod/ gzhan yang zhu mthigs sogs la byon pa'i* . . . The text here seems to be missing some words, since the complete *dbu can* manuscript copy preserved by the NGMPP (L855/29), part II, 31b5–6, reads: *gdung log ltar dangs shing lha sku dpag tu med pas gang pa phebs/ dang gdung lcags chod/ zhu mthigs sogs la byon pa'i* . . . My understanding of the expanded passage assumes some mistakes in spelling.
95. This is likely the mother of Nyukla Peṇchen, daughter of Norbu Zangpo, aunt of Dönyö Dorjé. See note 47.
96. This would seem to be another name of Nyukla Peṇchen.
97. This may refer to Künga Zangpo's disciple noted earlier as Chakchenpa Saraha.

EPILOGUE

98. I do not know if this printery—at *lho nyan dri legs* (or perhaps *lho gnyal*), three days south of Lhasa—used the original 1494 and 1537 woodblocks, or a set carved at a later time. It seems this printery may have specialized in works about the holy madmen, since it is recorded as housing woodblocks for biographies of the Madman of Ü, the Madman of Tsang, and Drukpa Künlé; Johan van Manen, "A Contribution to the Bibliography of Tibet," *Journal and Proceedings of the Asiatic Society of Bengal* 18, new series (1922): 485, 513.
99. NGMPP L855/29, 54b5–6.
100. See *The Holy Madmen of Tibet*, 115–19, 229–30.
101. See *The Holy Madmen of Tibet*, 65, 88, 215.
102. Michael Aris, *Hidden Treasures and Secret Lives: A Study of Pemalingpa (1450–1521) and the Sixth Dalai Lama (1683–1706)* (London and New York: Kegan Paul International, 1989), 54.
103. Sangs rgyas dar po, *Sangs rgyas dar po chos 'byung*, 78b6, 73a5.
104. Pad+ma dkar po, 'Brug chen IV, *Chos 'byung bstan pa'i pad+ma rgyas pa'i nyin byed ('Brug pa'i chos 'byung)*, published as *Tibetan Chronicle of Padma-dkar-po*, ed. Lokesh Chandra (New Delhi: International Academy of Indian Culture, 1968), 594.6; Khro ru mkhan po tshe rnam, *Dpal mnyam med mar pa bka'*

brgyud kyi grub pa'i mtha' rnam par nges par byed pa mdor bsdus su brjod pa dwags brgyud grub pa'i me long (Sarnath: WA Na bka' brgyud nyam skyong tshogs pa skabs so bzhi pas dpar skrun zhus, 2007), 103.

105. Sgam po pa mi pham chos kyi dbang phyug phrin las rnam rgyal dpal bzang po, also known as 'Dzam gling nor bu rgyan pa, *Gdan sa chen po dpal dwags lha sgam po'i ngo mtshar gyi bkod pa dad pa'i gter chen*, 32b–33a; in *Rare Texts from Tibet: Seven Sources for the Ecclesiastic History of Medieval Tibet*, ed. Per K. Sørensen and Sonam Dolma (Lumbini: Lumbini International Research Institute, 2007), 266.

106. Toni Huber and Tsepak Rigzin, "A Tibetan Guide for Pilgrimage to Ti-se (Mount Kailas) and mTsho Ma-pham (Lake Manasarovar)," in *Sacred Spaces and Powerful Places in Tibetan Culture: A Collection of Essays*, ed. Toni Huber (Dharamsala: Library of Tibetan Works and Archives, 1999), 137.

107. Chos kyi dbang phyug (1775–1837), *Grub pa'i gnas chen brag dkar rta so'i gnas dang gdan rabs bla ma brgyud pa'i lo rgyus mdo tsam brjod pa mos ldan dad pa'i gdung sel drang srong dga' ba'i dal gtam zhes bya ba bzhugs so*, 540.1–4 (which draws from page 427 in the 1972 edition of the *Life*). This is preceded by a single line stating that the Madman of Tsang had spent a month in Drakar Taso. I thank Andrew Quintman for directing me to this reference.

108. Roberto Vitali, *Early Temples of Central Tibet* (London: Serindia, 1990), 134.

109. Brag phug dge bshes dge 'dun rin chen, *'Gro ba'i mgon po chos rje kun dga' legs pa'i rnam thar rgya mtsho'i snying po mthong ba don ldan* (Kalimpong: Mani Printing Works, 1971), 87.1–6; Keith Dowman, *The Divine Madman: The Sublime Life and Songs of Drukpa Kunley* (Varanasi and Kathmandu: Pilgrims, 2000), 110.

110. Kenpo Könchok Namdak (*mkhan po dkon mchog rnam dag*), interview at Phyang Monastery, Ladakh, July 22, 2009.

The day before this interview I visited this same monastery, in order to set up my meeting with the *khenpo*, and to take in a major *cham* (*chams*) or monastic dance performance that was being held on that day. In the bazaar that had assembled outside the monastery gate, I purchased from a vendor a genuine human skull cup, which I had been hoping to buy for what was rather a long time. It felt like great fortune to have found such an ideal specimen, and at a fair price. To learn the very next day that the Madman of Ü's own skull may reside inside that same monastery remains one of the weightiest seeming coincidences of my life.

Personal and Place Names

The following keys reflect the ways these names and titles are spelled within the biography itself. Therefore, *sic* throughout.

Adrak Khung	*a brag khung*
Angé gorge	*ang+ge*
Apo	*a pho*
Apo Söpa	*a po bsod pa*
Asura cave	*a su ra'i brag phug*
Balok	*ba log*
Bangrimpa	*bang rim pa*
Bapmo	*'bab mo*
Bara	*'ba' ra*
Bara Döndrup Ding	*'ba' ra don grub sdings*
Barawa	*'ba' ra ba*
Barkor	*bar skor*
Bikché mountain	*ri bo 'big byed*
Bum Rapjampa Gendün Nyima	*'bum rab 'byams pa dge 'dun nyi ma*
Bumtso Dong	*'bum tsho gdong*
Celestial Palace	*mkha' spyod pho brang*
Chakchenpa Saraha	*phyag chen pa sa ra ha*
Changlung	*lcang lung*
Changlung Chöding	*lcang lung chos sdings*
Charnel Ground of the Nāga Queen	*dur khrod klu mo rgyal*
Chennga Tsültrim Bar	*spyan snga tshul khrims 'bar*
Chertong Repa	*gcer mthong ras pa*
Chiru Taktsé	*byi ru stag rtse*

Chödrak Gyatso	*chos grags rgya mtsho*
Chödzé	*chos mdzad*
Chöjung Puk	*chos 'byung phug*
Chokpu Puk	*lcog bu phug*
Chokro	*cog ro*
Chökyi Drakpa Yeshé Pelzangpo	*chos kyi grags pa ye shes dpal bzang po*
Chölung	*chos lung*
Chonglung Kyung	*'phyong lung khyung*
Chöying Namkhé Dzong	*chos dbyings nam mkha'i rdzong*
Chözang Nyida Drukdrak	*chos bzang nyi zla 'brug grags*
Chubar	*chu bar*
Chumik Ngombum	*chu mig sngo 'bum*
Chupurwa	*chu 'phur ba*
Chushül	*chu shul*
Chuwori	*chu bo ri*
Chuworipa	*chu bo ri pa*
Ḍāki Rechen	*DA ki ras chen*
Dakla Gampo	*dwags la sgam po, dags la sgam po*
Dakpa Shelri	*dag pa shel ri*
Dakpo	*dags, dags po, dwags po*
Ḍangka	*Dang+ka*
Danün Dorjé	*mda' bsnun rdo rje*
Daö Zhönnu	*zla 'od gzhon nu*
Daöpa	*zla 'od pa*
Dargyé	*dar rgyas*
Darpo	*dar po*
Dawa Gyeltsen	*zla rgyal*
Dechen	*bde chen*
Dechen Ding	*bde chen ldings*
Dechen Repa	*bde chen ras pa*
Densa Til, thel	*gdan sa thel*
Dingri Langkhor	*ding ri glang 'khor*
Dokhar	*mdo mkhar*
Döl Tashi Pelgang	*dol bkra shis dpal sgang*
Döndrup	*don grub*
Döndrupa	*don grub pa*
Doné	*ldo ne*
Dönyö Dorjé	*don yod rdo rje*
Doring	*rdo rings*
Dorjé Dzongkha	*rdo rje rdzong kha*
Dorjé Gyelpo	*rdo rje rgyal po*

Dorjé Tseten	*rdo rje tshe brtan*
Drak Yerpa	*yer pa*
Drakar Taso	*brag dkar rta so*
Drakchok	*brag lcog*
Drakchokpa	*brag lcog pa*
Drakjorpa	*grags 'byor pa*
Draklé	*brag le*
Drakmar	*brag dmar*
Drakmar Linga	*brag dmar ling nga*
Draksum Lung	*brag gsum lung*
Drakya Dorjé	*brag skya rdo rje*
Dramalung	*bra ma lung*
Dramozik	*khra mo gzig*
Drangyül Ölkha	*sbrang yul 'ol kha*
Dreshé	*'bras shes*
Dreyül Dzongkar	*'bras yul rdzong dkar*
Drikung	*'bri khung*
Drikung Rechen	*'bri khung ras chen*
Drikung Til	*'bri khung thel*
Drongpo Gang	*'brong po sgang*
Dröpa Cave	*grod pa phug, drod phug*
Droyetak	*sgro ye stag*
Dru Dorjé Den	*gru rdo rje gdan*
Drukpa Künlé	*'brug pa kun legs*
Durtröpa	*dur khrod pa*
Düsum Khyenpa	*dus gsum mkhyen pa*
Dzarangpa	*rdza rang pa*
Dzongkar	*rdzong kha*
Dzongkar Rechen	*rdzong kar ras chen pa, rdzong dkar ras chen*
Ewaṃ	*e waM*
Ewaṃ Rechen	*e waM ras chen*
Forest of Glorious Samantabhadra	*dpal kun tu bzang po'i nags khrod*
Fortress of the Expanse of Being	*chos dbyings nam mkha'i rdzong*
Gachil	*ga lcil*
Galo	*rga lo, rgwa lo*
Galo Cave	*rgwa lo phug*
Gampo Cave	*sgam po phug*
Gampo Nenang	*sgam po gnas nang*
Gampo Pel	*sgam po 'phel*

Gampopa	*sgam po*
Gampopa Mipam Chökyi Wangchuk Trinlé Namgyal Pelzangpo	*sgam po pa mi pham chos kyi dbang phyug phrin las rnam rgyal dpal bzang po*
Gang Tönting Gyelmo	*gangs mthon mthing rgyal mo*
Gangkar Rechen	*gangs kar ras chen, gangs dkar ras chen*
Gendün Pel	*dge 'dun dpal, dge 'dun 'phel*
Gendün Tashi	*dge 'dun bkra shis pa*
Gepel	*dge 'phel*
Geré	*ge re*
Gomdé Nangpa	*sgom sde nang pa*
Gomo Langtang	*sgo mo glang thang*
Gonak Chödzé	*mgo nag chos mdzad*
Gönpo gorge	*mgon po rong*
Gönpo Gyeltsen	*dgon po rgyal mtshan*
Götruk	*rgod phrug*
Götsangpa Gönpo Dorjé	*rgod tshang pa mgon po rdo rje*
Gyama	*rgya ma*
Gyangdrak	*rgyang grags*
Gyangom	*gyang sgom*
Gyantsé, rgyal rtse	*rgyal mkhar rtse*
Gyatso	*rgya mtsho*
Gyelchen Tsé	*rgyal chen rtse*
Gyel-la	*rgyal la*
Horkhang	*hor khang*
House of Dependent Connections	*rten 'brel gyi khang pa*
"Indian" Parping	*rgya gar pham thing*
Ja, bya	*bya yul*
Jak	*'jag*
Jamyang	*'jam dbyangs*
Jang Taklung	*byang stag lung*
Jangkha	*byang kha*
Jangsadam	*ljang sa dam*
Jetsün Drakpa	*rje btsun grags pa*
Jikmé Repa	*'jigs med ras pa*
Jikten Sumgön	*'jig rten gsum mgon*
Jokhang	*jo khang*
Jowo	*jo bo*
Jozang	*jo bzang*
Jozang Sthavira	*jo bzang gnas brtan*
Kala Dungtso	*ka la dung mtsho*

Karma Trinlepa Choklé Namgyel	*phyogs thams cad las rnam par rgyal ba*
Karmapa	*karma pa*
Kathmandu valley	*bal yul thil*
Kham	*khams, mdo khams*
Khamsum Zilnönpa	*khams gsum zil gnon pa*
Kharak	*kha rag, mkha' rag, mkha' reg*
Kharnak	*mkhar nag*
Khartsé	*mkhar rtse*
Khyenrap Yönten Penjung	*mkhyen rab yon tan dpal 'byung*
Khokhom	*kho khom*
Kongpo	*kong po*
Kuchuk Wenpa	*khu byug dben pa*
Künga Gyeltsen	*kun dga' rgyal mtshan pa*
Künga Lekpa	*kun dga' legs pa*
Künga Namgyel	*kun dga' rnam rgyal*
Künga Nyima	*kun dga' nyi ma*
Künga Nyingpo	*kun dga' snying po*
Künga Nyishar	*kun dga' nyi shar*
Künga Rinchen	*kun dga' rin chen pa*
Künga Tsepel	*kun dga' tshe 'phel ba*
Künga Zangpo	*kun dga' bzang po*
Küntu Zangpo	*kun tu bzang po*
Künzang Gönpo Rinchen	*kun bzang mgon po rin chen*
Künzang Nyida Pembar	*kun bzang nyi zla dpal 'bar*
Künzang Selwé Nyingpo	*kun bzang gsal ba'i snying po*
Kya-lhuk Cave	*phug pa skya lhug*
Kyangpen Namkha	*rkyang phan nam mkha'*
Kyapsé Jampel Gyatso	*skyabs se 'jam dpal rgya mtsho*
Kyemö Tsel	*skyes mos tshal*
Kyepo Dar	*skyes po dar*
Kyidé Nyima	*skyid lde nyi ma*
Kyimo	*skyid mo*
Kyirong	*skyi rong*
Kyishö	*skyid shod*
Kyitsel	*skyid tshal, skyid 'tshal*
Labar	*la bar*
Lagö	*brla gos*
Lajang	*la byang*
Lake Manasarovar	*ma pham*
Lapchi	*la phyi, lab phyi*
Latö	*la stod*

Latö Gyel	*las stod rgyal*
Lawateng	*gla ba steng*
Lazik Repa	*la gzigs ras pa*
Lekdenpa	*legs ldan pa*
Lekma	*legs ma*
Leu monastery	*sle'u dgon pa*
Lhasa	*lha sa*
Lhatong Lotsāwa Shényen Namgyel	*lha mthong lo tsA ba bshes gnyen rnam rgyal*
Lhatotori Nyensheltsen	*lha tho tho ri snyan shal btsan*
Lhündé	*lhun sde*
Lhünpo fortress	*lhun po rtse*
Lhünpo Palace	*pho brang chen po lhun po*
Lhünrap	*lhun rab*
Liberation Park	*thar pa gling*
Ling	*gling*
Lingré Nyida Öbar	*gling ras nyi zla 'od 'bar*
Lingrepa	*gling ras*
Lo monastery	*lo dgon pa*
Lochen	*lo chen*
Lochen Künchö	*lo chen kun chos*
Loden Dorjé	*blo ldan rdo rje*
Lohipa	*lo hi pa*
Longpo	*long po*
Lopa Chennga	*lo pa spyan snga*
Lopön Jetsünpa	*slob dpon rje btsun pa*
Lowo Möntang	*glo bo*
Lungshö Trakha	*klungs shod khra 'kha*
Lünpa	*lun pa*
Machik Lapdrön	*ma gcig lab sgron*
Madman of the Drukpa	*'brug smyon*
Madman of Tsang	*gtsang smyon*
Madman of Ü	*dbus pa smyon pa, dbus smyon*
Marnak Rakta	*dmar nag rak+ta, dmar nag rak ta*
Medro	*mal gro*
Medro Rapjampa	*mal gro rab 'byams pa*
Mikyö Dorjé	*mi bskyod rdo rje*
Milarepa	*mi la*
Minkyuk Drip	*smin khyugs grib*
Minyak Rapjampa	*mi nyag rab 'byams pa*
Misö	*mi gsod*

Miyowa	*mi g.yo ba*
Mön	*mon*
Mönkyiné	*smon skyid nas*
Mount Kailash	*ti se*
Mount Shampo	*sham po'i gangs*
Nakartsé	*sna dkar rtse*
Namkha Lekpa	*nam mkha' legs pa*
Namkha Lodrö	*nam mkha' blo gros*
Namkha Sönam Penjor	*nam mkha' bsod nams dpal 'byor*
Namkha Zangpo	*nam mkha' bzang po*
Nāropa	*nA ro pa*
Nedong	*sne'u gdong*
Nenying	*gnas rnying*
Nepal	*bal yul*
Neudzong	*sne'u*
Ngaki Wangpo	*ngag gi dbang po*
Ngari Dzongkar	*mnga' ris rdzong kha*
Ngari Gungtang	*mnga' ris gung thang*
Ngawang Chödrak Gyeltsen	*ngag dbang chos grags rgyal mtshan*
Ngawang Döndrup Namgyel	*ngag dbang don grub rnam rgyal*
Ngawang Drakpa	*ngag dbang grags pa*
Ngawang Drakpa Pelzangpo	*ngag dbang grags pa dpal bzang po, ngag gi dbang po grags pa dpal bzang po*
Ngawang Khyenpé Pel	*ngag dbang mkhyen pa'i dpal*
Ngawang Lekpa	*ngag dbang legs pa*
Ngawang Namgyel	*ngag dbang rnam rgyal*
Ngawang Tashi Drakpa	*ngag dbang bkra shis grags pa*
Ngendzongpa	*ngan rdzong, ngam rdzong*
Ngodro Rapjam Khyenrap Namgyel	*ngo gro rab 'byams mkhyen rab rnam rgyal ba*
Ngok	*rngok*
Niguma, ni gu	*ni gu ma*
Norbu Ling	*nor bu gling*
Nupchölung	*nub chos lung*
Nyanam	*gnya' nam, snye nam*
Nyang, lower	*nyang smad*
Nyang, upper	*nyang stod*
Nyangkhöl	*nyang khol*
Nyangpo	*nyang po*
Nyangpo Rechung	*nyang po ras chung*
Nyatsel	*nya tshal*

Nye	*snye*
Nyel	*gnyal*
Nyelpa Jatang	*gnyal pa bya btang*
Nyemo	*snye mo*
Nyentrö Rechen	*gnyan khrod ras chen*
Nyernyipa	*nyer gnyis pa*
Nyida Drukdrak Śākya Chöpel	*nyi zla 'brug grags shAkya chos 'phel*
Nyida Pembar	*nyi zla dpal 'bar*
Nyida Rapjampa	*nyi zla rab 'byams pa*
Nyima Rapjampa	*nyi ma rab 'byams*
Nyishang	*gnyi shangs*
Nyukla	*snyug la, smyug la*
Nyukla Peṇchen	*smyug la paN chen*
Nyukpa	*nyuk pa*
Odé Gungyel	*'o de gung rgyal*
Ölkha	*'ol kha*
Ölkha Chöjung	*'ol kha chos 'byung*
Ölsang Ngowo	*'ol sangs ngo 'o*
Ön	*'on*
Özang	*'od bzang*
Özang Sega	*'od bzang srad ga, 'od bzang srad ga ma*
Padampa Sangyé	*pha dam pa sangs rgyas*
Pakmodrupa	*phag mo gru pa*
Pangchung	*spang chung*
Pangchung Urgyen Ling	*spang chung u rgyan gling*
Pawo	*dpa' bo*
Pelmo	*dpal mo*
Pelmopel	*dpal mo dpal*
Pelnam Zhung	*dpal nam gzhung*
Pema	*pad+ma*
Pema Lingpa	*pad+ma gling pa*
Peṇchen of Nyukla	*smyug la paN chen*
Penjor Drakpa	*dpal 'byor grags pa*
Penjor Gyatso	*dpal 'byor rgya mtsho*
Penyül	*'phan yul*
Pönpa Tak	*dpon pa thag*
Rakma Jangchup	*rag ma byang chub*
Ramchung Dzago	*ram chung rdza sgo*
Ramoché	*ra mo che*
Rangjung Dorjé	*rang byung rdo rje*

Rapjampa of Changra	*lcang ra rab 'byams pa*
Rapjampa of Minyak	*mi nyag rab 'byams pa*
Rapjampa of upper Tsang	*gtsang stod rab 'byams pa*
Rapjampa Ngawang	*rab 'byams pa ngag dbang pa*
Rapjampa Tönpa Yarkhur	*rab 'byams pa ston pa yar khur*
Rapjampa Yönten Rinchen	*rab 'byams pa yon tan rin chen*
Raptang	*rab thang*
Rechen of upper Nyang	*nyang stod ras chen*
Rechung Cave	*ras chung phug*
Rechungpa	*ras chung*
Renda	*ras mda'*
Renga	*ras rnga*
Reting, ra sgreng	*ra sgreg*
Rikdzin Nyima	*rig 'dzin nyi ma*
Rinchen Gang	*rin chen sgang*
Rinchen Jampa Chönyipa	*rin chen byams pa chos nyi pa*
Rinchen Pelzang	*rin chen dpal bzang po*
Rinchen Samten	*rin chen bsam gtan pa*
Rinchen Zangpo	*rin chen bzang po*
Rinchentsé	*rin chen rtse*
Rinpung	*rin chen dpungs*
Ritrö Wangchuk	*ri khrod dbang phyug pa*
Riwo Ganden	*ri bo dga' ldan*
Rugönsar	*ru dgon gsar*
Sakya Chöjung	*sa skya chos 'byung, sa skya chos 'byung pa, sa skya chos 'byung ba*
Śākya Chokden	*shAkya mchog ldan*
Sakya Dükar Rechen	*sa skya bdud dkar ras chen*
Sakya Paṇḍita	*sa paN*
Samdé	*bsam bde*
Samdrup Dechen	*bsam grub bde chen*
Samten Ling	*bsam gtan gling*
Sangyé Gyeltsen	*sangs rgyas rgyal mtshan pa*
Sangyé Kyap	*sangs rgyas skyabs*
Sapmo Drak	*sab mo brag, gsab mo brag*
Sarahapa	*sa ra ha pa*
Śawaripa	*sha ba ri*
Sengé Repa	*seng ge ras pa*
Serkhang	*gser khang*
Serma Rapjampa	*gsar ma rab 'byams pa, gser ma rab 'byams pa*

Shakpa	*bshag pa*
Shang	*shangs*
Shara Rapjampa Sangyé Sengé	*sha ra rab 'byams pa sangs rgyas seng ge*
Sharmé	*shar smad*
Sharmepa	*shar smad pa*
Sheldrong	*shel grong, shel rdzong*
Shelpuk Chushing	*shel phug chu shing*
Shényen Namgyel	*bshes gnyen rnam rgyal*
Shigatsé	*bsam grub rtse*
Shinjé Dongkha	*gshin rje dong kha*
Sinpori	*srin po ri*
Six Fortresses of Milarepa	*mi la'i rdzong drug*
Sönam Gyeltsen	*bsod nams rgyal mtshan*
Sönam Gyeltsen Pel	*bsod nams rgyal mtshan dpal*
Sönam Tashi	*bsod nams bkra shis*
Sönam Tashi Gyeltsen Pelzang	*bsod nams bkra shis rgyal mtshan dpal bzang*
Sönam Wangchuk	*bsod nams dbang phyug*
Sönam Zangmo	*bsod nams bzang mo*
Sönam Zangpo	*bsod nams bzang po*
Songtsen Gampo	*srong btsan sgam po*
Śrī Bariko	*shri ba ri sko*
Śrī Samten Ling	*shrib [sic] bsam gtan gling*
Swayambhūnāth stūpa	*'phags pa shing kun*
Taklung	*stag lung*
Takshel	*stag shel*
Taksher Repa	*stag gsher ras pa*
Taktsang	*stag tshang*
Taktsé	*stag rtse*
Talam	*rta lam*
Tamdrin Tseten	*rta mgrin tshe brtan, rta 'drin tshe brtan*
Tanak	*rta nag*
Tangsak	*thang sag*
Tapa Chöjé	*mtha' pa chos rje*
Targyé Chödzepa	*mthar rgyas chos mdzad pa*
Tarma	*thar ma*
Tarpa Gyeltsen	*thar pa rgyal mtshan pa*
Tarpa Ling	*thar pa gling*
Tarpa Nyima Rechen	*thar pa ba nyi ma ras chen*
Tartsa	*mthar rtsa*
Tashi Dargyé	*bkra shis dar rgyas*

Tashi Dargyé Lekpé Gyelpo	*bkra shis dar rgyas legs pa'i rgyal po*
Tashi Lhünpo	*bkra shis lhun po*
Tashi Rinchen	*bkra shis rin chen*
Tashigang	*bkra shis sgang*
Tatok Khar	*rta thog mkhar*
Tekchen fortress	*theg chen rtse*
Tibet	*bod*
Tilopa	*tai lo pa*
Tölung	*stod lung*
Tongmön	*mthong smon*
Tongshong	*stong shong*
Trabkha	*khrab kha*
Trangpo Dar	*sprang po dar*
Tri Künzang Nyida Drak	*khri kun bzang nyi zla grags*
Tri Relpachen	*khri ral pa can*
Trinkyi Shukchen Norbu Yangdong	*sprin gyi shugs can nor bu g.yang mdongs*
Trisong Detsen	*khri srong lde'u btsan*
Tropu	*khro phu*
Tsachungpa	*tsha chung pa*
Tsang	*gtsang*
Tsangpo	*gtsang po*
Tsari, tsA ri	*tsa ri*
Tsari Rechen	*tsa ri ras chen*
Tsari Yöndrel	*tsa ri g.yon gral*
Tsel Gungtang	*mtshal gung thang*
Tsembupa	*tshim bu*
Tseringma	*tshe rings ma*
Tsetar	*tshe thar*
Tseten Dorjé	*tshe rtan rdo rje*
Tsibri	*rtsibs ri*
Tsikpa Kangtil	*brtsig pa rkang mthil*
Tsimar Pel	*rtsi dmar dpal*
Tsokyé Dorjé	*mtsho skyes rdo rje*
Tsopé	*tso pe*
Tsuklak Trengwa	*gtsug lag phreng ba*
Tsünmo Tsel	*btsun mo tshal*
Tsurpu	*mtshur phu*
Tungchö	*'thung gcod*
Tupten Kyetsel	*thub bstan skyed tshal*
Tupten Serdokchen	*thub bstan gser mdog can*
Turquoise Lake	*g.yu mtsho*

Ü	*dbus*
Uma Drakar	*dbu ma brag dkar*
Umé fortress	*dbu ma'i rdzong*
Üpa Rechung	*dbus pa ras chung*
Ur	*dbur*
Urgyenpa	*u rgyan pa*
Uru	*dbu ru*
Utö	*dbu stod*
Virūpa	*bi ru pa, birba pa*
Vulture Peak	*bya rgod phung po'i ri*
White Mausoleum	*sku gdung dkar po*
Wönpo Dorgyel	*dbon po rdor rgyal*
Wonré Sönam Namgyel	*dbon ras bsod nams rnam rgyal*
Ya lake	*g.ya' mtsho*
Yakdé	*g.yag sde*
Yamda	*yar mda'*
Yamdrok	*yar 'brog*
Yangleshö	*yang le shel*
Yanggönpa	*yang dgon pa*
Yargyap	*yar rgyab*
Yarlung	*yar lung*
Yartö	*yar stod*
Yöl	*yol*
Yöl Rinchen Ling	*yol rin chen gling*
Yöndrel Bechungpa	*g.yon gral sbad chung pa*
Yöngompa	*yon sgom pa*
Yönten Penjung	*yon tan dpal 'byung*
Yülgyel	*g.yul rgyal*
Yülmé	*yul smad*
Zambulung	*zab phu lung, zam bu lung*
Zangtel Puk	*zang thal phug pa*
Zhoklha Chukpo	*zhogs lha phyug po*
Zhokpu Jomo-nying	*zhogs phu jo mo snying*
Zholung Tsokha	*zho lung mtsho kha*
Zilung	*zi lung*
Zurkhang Sharpa	*zur khang shar pa*

Tibetan Texts Referred to in the Biography

Alphabet Dohā, ka kha'i do ha
Application of Accomplishment, sgrub pa'i lag len
Brilliant Rays That Open the Eyes, mig 'byed 'od stong
Buddhasamayoga Tantra, sangs rgyas mnyam sbyor
Cakrasaṃvara Tantra, bde mchog gi nyung ngu'i rgyud
Collected Sayings of the King, rgyal po bka' 'bum
Collected Songs of Milarepa, mi la'i mgur 'bum
Commoners' Dohā, dmangs kyi do ha
Completely Non-abiding Mahāmudrā, phyag rgya chen po rab tu mi gnas pa
Condensed Meaning of the Hevajra Tantra, brtag gnyis kyi bsdus don
Condensed Perfection of Wisdom Sūtra, shes phyin sdud pa
Consecration Tantra, rab gnas kyi rgyud
Defeating Conceptuality, rtog pa 'bur 'joms
Dispelling the Darkness of Ignorance, ma rig mun sel
Dohā on Dying, 'chi kha ma'i do ha
Dohā on Paying No Attention to Body, Speech, or Mind, sku gsung thugs yid la mi byed pa'i do ha
Dohā That Is Like the Flame of a Butter Lamp, mar me'i rtse mo lta bu'i do ha
Dohā Trilogy, do hA skor gsum, do ha skor gsum
Drop of Ambrosia, bdud rtsi thigs pa
Earlier and later *Primers*, ka dpe snga phyi
Essence of Accomplishments, grub snying
Extensive Perfection of Wisdom Sūtra, yum rgyas pa
Finding Ease in the Nature of Mind, sems nyid ngal bso
Four-Fold Scroll of Marpa, mar pa'i shog dril bzhi
Garland of Vajras, rdo rje phreng ba

Glorious Unpolluted Tantra, dpal rnyog pa med pa'i rgyud
Golden Rosary of the Kagyü, bka' brgyud gser phreng
Great All-Perfect Yard, kun rdzogs stong ra chen mo
Great commentary on the *Hevajra Tantra* by Nāropa, na ro 'grel chen
Guhyasamāja Tantra, gsang ba 'dus pa [*sic*]
Guiding Instructions on the Madhyamaka View, dbu ma lta khrid
Heart Essence of Profound Meaning, zab don thugs snying
Hevajra Tantra, the "Two-Parted," brtag gnyis, brtag pa gnyis pa, dgyes rdor, kye rdor gyi rgyud
Immortal Vajra, 'chi med rdo rje
Jewel Ornament Commentary, rin chen rgyan 'dra
Kālacakra Tantra, dus 'khor
King's Dohā, rgyal po do ha
Life of Milarepa, mi la'i rnam thar
Mahāmudrā Drop, phyag chen thig le
Mañjughoṣa Vajra, 'jam dbyangs rdo rje
Mountain Dharma, ri chos
Mountain Dharma That Is the Origin of All Attainments, ri chos yon tan kun 'byung
Nāropa–Maitripa *dohā*, nA ro pa/ mai tri pa gnyis kyi do ha
Peacock in the Poison Grove, rma bya dug 'joms
Queen's Dohā, btsun mo do ha
Quintessence of the Great Perfection, rdzogs chen snying tig
Secret Practice of India, rgya gar gsang spyod
Seven Points of Mind Training, blo sbyong don bdun ma
Ship of Liberation, thar gru
Six Dharmas in Pure Gold, chos drug gser zhun ma
Six Treasuries, mdzod drug
Song of the Esoteric Oral Instruction of the Inexhaustible Treasury, Completely Full, mi zad pa'i gter mdzod yongs su gang ba'i man ngag gi glu
Stages of Bodhisattvahood, sems pa'i rim pa
Summation of the Equalization of Taste, ro snyoms sgang dril
Sun of the Little Collection, nyi ma 'bum chung
Synopsis of the Empowerments, dbang mdor bstan
Tantra for the Accomplishment of the Single Hero, dpa' bo gcig sgrub kyi rgyud
Thousand Rays Clarifying the Great Bliss, bde chen gsal ba'i 'od zer stong ldan
Tiger Encountering the Lion, stag seng kha sprod
Unborn Vajra, skye med rdo rje
Vajra Songs of the Six Dharmas, chos drug rdo rje'i mgur
Vajra Verses on the Aural Tantra, snyan rgyud rdo rje'i tshig rkang
Valid Understanding of the Authentic Word, bka' yang dag pa'i tshad ma
Wheel of Sharp Weapons, mtshon cha'i 'khor lo
Wish-Fulfilling Jewel of Mind Instructions: The Rain Cloud That Fulfills Every Need and Want, sems khrid yid bzhin nor bu'i khrid yig dgos 'dod char 'bebs

Works Cited

NGMPP: Nepal–German Manuscript Preservation Project

EDITIONS OF *THE LIFE OF THE MADMAN OF Ü*

Smyug la paN chen ngag dbang grags pa (1458–1515) and Lha mthong lo tsA ba bshes gnyen rnam rgyal (born 1512). Part I, *Dpal ldan bla ma dam pa grub pa'i khyu mchog phyogs thams cad las rnam par rgyal ba'i spyod pa can rje btsun kun dga' bzang po'i rnam par thar pa ris med dad pa'i spu long g.yo byed.* Part II, *Rje btsun kun dga' bzang po'i rnam par thar pa ris med dad pa'i spu long g.yo byed ces bya ba las/ rim par phye ba gnyis pa phrin las rgyan gyi rnga sgra.* The following three editions were used in making this translation: (1) an edition from the 1494 woodblocks for the first part of the biography, in fifty-one folios, preserved by the NGMPP, E1581/11; (2) an *dbu can* manuscript of the complete biography, in eighty-six folios, preserved by the NGMPP, L855/29; (3) a reprint of the complete biography, in *Bka' brgyud pa Hagiographies: A Collection of Rnam Thar of the Eminent Masters of Tibetan Buddhism,* compiled and edited by Khams sprul don brgyud nyi ma, vol. 2: 383–660. Palampur, Himachal Pradesh: Sungrab Nyamso Gyunphel Parkhang, Tibetan Craft Community, 1972.

The following two editions have been examined, but were not used in making this translation: (1) an *dbu can* manuscript of the first part of the biography, in fifty-one folios, preserved by the NGMPP, L117/1; (2) a reprint of the first part of the biography, mislabeled as *Dbus smyon kun dga' bzang po'i mgur 'bum,* made in Delhi, 1973.

TIBETAN-LANGUAGE SOURCES

Khro ru mkhan po tshe rnam. *Dpal mnyam med mar pa bka' brgyud kyi grub pa'i mtha' rnam par nges par byed pa mdor bsdus su brjod pa dwags brgyud grub pa'i me long.* Sarnath: WA Na bka' brgyud nyam skyong tshogs pa skabs so bzhi pas dpar skrun zhus, 2007.

Rgod tshang ras pa sna tshogs rang grol (1482–1559). *Gtsang smyon he ru ka phyogs thams cad las rnam par rgyal ba'i rnam thar rdo rje theg pa'i gsal byed nyi ma'i snying po* [The *Life* of the Madman of Tsang]. Edited by Lokesh Chandra. New Delhi: Sharada Rani, 1969.

Sgam po pa mi pham chos kyi dbang phyug phrin las rnam rgyal dpal bzang po (1589–1633). *Gdan sa chen po dpal dwags lha sgam po'i ngo mtshar gyi bkod pa dad pa'i gter chen*. In *Rare Texts from Tibet: Seven Sources for the Ecclesiastic History of Medieval Tibet*, edited by Per K. Sørensen and Sonam Dolma, 51–52, 248–273 (Text G). Lumbini: Lumbini International Research Institute, 2007.

Chos kyi dbang phyug (1775–1837). *Grub pa'i gnas chen brag dkar rta so'i gnas dang gdan rabs bla ma brgyud pa'i lo rgyus mdo tsam brjod pa mos ldan dad pa'i gdung sel drang srong dga' ba'i dal gtam zhes bya ba bzhugs so*. 485–593 in vol. 10 (*tha*) of his *Collected Works, Kun mkhyen brag dkar ba chos kyi dbang phyug mchog gi gsum 'bum*. Kathmandu: Gam-po-pa Library, 2011.

Na ro'i chos drug las/ gtuH mo bde drod rang 'bar gyi lam gyi cha lag 'khrul 'khor rtsa tshig zin bris gsal ba'i me long. Undated manuscript in five folios. NGMPP E829/1.

Pad+ma dkar po, 'Brug chen IV (1527–1592). *Chos 'byung bstan pa'i pad+ma rgyas pa'i nyin byed ('Brug pa'i chos 'byung)*. Published as *Tibetan Chronicle of Padma-dkar-po*, edited by Lokesh Chandra. New Delhi: International Academy of Indian Culture, 1968.

Dpa' bo gtsug lag phreng ba (1504–1564/6). *Chos 'byung mkhas pa'i dga' ston (Dam pa'i chos kyi 'khor lo bsgyur ba rnams kyi byung ba gsal bar byed pa mkhas pa'i dga' ston)* [*Scholar's Feast*]. Beijing: Mi rigs dpe skrun khang, 1986, 2006.

Brag phug dge bshes dge 'dun rin chen [Geshé Chapu] (1926–1997). *'Gro ba'i mgon po chos rje kun dga' legs pa'i rnam thar rgya mtsho'i snying po mthong ba don ldan*. Kalimpong: Mani Printing Works, 1971

'Brug pa kun legs (born 1455). *'Brug pa kun legs kyi rnam thar*. Beijing: Bod ljongs mi dmangs dpe skrun khang, 2005.

Ma gcig lab sgron. *Shes rab kyi pha rol tu phyin pa gcod kyi gzhung dang man ngag mtha' dag gi yang bcud zab don thugs kyi snying po*. In the *Gdams ngag mdzod*, compiled by 'Jam mgon kong sprul blo gros mtha' yas (1813–1899), vol. 14 (*pha*): 9a1–11b5 (17–22). Delhi: Shechen Publications, 1999.

Ma pham rdo rje. *Rnal 'byor gyi dbang phyugs grags pa mtha' yas dpal bzang po'i rnam thar mgur 'bum ngo mtshar nor bu'i 'phreng ba*. Gangtok: Gonpo Tseten, 1977. (Reproduced from tracings from prints of the central Tibetan woodblocks.)

Sangs rgyas dar po. *Sangs rgyas dar po chos 'byung* (*Bka' brgyud chos 'byung rin po che spungs pa'i 'od stong 'khyil* or *Bde gshegs bstan pa'i gsal byed bka' rgyud chos kyi 'byung gnas rin po che spungs pa'i 'od stong 'khyil ba*) [*History of the Kagyü: The Combined Luster of a Heap of Jewels*]. Undated block print. NGMPP L392/14. A copy lent by Tashi Tsering (Dharamsala) was used during research.

Si tu paN chen chos kyi 'byung gnas (1699/1700–1774) and 'Be lo tshe dbang kun khyab. *Bsgrub brgyud karma kaM tshang brgyud pa rin po che'i rnam par thar pa rab 'byams nor bu zla ba chu shel gyi phreng ba*. New Delhi: D. Gyaltshan and Kesang Legshay, 1972.

WESTERN-LANGUAGE SOURCES

Aris, Michael. *Hidden Treasures and Secret Lives: A Study of Pemalingpa (1450–1521) and the Sixth Dalai Lama (1683–1706)*. London and New York: Kegan Paul International, 1989.

DiValerio, David. *The Holy Madmen of Tibet*. New York: Oxford University Press, 2015.

Dowman, Keith. *The Divine Madman: The Sublime Life and Songs of Drukpa Kunley*. Varanasi and Kathmandu: Pilgrims, 2000.

Ehrhard, Franz-Karl. "The Holy Madman of dBus and His Relationships with Tibetan Rulers of the 15th and 16th Centuries." In *Geschichten und Geschichte: Historiographie und Hagiographie in der asiatischen Religionsgeschichte*, edited by Peter Schalk, 219–246. Uppsala: Uppsala University Library, 2010.

Huber, Toni, and Tsepak Rigzin. "A Tibetan Guide for Pilgrimage to Ti-se (Mount Kailas) and mTsho Ma-pham (Lake Manasarovar)." In *Sacred Spaces and Powerful Places in Tibetan Culture: A Collection of Essays*, edited by Toni Huber, 125–153. Dharamsala: Library of Tibetan Works and Archives, 1999.

Okawa, Tami. "'We're All Mad Here . . .': The Divine Madmen of 15th-Century Tibet." Unpublished research paper. School for International Training, Tibetan Studies, Kathmandu, Spring 1999.

Sernesi, Marta. "A Manual on Nāropa's Six Yogas by sPyan snga Nyer gnyis pa (1386–1434): Tucci Tibetan Collection 1359." *Indo-Iranian Journal* 53 (2010): 121–163.

Stein, R. A. *Vie et chants de 'brug-pa kun-legs le yogin*. Paris: G.-P. Maisonneuve et Larose, 1972.

"The Three Divine Madmen." In *The Dragon Yogis: A Collection of Selected Biographies and Teachings of the Drukpa Lineage Masters*, 41–49. Gurgaon: Drukpa Publications, 2009.

van Manen, Johan. "A Contribution to the Bibliography of Tibet." *Journal and Proceedings of the Asiatic Society of Bengal* 18, new series (1922): 485, 513.

Vitali, Roberto. *Early Temples of Central Tibet*. London: Serindia, 1990.